WONG TAI-CHEE &
YAP LIAN-HO ADRIEL

FOUR DECADES OF TRANSFORMATION

Land Use in Singapore, 1960 – 2000

EASTERN UNIVERSITIES PRESS
by Marshall Cavendish

© 2004 Marshall Cavendish International
(Singapore) Private Limited

Published 2004 by Eastern Universities Press
An imprint of Marshall Cavendish International
(Singapore) Private Limited
A member of Times Publishing Limited

Times Centre, 1 New Industrial Road,
Singapore 536196
Tel:(65) 6213 9288
Fax: (65) 6284 9772
E-mail: tap@tpl.com.sg
Online Book Store:
http://www.timesacademic.com

All rights reserved. No part of this publication may be reproduced, stored in a retrieval system, or transmitted, in any form or by any means, electronic, mechanical, photocopying, recording or otherwise, without the prior permission of the publishers.

ISBN: 981-210-270-1

A CIP catalogue record for this book is available from National Library Board (Singapore).

Printed by Times Graphics Pte Ltd, Singapore on non-acidic paper

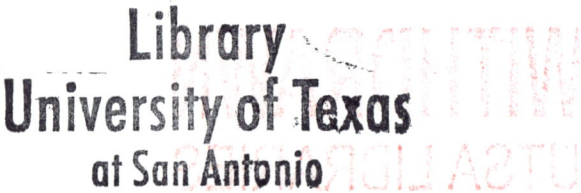

London • New York • Beijing • Shanghai
• Bangkok • Kuala Lumpur • Singapore

Contents

Preface	vii
Acknowledgements	x
List of Tables	xi
List of Figures	xiii
List of Abbreviations	xiv
Introduction	1
Chapter 1 **The Transformation of Singapore's Central Area: From Slums to a Global Business Hub**	8
Process and Agents of Change	10
Phase 1: Prelude to Urban Renewal, 1945–1959 Dilapidated Housing Stock Master Plan Preparation	11
Phase 2: Early Stage of Urban Renewal, 1960–1970 Urban Renewal in Concept and Action Urban Renewal: Ending the Effect of the 1947 Rent Control Act From the 1958 Master Plan to the 1971 Concept Plan	16
Phase 3: Concept Plan Implementation— Urban Redevelopment, 1971–1990 Concept Plan Implementation Conservation Concept Plan Revision	22
Phase 4: Post-Revised Concept Plan, After 1991 The New Downtown Core Singapore's New CBD in Search of a Global City	30
Concluding Remarks	36

Chapter 2
Infrastructure as a Modernising Agent: The Transition from Physical Infrastructure to Infostructure
34

Introduction — 34
Scope of Infrastructure
Linkage of Infrastructure to Economic Growth

Infrastructure and Modernisation — 11

Physical Infrastructure Development in Singapore — 41
Transport and Communications Infrastructure
Other Public Utilities

Towards Infostructure: The Knowledge-Based Economy — 50
Singapore's IT Plans and Implementation
Spatial Integration of ICTs and Research Institutions

Concluding Remarks — 56

Chapter 3
Industrialisation, Multinationals and Land-Use Development
59

Introduction — 59

Industrialisation Drive and the Role of the State — 61
Role of the State
Educational Upgrading

The Industrialisation Strategy and its Implementation — 66
The Import-Substitution Industrialisation
The Export-Oriented Strategy

Physical Development of Industrial Estates — 78
Industrial Estates in Singapore
Future Developments

Concluding Remarks — 86

Chapter 4
From Universal Public Housing to Meeting Aspirations for Private Housing
91

Introduction
91

Public Housing as Mass-Produced Public Consumer Goods?
92
Public Housing Since 1960
Universal Provision of Public Housing

Rising Aspirations for Private Housing
101
Income Change
Survey Method
Survey Results

The Land Issue, Perception of Private Housing Status and Quality
108
Private Property Aspirations versus the Price Spiral
The State as a Facilitator to Support Aspirations and the Construction Industry
Whither Private Housing?

Concluding Remarks
116

Chapter 5
Development of Recreational Spaces
120

Introduction
120

Conceptual Relationship Between Recreation and Quality of Life
122

Urbanisation and Land-Use Transformation in Singapore
124
Recreational Areas and the National Parks Board
Park Connectors
Waterbodies
Vision of the 1991 Revised Concept Plan

Recreational Pursuits and their Implications for Sustainability and Quality of Life	135
The Triangular Relationship Between Growth, Environment and Equity	
Heading for Creative Conservation in an Intensively Built-Up Urban Environment?	
Concluding Remarks	138
Conclusion	141
Bibliography	149
Index	165

Preface

The transformation of every aspect of Singapore—physical, social and economic—over the past 40 years has been truly dramatic. I have had the chance to observe this transformation over frequent visits since first spending a month here as a PhD student in 1963. At that time, Singapore already had quite a jump on its neighbours in living levels, but it was still nevertheless a gritty port city. Tourists loved it, perhaps more than many of its residents did. The charm of its Chinatown reflected the crowded and unsanitary housing and the consequent colourful street life; the charm of the Singapore river (which announced its presence to the nose well before being observed by the eyes) lay in its picturesque, almost Brueghelesque, "busyness"—the backbreaking work for longshoremen unloading goods from the *tongkangs* and *tua kows* into the godowns lining Boat Quay. Singapore possessed a Third World airport and an adequate but basic road system.

It is unlikely that there is another city anywhere in the world whose transformation over 40 years has been so complete. Every visit one made was marked by revelations of the scale of the change: the wrecking ball demolishing HDB apartments in Queenstown that were considered incapable of upgrading to the standards expected by even the lower-income end of an increasingly affluent population; the building of prestigious flagship projects, such as Suntec City in Marina Centre, on reclaimed land where ships lay at anchor in 1963; the mutation of Boat Quay from working river to yuppie nightlife centre; the further expansion, seemingly at every visit, of the MRT network; and the construction of one of the world's most advanced airports.

The documentation through maps and tables of aspects of a changing Singapore is one of the fascinating aspects of this book. Many younger Singaporeans will no doubt be surprised to follow, through dotted lines on the maps, the earlier location of the Singapore coastline, but it will help them to understand why the Seaview Hotel overlooks nothing other than more land and buildings. They will also see that the Southern Islands have been amalgamated into one Jurong Island, housing a vast petrochemical industry. Other maps show the constant spread of HDB estates into the further reaches of the island—places such as Pasir Ris, Punggol and Choa Chu Kang.

This book, however, does more than document and describe. It traces the policy changes, the planning and bureaucratic arrangements for dealing with change, the restless re-thinking and modification of approaches by a government with a supreme confidence in its ability to orchestrate change in the interests of its citizens' welfare, not to mention the perpetuation of its own role as the benevolent "guiding hand". From the very beginning, the new government rejected the colonial government's planning assumptions of slow and steady social and economic change: the passive role of government in the economy; and preservation of the achievements and institutions of the past as the main objective of all planning. Instead, it sought a drastic transformation of the city-state. There are downsides to all this. The trade-off of political freedom for economic well-being in Singapore is a much-debated issue. Controversy, too, surrounds the kind of nation and society Singapore should become by 2030, the target year for some of Singapore's longer-term planning. The benevolence and technocratic approaches in planning have not prevented mistakes, indeed blunders, from occurring. The present book does not resile from discussing such issues.

One of the most interesting issues discussed is the politicisation of public housing services, in a context in which the extraordinarily high proportion of Singaporeans dependent on public housing locks the state and the population into a dependent-supplier relationship from which neither can easily extract themselves. Nevertheless, there is a rising demand for private housing, and the aim of raising the share of private housing has become a government goal since 1990.

One interesting chapter of this book is devoted to the development of recreational spaces. The "garden city" objective had to be applied in a verticalised high-rise public housing landscape. Greenery was made an inseparable component of public housing estates. Some parks have been developed on reclaimed land, the most notable of them being East Coast Park. Natural vegetation has been retained in some of the ridge parks, whereas community and town parks are seen as havens in the heart of the city or within or between housing estates. "Park connectors" between major parks and nature areas are planned with multiple purposes, including provision of cycling and jogging tracks, and assisting birds to move between nature reserves and refuges and wetland habitats. This is an area of Singapore's planning where public interest groups have come to play an increasing part. Praise for the planners' success in providing varied recreational space must be tempered, however, by concern about busy Singaporeans' lack of time to enjoy it.

One dilemma facing Singapore's planners is the ever-increasing gap between the fertility rate necessary to reproduce the population over time, and the actual fertility rate of Singaporeans. This is not an issue confined to Singapore, but is common to most industrial and post-industrial societies. But Singapore's fertility rate is towards the lower end of rates prevailing in such societies. The hard fact is that the economic and social environment created in Singapore over the past 40 years is not one in which replacement-level fertility is even remotely approached. In time, then, Singapore will either have to accept a declining population and labour force, with all that may imply for its economic competitiveness, or rely increasingly on foreign workers, at all levels of the occupational spectrum, to keep it on its planned economic path. It will be ironic indeed if extraordinary successes of urban planning and material well-being achieved over the past 40 years come to be enjoyed predominantly by a foreign-born population permitted to stay only for limited periods, because Singaporeans themselves have adapted to the changing socio-economic context by drastically restricting their childbearing.

This book will provide invaluable material for anyone interested in the dynamics of the transformation achieved over the past 40 years, the mechanisms by which it has been achieved, and the constantly evolving issues in planning the Singapore of the future.

Gavin Jones
Professor
Asian Research Institute
National University of Singapore

Acknowledgements

We would like to gratefully acknowledge the help we received in successfully completing this book. First, it was the academic research fund (AcRF) granted by the National Institute of Education, Nanyang Technological University, that enabled us to pursue the project with necessary resources till its completion. Three important people reviewed the manuscript at different stages: Dr Cheng Lim Keak; the anonymous reviewer provided by the publisher, Times Media; and Professor Gavin Jones who also kindly wrote the preface for the book. Their comments have helped to produce a better book.

We also wish to express our appreciation for the moral support given by Professor Goh Kim Chuan when he was head of the Geography Division, and Dr Christine Lee, the current head. Finally, specific acknowledgement must go to the three journal publishers for permission to reprint their materials, though modifications have been made in response to reviews and in updating. These materials appear in the following chapters:

- Chapter 1—"The Transformation of Singapore's Central Area: From Slums to a Global Business Hub?" *Planning Practice and Research*, Vol. 16, No. 2 (2001), pp. 155–170;
- Chapter 2—"The Transition from Physical Infrastructure to Infostructure: Infrastructure as a Modernising Agent in Singapore", *GeoJournal*, Vol. 49, No. 3 (1999), pp. 279–288; and
- Chapter 4—"From Universal Public Housing to Meeting the Increasing Aspiration for Private Housing in Singapore", *Habitat International*, Vol. 27, No. 3 (2003), pp. 361–380.

List of Tables

Table 1.1　Land-Use Change in Singapore, 1967–1982
Table 1.2　Employment Distribution Trends of the Central Area by Sector, 1974–1989
Table 1.3　The Central Area's Share of Office Space in Singapore, 1979–1992
Table 2.1　Public Roads in Singapore, 1961–2000
Table 2.2　Access of Urban Population to Drinking Water and Sanitation—Singapore and Other Selected East Asian Economies, 1980–1996
Table 3.1　Industrial Land Requirements Proposed in Winsemius Report, 1960–1980
Table 3.2　GDP and Manufacturing Growth of Singapore, 1960–2000
Table 3.3　Output of Petrochemical Industries in Comparison with Other Selected Industries, 1966–2000
Table 3.4　Foreign and Local Equity Investment in Singapore's Manufacturing Industry, 1998
Table 3.5　Singapore's Investment Abroad, 1998–2000
Table 3.6　Principal Manufacturing Statistics, 1980–2000
Table 4.1　Change in Distribution of HDB Apartments by Type, 1980–2000
Table 4.2　Performance of the Housing and Development Board, 1960–2000
Table 4.3　Average Monthly Earnings of Income Earners in Singapore, 1980–1990
Table 4.4　Distribution of Singapore Household Expenditures as a Percentage, 1973–1998
Table 4.5　Rationale of Public Housing Owners for Upgrading/Not Upgrading to Private Housing
Table 4.6　Types of Housing that Public Housing Owners Wish to Move to
Table 4.7　Reasons Given by Public Housing Owners for Mortgaging/Not Mortgaging their Flats
Table 4.8　Change in Household Income, 1990–2000
Table 4.9　The Construction Industry Slump Since the 1997 Financial Crisis

Table 4.10 Share of Private Housing in Singapore, 1980–2000
Table 5.1   Land-Use Change in Singapore, 1960–1999
Table 5.2   Major Greenery Sites in Singapore

List of Figures

Figure 1.1	Population Distribution in 1947
Figure 1.2	Preliminary Island Plan, 1952
Figure 1.3	The 1958 Master Plan of Singapore
Figure 1.4	Ring Concept Plan
Figure 1.5	The Golden Shoe
Figure 1.6	CBD Zone Structure Plan, 2000–Year X
Figure 1.7	Expansion of the Central Area, 1958–1997
Figure 2.1	Infrastructure in 1958
Figure 2.2	Infrastructure in 1975
Figure 2.3	Infrastructure in 2000
Figure 2.4	Reservoirs and Catchment Areas in Singapore
Figure 2.5	Existing Sewage Treatment Plants and Deep Tunnel Sewerage System
Figure 2.6	Revised 1991 Concept Plan for Year X
Figure 3.1	Jurong in 1958
Figure 3.2	JTC Industrial Estates, 1970
Figure 3.3	Jurong in 1975
Figure 3.4	JTC Industrial Estates, 1980
Figure 3.5	JTC Industrial Estates, 1990
Figure 3.6	Business Parks, Industry Clusters and Institutes of Higher Learning
Figure 3.7	JTC Industrial Estates, 1998
Figure 3.8	Jurong in 1998
Figure 4.1	Public Housing in Singapore, 1960–2000
Figure 4.2	Private Property Price Index by Type, 1990–2000
Figure 4.3	Type and Distribution of Private Residential Units, 1999
Figure 5.1	Natural Areas and Parks, 1958 and 1975
Figure 5.2	Major Parks and Nature Areas in Singapore, 2000
Figure 5.3	Proposed Recreational Areas in Singapore by Year X
Figure 5.4	Concept Plan 2001
Figure 5.5	The Triangular Relationship Between Recreational Provision, Equity and Quality of Life

List of Abbreviations

ADSL	Asymmetric Digital Subscriber Line
ASEAN	Association of Southeast Asian Nations
CBD	Central Business District
CPF	Central Provident Fund
DGP	Development Guide Plan
DTSS	Deep Tunnel Sewerage System
EDB	Economic Development Board
EOI	Export-oriented Industrialisation
ESCAP	United Nations Economic and Social Commission for Asia and the Pacific
FDI	Foreign Direct Investment
GDP	Gross Domestic Product
GLC	Government Linked Company
GNP	Gross National Product
HDB	Housing and Development Board
HUDC	Housing and Urban Development Company
ICT	Information and Telecommunications Technology
IP21	Industrial Land Plan for the 21st Century
iParks	Industrial Parks of the 21st Century
ISI	Import-substitution Industrialisatiion
IT	Information Technology
JTC	Jurong Town Corporation
LTA	Land Transport Authority
MNC	Multinational Corporation
MND	Ministry of National Development
MPA	Maritime and Port Authority of Singapore
MRT	Mass Rapid Transit
MTI	Ministry of Trade and Industry
NCB	National Computer Board
NPB	National Parks Board
NSS	Nature Society (Singapore)
OECD	Organisation for Economic Cooperation and Development
PAP	People's Action Party
PRD	Parks and Recreation Department
PSA	Port of Singapore Authority

PUB	Public Utilities Board
SIT	Singapore Improvement Trust
SLA	Singapore Land Authority
TEU	Twenty-foot Equivalent Units
UN	United Nations
URA	Urban Redevelopment Authority
URD	Urban Renewal Department

Introduction

> I believe that modernisation is inevitable and that the pressure in this direction is far stronger than the traditionalists are prepared to concede. The Asian Revolution has released social forces and implanted aspirations and hopes which make modernisation irresistible in the long run. This is because the people of Asia are appreciative of the fruits of modern progress and hunger for them...[But] modernisation demands its price. Modernisation requires a certain measure of hard work, sacrifice and discipline [and] we must make radical changes to our economic, social and political institutions and accept ideas and developmental attitudes necessary for the process of modernisation.
> **Rajaratnam, S. (1985),** *The Prophetic and the Political: Selected Speeches and Writings of S. Rajaratnam,*[1] p. 247.

Over the last four decades, land-use development and modernisation in Singapore is characteristically a shared outcome of modernism and developmentalism realised in a circumstantial pursuit for economic survival in the post-independence era. Specifically in the city-state, modernity has been deployed as an end whilst developmentalism serves as a means through which state programmes and social objectives require persistent justification in rationalisation and industrialisation (Nederveen Pieterse, 2001: 20–21). Thus, industrialisation through modernisation of the manufacturing industry executed in a rational manner is both a prerequisite and a searched outcome of modernisation.

Johnston and Gregory's (1981: 223) definition of modernisation is much action-driven and holistic. As a targeted force directed to reshape societies, they see modernisation as an agent that "involves social mobilisation, the growth of a more effective and centralised apparatus of political and social control, the acceptance of scientifically rational norms and the transformation of social relations". Progress and development are modernist concepts that have been strongly associated with economic growth, anti-traditional behaviours and social rationality in human history. Ideologically, this approach in the Singapore context may be interpreted as a dual policy of a "middle-class progressive regime" to justify political mandate and commitments, as well as a "regime devoted to lower-class opportunity expansion" characterised by a constant need to improve the general progress of the populace.

Whilst modernisation is more of a conceptual and ideological guide that leads one away from the traditional to modern norms often classified as progress and advancement, developmentalism needs state actions and competence to fulfill modernist targets and ambitions. Developmentalism carries with it a momentum of aspiration, which operates on the basis of rationalisation to fulfill the expectations of modernist faith. Having religious origins in early nineteenth-century Europe, the outfit of developmentalism was freed from church bureaucracy as a result of waves of social revolutions. The shift had empowered the rising capitalist states to consolidate their political power with the development of technology and scientific knowledge. With the expansion of colonialism, developmental spirit diffused and grew over space towards a more secular and material-based pursuit overseas (Nederveen Pieterse, 2001; Mackintosh, 1992).

The ideology of developmentalism and interventionist state was an ingredient in the post-World War Two era that many newly independent states, including Singapore, had adopted as a development path to assume mandate of governance. Preston (1996) above all sees the key role played by the "replacement elites" in post-independent states in their pursuit of an "effective nationstatehood", using the available interventionist Keynesian theories of growth and welfare. Accordingly, in the process of a peaceful transition of power, the new nationstatehood framework was set up through reworking the long-established colonial relationships to install developmentalist ideas. Arguably, the ideas were guided by two imperatives—material progress and efficiency—that characterised and matched the post-war meaning of modernisation, and justified governance when nationalism was indistinct and weak. This was a case in point when national independence was institutionalised extrinsically in Singapore in the early 1960s rather than derived from intrinsic and inherent origins.

In the 1960s, the Singapore city-state initiated an urban-industrial, liberal capitalist and market-led approach to lead the modernist movements. Its role had also been extended as a regulator of labour, foreign exchange, capital markets and multinational corporations' involvement to promote development and bolster growth (Potter *et al.*,

1999: 173; Wong, 1999a). Organised through a set of disciplined governmental institutions and legitimised power and a strong trade link with the developed economies, much progress has been made in the last four decades. Motivated by improved material well-being, and impressed by what an isolated city-state could do, the people have returned their electoral support repeatedly to the ruling party. Undeniably, the main contributing factor has been the international market rather than the state, which is seen as the prime mover in economic development. Linking to this marketplace and achieving high economic growth rates, however, would not have been that effective without the early shaping and foundation laid by international organisations such as the United Nations, World Bank, and the developed world's official development aid programmes and agendas. International agencies' contributions in the early stages of land-use modernisation and planning comprised a forum of guidance and directional change. Singapore, as an aid recipient, responded vigorously and adjusted under local conditions. It is the Singapore state's effectiveness in adopting the modernisation path orientated around the world market mechanism that has been responsible for the continued growth from which political support is gathered. In the process, state-sponsored institutions and functions are made accountable and responsive to public needs and market operations on the basis of economic efficiency. Identifying the specific points of intervention and bridging the gap from the traditional to the modern were other attributes that allowed the state to regulate and moderate constantly the development path towards the superimposed values of an industrial society.

Throughout the modernisation campaign guided by developmentalism and, to a great extent, paternalism, Singapore has gone through a dramatic transformation. In spatial terms, this modernisation of the space economy was expressed by Peter Gould (1970) as a "modernisation surface" over 30 years ago in his analysis of Tanzania's progress to modernity. Indicators of modernity used were the mapping of the spatial distribution of schools, health services, modern roads and railways, telecommunications, office headquarters, etc.

Quite similar to Gould's description of Tanzania's modernisation surface that went through a process of hierarchical diffusion from the initial centres of colonial contact (Gore, 1984), Singapore's Central Area adjacent to the seaport and the estuary of the Singapore River became the take-off point of modernisation following the city-state's independence in the 1960s. Modernisation was translated into action plans by socio-economic forces, notably industrialisation, public housing and infrastructure provisions, through a series of centralised planning efforts. Alongside the radial-patterned diffusion from the Central Area to the rest of the island, the spread and establishment of a modern framework of political, social and economic institutions island-wide during the last four decades have become highly noticeable.

Another area of investigation covered by the book is how the transformation and changing trends are translated or reconstructed in the regulated spatial dimension. As widely acknowledged, land-use planning is instrumental in shaping the intended change and realising the strategic goals by stages and according to demographic, social, economic and environmental needs on par with technological and infrastructure improvements.

As a modernisation tool, Singapore's land-use planning cannot strictly be separated from its colonial British ties and planning traditions. Particularly in the early stages, there was a strongly forged link. For instance, the study by Colin Buchanan (Ministry of Transport, 1963) inevitably had a long-standing impact on Singapore's physical planning. As the chief consultant in studying London's transport system in the early 1960s, Buchanan predicted the rapid increase in the number of private motor vehicles. Recommending redevelopment and giving priority to pedestrians, he criticised automobile dependence and urban sprawl, and the intrusion of freeways through the old city areas (Ward, 2002).

In the early 1960s, slum clearance and redevelopment for public housing development proceeded in parallel in both Britain and Singapore. One has to note that Buchanan's perception of the need for restructuring city roads was well-reflected in new patterns of development. Nonetheless, fate had differed between the old metropolis and the former colony. Whilst slum clearance and redevelopment in Britain were wound down in the 1970s as a result of growing domestic criticism against the destruction of the working-class communities, clearance had continued in Singapore in the city centre to make room for modern commercial and office buildings (*ibid.*: 241–243). In this sense, the city-state has proved that in being equipped with a more centralised and powerful planning system, justified by survival economism and a genuine land scarcity argument, what was believed to be the right course of action by the ruling party could be undertaken. Dale (1999: 98–99) asserts that such a performance was in practice a moral contract set implicitly between the ruling party and the ruled masses. Given that a competent and honest government will be preoccupied with the provision of welfare, jobs, growth and prosperity, it does not need to be committed to a pluralistic democracy. In other words, priorities of individuals ought to be placed below the interests of the social entity that encompasses all members of different ethnic groups. The paternalistic ruling party is supposed to strive towards the common goal of collective security and welfare.

Furthermore, the uniqueness of being a city-state has exempted Singapore from planning considerations of spatial equity in the context of rural-urban disparity. Its development has thus been mainly determined by island-wide plans set by the 1970 Concept Plan, which aimed to transform the island into a world-class city with a strong central business district, and one of the command centres in the Asia-Pacific. Through effective global integration and industrialisation, Singapore has enabled itself to deploy accumulated revenues and surpluses towards land-use transformations. During the early period from the 1960s to the 1970s, urban renewal by means of a massive slum clearance in the downtown zone and its fringes, and new town development in outlying zones supplemented by corresponding services and infrastructure were most symbolic of land-use modernisation. Suburban zones surrounding the Central Area of the 1950s gave way systematically to new housing and urban development projects. Expansion of public housing estates continued into the 1980s and the 1990s. Phase after phase, "traditional" forms of rural and low-value land use gave way to changing patterns of public housing estates, schools, health services and local shops serving newly established nuclear families. By 2000, urbanisation was virtually complete as a modernisation process, leaving rurality behind in history.

In balancing the modernised landscapes, conservation areas representing the three key ethnic groups (Chinatown, Little India and Kampong Glam) stand in sharp contrast side by side. They reconcile modernity with their historic and cultural heritage, seen as being essential to the identity and nation-building of a relatively new nation-state that cannot ideally modernise by neglecting its past.

This book specifically examines the period from 1960 to 2000, a spectacular phase of far-reaching mutations that marked a significant departure from Singapore's colonial past. Chapter 1 deals with the transformation of Singapore's Central Area that saw the replacement of slums by a dynamic business hub. This morphological change is virtually an elimination of dualism in physical structure typical of a colonial port city within the old core-periphery framework. Through the removal of the inherited colonial urban land-use structure and the built form, Singapore has seen a functional transition from a low-ordered service-oriented central place to an increasingly higher-ordered service centre. Since the early 1990s, however, globalisation and the widespread use of the Internet and other advanced telecommunications between Singapore and global cities such as New York, London and Tokyo have called for a constant adaptation to the dynamic capitalist business world. Particularly due to the decentralising and deterritorialising effects of Information and Communications Technology (ICT), the new downtown core of Singapore is also subjected to a new challenge that makes the orientation of change uncertain.

Chapter 2 examines infrastructure as a modernising agent, from the earlier emphasis on physical infrastructure to infostructure (ICT), a new commodity and a key product of the globalisation process. Infrastructure has been widely recognised by post-war developmentalist states as a precondition for economic take-off. It supports and facilitates the government administration, private business operations and daily activities of the general public. In Singapore, it has also served in the last three decades to attract multinational corporations whose leading technology, global marketing networks and competitive products have bolstered the city-state's export-led economy. The shift to infostructure in the 1980s served the medium- to long-term goals to transform Singapore into a regional trade, financial and knowledge-based information hub. Indeed, the ICT plan is a key strategy of advanced global integration aimed at lifting Singapore from a semi-peripheral economy to the heartland of the core-dominating marketplace.

Chapter 3 focuses on Singapore's industrialisation, an engine of growth dependent on multinationals. Dependency is perceived here as a relative term associated with whether the end could justify the means. If the development process has led to a sharp rise in material living standards that warrants a sustained political governance, using multinational corporations equipped with high technology and world-class management skills as a means to lead a dynamic industrialisation drive to achieve that end is conceivably justifiable. The first section of the chapter presents the theoretical framework and the rationale of industrialisation as a basis for economic development, and the role of the state as an initiator and facilitator. After 1965, Singapore's deep-rooted primary resource-based *entrepôt* trade was modified into a manufacturing-based export-led trade, with heavy input from the MNCs. The second section investigates the industrialisation strategy and the circumstances in the shift from the labour-intensive model in the 1960s and 1970s to the knowledge- and skill-intensive model after the mid-1980s.

Chapter 4 investigates housing development. Housing policy is indeed a real test of state determination, persistence and vigour as it involves voters' welfare and basic needs. With effective implementation and promotion of homeownership by the Housing and Development Board, housing has largely been resolved as a basic-need issue. Nonetheless, by nature of its varied quality, housing reflects different levels of comfort to different users and, to many, social status. Consequently, despite continued state efforts to upgrade public housing quality, housing has a social representation that motivates household mobility as an implicit part of the social upgrading process. General affluence and rising numbers of the middle class have increasingly exerted pressure for more private housing distinctively different from public housing. This rising demand has met with response from the state that sees a necessity to facilitate access as a negotiating term for support of the government's economic priority model. The effectiveness of this model relies essentially on material incentives offered by the government that seeks to renovate itself frequently in response to popular demand. Rising aspirations for private housing are, however, hindered by the price spiral and a limited land supply.

Development of recreational spaces is the focus of Chapter 5. Rapid urbanisation and nature conservation are two contrasted issues that have conflicting objectives. Even with limited land space, Singapore has to fulfill its multiple status as a city-state, global city and nation-state. To accommodate economic growth, nature has to give way to the expanding built environment. As an alternative, man-made greenery is increasingly seen as an aesthetic representation of nature and quality of life that can counter the debilitating effects of pollution and a congested and impersonal urban life. The chapter looks at the conceptual relationship between recreation and quality of life as well as the complex triangular relationship of growth, equity and environmental preservation.

ENDNOTES

1. Speech entitled "The Modernisation Revolution—Asia's Unfinished Revolution" delivered on 2 June 1966 at the VIII Congress of the International Union of Socialist Youth in Vienna. S. Rajaratnam was then the Foreign Minister of Singapore.

CHAPTER 1

The Transformation of Singapore's Central Area: From Slums to a Global Business Hub

INTRODUCTION

Urban morphological change, particularly in the city centre, is a historical process (Whitehand, 1983; Carter, 1995) often reflective of political and economic priorities and, more recently, planning directions. These priorities and planning directions are respectively influenced by prevailing ideological thinking and planning concepts available at the time. In open societies, the scope and scale of change, however, are strongly associated with the urgency of the development agendas, subjected to domestic policy and international circumstances.

An ex-colony and a strategic *entrepôt* of Britain in the Far East until its independence in 1965, Singapore has since adopted a developmental approach to boost its export-led production system through intensive trade links with the developed world. It is the developed countries that the city-state has been strongly dependent upon for multinational investments, market exports and, to a substantial extent, transfer of technology and workforce upgrading.

During the colonial period, the Central Area, located adjacent to the seaport in the south of the island, had a typical colonial downtown pattern of a dualistic character. The scenario showed a sharp contrast of a high concentration of the working class living in degenerated housing conditions in coexistence with a small number of modern trading and financial enterprises (McGee, 1967). On the eve of independence in the 1950s, the ruling party, the People's Action Party, had built up its grassroots support through anti-colonial labour movements. Party leadership was predominantly controlled by an English-educated middle-class elite. In the nation-building process, the formation of a grassroots cum middle-class coalition paved the post-independence path towards a strong developmental and modernist approach (Wong, 1999a). Ideologically, this approach may be interpreted as a dual policy of a "middle-class progressive regime" and a "regime devoted to lower-class opportunity expansion" (see Taylor, 1998: 142). The latter devotion would be translated subsequently into an array of action plans, aimed at transforming the habitat of the lower-class workers. In parallel, the middle-class political leadership, conscious of the need to improve the general progress of the populace and justify political mandate and commitments, set off to build a thriving Singapore. Thus, elimination of dualism in physical structure in the Central Area became a priority of the initial agenda of action.

Starting with slum clearance, the process of change has been dramatic in the subsequent three decades. Through the removal of the inherited colonial urban land-use structure and the built form, Singapore has seen a functional transition from a low-ordered service-oriented central place to an increasingly higher-ordered service centre.

Since the early 1990s, globalisation has been further accelerated. Typical of this phenomenon is the increasing centrality of the financial structure and the rise of financial power over production in developed economies. While widespread use of the Internet and other advanced telecommunications by virtual networks between Singapore and global cities such as New York, London and Tokyo has underplayed the importance of a central place, this is countered by an opposing concept that centres are needed to develop the critical mass of knowledgeable people for daily discourse and face-to-face interactions in response to the demand for new market patterns. There is therefore a need for a modern city to constantly adapt itself to the dynamic capitalist business world marked by rapid technological advances and accelerated capital circulation, information and images (Amin and Thrift, 1995; Sassen, 1998). This new challenge has compelled Singapore to seek an enlarged participation in the increasingly competitive global marketplace. Consequently, the new downtown core of Singapore is also subject to new challenges, which have never been encountered before.

This chapter examines Singapore's post-war transformation of its downtown core from a dualistic and "traditional" pattern into a Western-modelled new financial district. The chapter also traces the agents of change during 1945 to 2000. The period 1945 to 1959 is included as this was a crucial transitional period characterised by political unrest and inaction of the colonial government under pressure for the transfer of political power to local elites. The discussion is divided into four phases, each of which is marked by a specific character. Particular attention is focused on planning as an endorsing force in matching the political will to modernise the Central Area. Finally, in the light of the potentially strong decentralising and deterritorialising effects of information and communications technology which is increasingly being used, the feasibility of the current ambitious downtown expansion plan is investigated.

PROCESS AND AGENTS OF CHANGE

As suggested above, political imperatives and convictions about the improvement of material standards of living as a symbol of good governance are often a key driving force towards changing the old for the new. Locational patterns of land use follow logically the economic forces in the spatial organisation, including the most strategic points such as the central area of cities where the potential of economic returns on investment is highest (Berry, Conkling and Ray, 1997). Classical views of Brian Berry, a reputed economic geographer, have provided evidence to support this operational mechanism, using land value as the common denominator and based on transport and telecommunications technology of the immediate post-war era (see also Murphy, Vance and Epstein, 1955; Garner, 1967).

The rise to power in the late 1950s of an elite group of Western-trained Singaporeans, supported by a large number of incoming talents from Malaya, marked the start of the implementation of a modern Singapore. The planning backdrop was, however, designed by a United Nations mission providing technical assistance to newly independent nations against poverty and deprivation (United Nations, 1962b) as part of a Cold War strategy by the United States to counter Soviet expansion. Administered under the United Nations' Economic and Social Council, the mission's key task was to help national governments incorporate low-cost housing, urban and basic community development programmes. In the early 1960s in Asia and the Far East, 40% of the urban population and 50% of the rural population were then found to be inadequately housed, "living in unsanitary and overcrowded conditions...[their] economic, social and physical development need to be developed comprehensively and in an integrated way" (United Nations, 1962b: 11–

12). Among the United Nations experts, a prominent figure who later led a multinational team to examine Singapore's Central Area slums was Charles Abrams.[1] His recommendations were to have strong repercussions in subsequent years in the redevelopment of Singapore's downtown slums (see Abrams, Kobe and Koenigsberger, 1963).

In parallel with the urban renewal introduced by the United Nations, major intervention in the newly independent nation-state was decisive. Two courses of action were taken. The first, classified as market-critical, was aimed at correcting market inefficiencies inherited from the British colonial economy characterised by a large low-productive informal sector highly concentrated in the Central Area. The second was targeted at physical transformation, using planning as a vehicle to address the "derelict" areas or slums marginally but positively attached to the world economy (Taylor, 1998; Goldblum, 1998). These two courses of action went hand in hand with the large-scale industrial development led by multinational corporations (MNC), modernisation of the administrative system and infrastructure provision from the mid-1960s, laying the foundation in uplifting Singapore to become a newly industrialising economy in East Asia in the 1980s.

PHASE 1: PRELUDE TO URBAN RENEWAL, 1945–1959

Since the early nineteenth century, the seaport and the adjacent Singapore River estuary became the lifeline of the *entrepot* economy. It was around here that the Central Area was strategically developed and grew, with masses of immigrants and their descendants serving directly and indirectly the port economy and British military base that once used Singapore as a key bastion in the Far East. Before the outbreak of World War Two, the rural-urban divide between the urbanised Central Area and the outlying rural zones was distinct; the latter were either in the natural state or village sites surrounded by farmlands and cottage industries.

The Central Area was then a congested core filled with "coolies" and petty traders who were interspersed with a small number of white-collar employees working in more dominating government buildings, banks, trading agencies and merchant houses. The most popular and affordable residence for the low-income masses was in the poorly serviced village-like squatter areas, and in the second and third floors of shophouses rented out to families or single persons.[2]

Dilapidated Housing Stock

Little was done to the dilapidated housing stock in the Central Area inherited from World War Two, which had worsened for lack of maintenance and an expansion of the slums. In 1947, out of Singapore's population of 938,000, 700,000 were living in the municipality area of about 8,100 hectares with 38,440 buildings (see Figure 1.1). When the Housing Committee was set up by the colonial government in the immediate post-wartime to investigate housing conditions, it was found that about 300,000 people were "herded into about 1,000 acres [400 hectares] in the heart of the city...and with numbers of large blocks of houses, often back to back, with densities [of] 1,000 or more to the acre.". Overcrowding was logically interpreted by the Housing Committee as responsible for the spread of diseases, notably tuberculosis. Death rates from tuberculosis, about 235 per 100,000, accounted for one-sixth of all deaths in 1947 in Singapore. The 1948 Housing Committee report estimated that about 20,000 families, or 10% of the total population, were living in deplorable conditions (Housing Committee, 1948: 1).

Even as late as 1961, extensive squatter settlements were still in existence; they were characterised by a lack of "sanitation, water or any of the elementary health facilities. [Many people] lived in huts made of *attap*,[3] old wooden boxes, rusty corrugated iron sheets and other such salvage material" (HDB, 1963: 2–3). One reason for the continuation of this deplorable state of housing was the Rent Control Act of 1947, which, for goodwill, aimed at protecting tenants from exorbitant landlords and securing social stability, but had also discouraged landlords from improving their properties.[4] Population densities in certain quarters were so high that overcrowding threatened the health of the residents. In the two- to three-storey shophouses of residential blocks, population densities reached between 1,220 and 1,700 people per hectare (URA, 1989: 10–11).

Such overcrowding was a consequence of subletting by tenants or landlords who partitioned living space into cubicles for rent to low-income households. To save living expenses, a whole family might then be living in a cubicle smaller than 10 square metres. Space for laundry, cooking and dishwashing was shared outside the cubicles. Hawking, petty trading and selling labour as a "coolie" were the main livelihoods and apparently the only outlets for many who had little skill and savings. High-density living was hence a physical absorption of the masses into a low value-added and lower-circuit urban economy, a situation well-illustrated by Brenda Yeoh (1996: 137) in her accounts of the pre-independence downtown Singapore. The incessant pressure of a rapidly rising population on a dwindling supply of space also revealed the need of the people to live within reach of their workplace. This necessity grew even more acute following each wave of immigrants who tried to fit in the predominantly informal sectors of an unchanged port-dependent economic base.

Under colonial rule, housing for the public was basically a "private affair". The Singapore Improvement Trust (SIT), which was formed in 1927, had a limited role focused on the control of land subdivision, land and building use, and sanitary improvement. It had no statutory powers of a general housing authority, but concentrated on such tasks as reclaiming swampland to eliminate mosquito breeding. Among the limited numbers of public residential blocks it built, there was a provision of backlanes to give rear access to buildings for the installation of modern sanitary facilities and garbage clearance and other maintenance purposes (Singapore Improvement Trust, 1958).

In its 32 years of existence, SIT built less than 30,000 units of low-cost public housing, the most notable of which were the modern low-rise houses developed in the Tiong Bahru Estate in the late 1930s. Though SIT failed to impress in quantitative terms, it contributed the notion of design principles and the offer of minimum standards of hygiene and comfort. These were to be followed as a norm by its succeeding authority when the HDB initiated a mass-production mechanism to construct quickly and cheaply affordable housing units in the 1960s.

Master Plan Preparation

Though little attention was given to public housing, the 1950s saw a preparatory effort for a major planned development by the use of a master plan. While it is argued that colonial administrators might not be visionary with regard to looking after the long-term interests of colonies, they nonetheless followed courses of action initiated and exercised back home. Physical land-use planning was a typical example in Singapore.

With the start of the Cold War and the coming into power of the Labour government in Britain in the late 1940s, the welfare of colonies received slightly greater attention. For practising planners, colonised territories abroad were the testing grounds for new planning concepts from home (see Bristow, 2000: 139). Overcrowding in Singapore's downtown area characterised by high population density, dense spatial organisation of building blocks, and a general lack of open space, privacy and proper ventilation had become increasingly unacceptable for living (Yeoh, 1996; Choe, 1969). This situation was no doubt seen by the colonial government as a human plight that needed improvement. Spatial reorganisation would mean use of the planning instrument in readjusting the spatial state of affairs. An island-wide Master Plan was conceived as necessary for more systematic growth and development. Under such circumstances and devoid of a planning authority, the low-profile and capacity-deficient SIT was required under the Singapore Improvement Ordinance in January 1952 to form a Preliminary Island Plan team to conduct a diagnostic survey for the first master plan to guide future development.

For the Central Area, a detailed survey was carried out to record the structural conditions of buildings and their materials, existing land use and population density. The objective was primarily to identify areas (570 hectares) most needed for redevelopment, involving 142,000 residents or 45% of the population in the Central Area.

Outside the Central Area, self-contained communities were planned in the suburbs,[5] supplemented by shopping areas, schools and recreational spaces. Conceptually, in keeping much of the island as rural areas, the Preliminary Island Plan had retained the classical pre-war core-periphery relationship where industry was not to become a major employer of the workforce in the colonies. It may be also argued that the team found little evidence that large-scale capital formation and technical and management training of the local workforce were available in Singapore to cope with growth from massive industrialisation. Consequently, the Diagnostic Survey team drafted a plan which emphasised self-support in terms of food supply to "its fullest extent", so as to cut down food imports and as a means to absorb surplus labour, as shown in Figure 1.2 (Colony of Singapore, 1952: 32–36).

The Preliminary Island Plan was drafted by a group of colonial officers whose role was not to produce a blueprint for an emerging nation-state, but to test the feasibility of a large-scale plan as a prototype in anticipation of more efficient management thereafter. The Preliminary Island Plan, submitted as a draft plan in 1955, rejected tall buildings due to cost considerations and their liability to generate traffic congestion. This view was discarded in 1958 when the Master Plan was formally adopted as a guiding plan for land-use development (see Figure1.3). The Plan had, however, reinforced the zoning concept introduced in the 1920s (Yeoh, 1996), in anticipation of traffic congestion in the Central Area.

PHASE 2: EARLY STAGE OF URBAN RENEWAL, 1960–1970

This phase marked the beginning of the Singapore government's highly interventionist self-governing approach in 1959, which replaced the *laissez-faire* attitude of the colonial government (Teo and Savage, 1991: 327). Following this, the Housing and Development Board was created in 1960 to replace the SIT and to assume the state's role as the main public housing developer. With a tight schedule, the HDB's option for a comprehensive redevelopment was the follow-up of the key recommendation of the 1958 Master Plan. This was perceived administratively by the public authority as an effective means of regenerating housing stock, equipped with updated, easy-to-manage facilities and infrastructure,[6] while private interests were encouraged in other commercial undertakings. It was in 1967 that the Urban Renewal Department of the HDB first introduced the programme for the sale of sites to allow private investments through the public tender system.

In need of medium- to long-term planning strategies, a Planning Department was set up under the direct jurisdiction of the Prime Minister's Office in February 1960 to oversee island-wide planning matters.[7] Replacing the Singapore Improvement Ordinance of the colonial government, the Planning Department took over all planning roles previously assumed by the Singapore Improvement Trust (MND, 1963). The HDB's first task was to initiate a series of renewal and resettlement programmes beginning with the Central Area, with the strong support of the United Nations team led by Abrams, Kobe and Koenigsberger (1963), who visited Singapore in 1963 and recommended a comprehensive urban renewal programme.

Urban Renewal in Concept and Action

Urban renewal was seen as a post-war modernist idea and one of the mainstream urban planning concepts of progressive change (Oc and

Tiesdell, 1997). Moreover, it was a social housing reform for the urban poor, involving a drastic transformation of the built form. The post-war clearance of residential slums was partly argued on the grounds of their structural degeneration, vulnerability to fire and health hazards and other negative externalities such as environmental pollution. More importantly, it arose from their functional obsolescence, and their weaknesses in responding to the challenges of a modern city epitomised in the revaluation of prime lands with profit maximisation being the yardstick of city performance (Sim, 1982; Smith *et al.*, 1991).

In efficiency and modernist terms, comprehensive redevelopment was a preferred action to cut down delay of deliverables rather than rehabilitation measures. Correspondingly, more modern and higher-density, higher rent-paying buildings matching the rising land values justified the replacement of lower-density shophouses and slums. The pre-war two- to three-storey shophouses and low-value shelters were thus seen as an obstacle to progress and economic efficiency in the government's attempts to exploit functionally and rationally the new opportunities that a modern city could offer (Oc and Tiesdell, 1997: 6; Jensen-Butler and van Weesep, 1997).

Hence, slum clearance became a direct response to accommodate the new user demand with a more functional built form. The user demand was a representation of international and regional central area market values in which the agents of spatial change included Singapore's profit-oriented government-linked companies, local private developers and international investors. The redevelopment of the Central Area in the 1960s was accompanied by a two-pronged strategy in line with the newly set up Economic Development Board's industrialisation objectives. First, dispersal was a force of change symbolising opportunities for better quality of housing and improved provision of basic social services to the populace. Second, there was a need to decentralise the overcrowded population in the city centre to newly planned industrial estates in both Jurong and other smaller light industrial estates adjoining the outlying new towns. The renewal was perceived not as an action in isolation but as having "an island-wide scale...and be integrated with housing, trade, and industrial development programmes" (URA, 1989: 13).

In the Central Area itself, attention was focused on transforming the largely low-skilled, labour-intensive sectors through intensification of commercial and business activities (Dale, 1999; Yeoh, 1996). The process was expedited following the adoption of an export-oriented strategy when Singapore became an independent city-state in 1965 after losing Malaysia as a potential hinterland for manufactured exports. Slum clearance became strongly justifiable under the circumstance of economic survival dependent on trade and multinational investments to create jobs badly needed to fight double-digit unemployment rates of the time (Lee, 2000). For Alan Choe (1969: 161), a practising planner, urban renewal conveyed a very practical meaning such as arresting blight, clearing slums, revitalising the city centre, and improving the city's environment, services, amenities, circulation and its car-parking facilities. Other prospects in perspective comprised greater employment opportunities and a larger scope for private participation in businesses, thus increasing the tax base of the city as a whole.

Under the HDB, clearance was executed by its Lands Department, assisted by its Building and Resettlement Departments. The first HDB Five-Year Plan (1960–1965) estimated that one-quarter million inhabitants in Chinatown, part of the Central Area, would require immediate rehousing. Another one-quarter million in degenerated housing areas from Telok Blangah in the west to Geylang Serai in the east would be gradually rehoused. A further one-quarter million living at the fringes of the Central Area would be resettled in a number of phases (Teo and Savage, 1991).

Only a small proportion of the households would be resettled in the HDB estates within the Central Area; the "surplus population" would be shifted to outlying areas in self-sufficient new towns. Small industries, almost all family-based, were offered resettlement sites when they had to be cleared for redevelopment. New industrial sites in Redhill and Tanglin Halt Industrial Estate, Alexandra Industrial Estate, at Leng Kee Road, Bendemeer Road, Kampong Empat and Kallang Reclamation site, Tanjong Rhu and Toa Payoh were used to resettle affected small industries (HDB, 1963: 26–27).

Land acquisition, a facilitator and catalyst in urban change, began with the setting up of the Urban Renewal Unit in 1964 as part of the HDB, the year when renewal commenced with the actual demolition of slums. This Unit was upgraded in 1966 to become the more powerful Urban Renewal Department (URD) in the acquisition of private lands following the amendment of the colonial government's Land Acquisition Act that year. The URD undertook two pilot projects on state lands at the peripheral precincts of the Central Area, known as North 1 and

South 1, to resettle families affected by clearance in the heart of the Central Area.

Urban Renewal: Ending the Effect of the 1947 Rent Control Act

As stated earlier, the Act was introduced by the colonial government in the immediate post-war era to protect tenants at a time of severe housing shortage. Thus, the urban renewal in the Central Area would be ineffective unless landlords were motivated to redevelop their land parcels and subsequently maintain the premises. Further to the 1961 amendment of the Act, the Singapore government adopted a new Control Premises (Special Provision) Act in 1969. The new Act allowed landlords to terminate tenancy and repossess their property in areas gazetted by the Ministry of National Development. In return for the incentive given, however, landlords had to submit plans for areas gazetted for redevelopment for approval. The rental decontrol provided incentives to business interests in the Central Area, and was a prelude to a new phase of development forwarded by a more ambitious Concept Plan prepared with the assistance of another United Nations team (MND, 1970).

From the 1958 Master Plan to the 1971 Concept Plan

The 1958 Master Plan prepared by the colonial government was largely rejected by both the United Nations teams[8] and the Singapore government. The first team found the 1958 plan "conceptually too conservative because of its passive acceptance of the extent of conditions of the early 1950s" (URA, 1989: 12). The 1963 team found the 1958 plan wanting, partly because of its Euro-centric assumptions, which comprised "a slow and steady rate of social and economic change; the passive role of government in the economy as providing welfare relief to the distressed; and a conservative disposition which considered the preservation of the achievements and institutions of the past as a main objective of all planning" (URA, 1989: 13). What was required was:

> ...the need for the public authorities to take the initiative: Instead of using the Master Plan essentially as a development control

mechanism, the planning authority should adopt a "positive policy of guiding, encouraging and giving aid to private redevelopment within the framework of comprehensive renewal schemes".
(The Lorange Report, p. 26, cited in URA, 1989: 12)

Concurring with the recommendations of the United Nations team, the Singapore government wanted to pursue a drastic transformation of the city-state rather than conserve much of the colonial past. The UN consultants, Abrams, Kobe and Koenigsberger (1963: 57–58), criticised the 1958 plan as being out of date and inappropriate for a modern metropolis with a rapid growth of cars. Both parties agreed that a series of action plans were needed to expedite the city-state's industrialisation programme which would require strong support by the financing system. An efficiently run financial business district was seen as being crucial for attracting foreign capital and mobilising local savings. This financial district must be ideally built on the basis of the existing infrastructure in the Central Area around Shenton Way, Raffles Place and Cecil Street.

The UN team had confidence that Singapore, given its dynamics, would grow economically and demographically. Too rapid a population growth was, however, their worry as a high dependency ratio would cancel off available resources needed to support economic growth (Abrams, Kobe and Koenigsberger, 1963). Singapore's separation from Malaysia in 1965 proved a "blessing in disguise" in terms of urban planning in later years (Chua, 1996: 208). It made slum clearance later an easier task because rural-urban migration, a common phenomenon in Third World primate cities, made control of the expansion of slums almost impossible. Singapore avoided this by introducing restrictive measures to minimise inflow of unskilled labourers from its neighbours—demand was constantly regulated on the basis of economic performance whilst its own rural areas were being urbanised rapidly.

In September 1967, the Singapore government signed a Plan of Operation with the United Nations to prepare a comprehensive long-range island-wide Concept Plan. Under this State and City Planning Project, a UN team was sent to work with local counterparts seconded from the Planning Department, Public Works Department and the HDB. In 1969, the State and City Planning Project produced a Ring Concept Plan functionally linking the whole island by a dense network of communication lines between new towns, as well as other active sectors such as the Jurong Industrial Site in the west (Figure 1.4). A Sub-Project was formed in May 1970 to study detail planning of the Central Area as an extension of the island-wide planning work. This Central Area Sub-Project was, however, attached to the Urban Renewal Department of the HDB. The Central Area Concept Plan, also known as the Structural Concept Plan, constituted a specially designed topic within the overall Concept Plan study. It focused on the distribution of different activities such as communication, institutional processes, commerce and banking which were planned as central activities (MND, 1970: 19–27). The Concept Plan, adopted by the government in April 1971, was to produce longstanding impacts on land-use development in Singapore.

PHASE 3: CONCEPT PLAN IMPLEMENTATION— URBAN REDEVELOPMENT, 1971–1990

The approval of the Concept Plan in 1971 provided a legal blueprint, paving the way for a progressively planned redevelopment of the Central Area. The state's role shifted from a strongly regulatory one to that of a law enforcement agency, and occasionally arbitrator, in the pursuit of a world-class Central Business District (CBD). The Urban Renewal Department's renewal activities grew over the subsequent years to cover the development and management of commercial properties in the Central Area. In 1974, the URD was detached from the HDB to become the Urban Redevelopment Authority, an autonomous statutory board under the Ministry of National Development. By the mid-1970s, following large-scale resettlement and the erection of public housing and higher-income private residential blocks as well as retail and office premises, the Central Area's population had declined correspondingly in line with the decentralisation process. In 1980, the Central Area saw its population dropping to 155,800 or 6.5% of the national population, with close to two-thirds living in public housing (Dale, 1999: 232). Concomitant with this, the incorporation of higher value-added business-related activities saw at the same time a resettlement of industries and warehousing from the Central Area to the Jurong industrial zone and other light industrial estates adjacent to HDB new towns.

Higher environmental standards such as the greenery concept were infused in the resettlement process. Sizeable tracts of open space were incorporated in the Central Area as a softener and harmoniser in the midst of tall concrete blocks of residential or office areas[9] (URA,

1976/77: 32). The most drastic changes occurred in the Golden Shoe area where the financial and banking sector was concentrated (see Figure 1.5). A new Act, the 1969 Control Premises (Special Provision) Act that replaced the 1947 Control of Rent Premises Act, had given private landowners incentives to redevelop their lands. The results were positive. In 1979, the Golden Shoe area was further redeveloped in anticipation of rising demand for office space. Developments took place at Raffles Place, Cecil Street, Robinson Road and Shenton Way. Landmark buildings in these areas such as the DBS Building (1975), OCBC Building (1976), Chartered Banking Building (1984), Overseas Union Bank Centre (1988), Treasury Building (1986), Monetary Authority of Singapore Building (1985), Raffles City (1984) and Marina Centre (1984), etc. were erected. During this time, the Orchard Road Corridor was transformed into the main tourist and shopping district. Aesthetic and architectural norms were applied as a means of redevelopment control to ensure a "systematic approach to beautify the urban environment and promote a more gracious life style" (URA, 1982/83).

The early 1980s also saw land reclamation completed at the Marina Centre and Marina South. At the end of 1983, 17 hectares of land at the Marina Centre was sold by the URA through its Sale of Sites Programme to build a large hotel, shopping complexes and convention facilities. By 1984, the Central Area had transformed itself into an area that was completely different from that in the 1960s. In the words of the URA chairman, Kor Cher Siang, the Central Area had become a place where Singaporeans (URA, 1983/84: 2):

> ...eat in clean and hygienic cooked food centres, shop in modern complexes, relax in landscaped gardens and walk along tree-lined pedestrian malls segregated from heavy vehicular traffic. They go to work in modern, well-designed office buildings and park their cars in multi-storey stations in Central Area. A decade ago, all these developments were almost non-existent.

Concept Plan Implementation

In 1982, the Planning Department completed a comprehensive Land and Building Use Survey covering the whole island. The survey showed that substantial change had occurred in the island-wide land-use distribution as a result of rapid industrialisation over the period 1967–1982, as indicated in Table 1.1. The table shows that sustained economic development and expansion of the HDB new towns had required more road construction and other related facilities which used up a substantial amount of land, including areas previously used for agriculture and as natural habitats. There was, however, a low 16% of additional land-take for housing and this was attributed to the construction of high-rise HDB apartments, despite a large relocation of population from the Central Area and a population growth of more than one-quarter. By 1990, decentralisation in the Central Area itself had further reduced its population to only 100,000 (Dale, 1999: 233).

TABLE 1.1: LAND-USE CHANGE IN SINGAPORE, 1967–1982

Main Land-Use Categories	1967 Land Area (ha)	1982 Land Area (ha)	Change in Percentage
Residential	7,485	8,715	+ 16.5
Industrial	730	3,345	+ 359.4
Transportation	2,655	7,455	+ 180.8
Swamp/Water /Wooded Area	8,350	5,930	- 29.0
Agricultural	14,280	8,100	- 43.3
Vacant incl. under Clearance	9,385	9,320	- 0.7

Source: MND (1983), p. 4.
Note: Figures are rounded to the nearest 5.

The survey also completed a Permissible Plot Ratio[10] study for the Central Area which prepared a basis for further intensification of building land-use. In sites less restricted by technical height clearance, a higher plot ratio was allowed. Buffer zone guidelines were introduced for the Central Area in early 1983. The sea adjacent to the Central Area was substantially reclaimed during this phase, including Marina East and Marina South, as extended land parcels of the Central Area for future expansion.

A key feature that had resulted from renewal and decentralisation during the period 1971–1990 was employment and office-space change.

By proportion, the decline in the share of employment in the Central Area in relation to the whole island was more significant than that of office space, as reflected in Tables 1.2 and 1.3. The success of the transformed CBD in attracting international and local investors had maintained a high percentage share in banking and financial services in the Central Area. In transport, storage and communications, the share dropped drastically from 75% in 1974 to 41% in 1989 following the completion of Changi Airport in the eastern end in the early 1980s and the expansion of Jurong Port in the western sector. Table 1.3 shows that the office space used by private enterprises was highly concentrated in the Central Area; this explains why it was imperative in the revised 1991 Concept Plan that there was a decentralisation of services to regional centres.

Alongside the destructive urban renewal, there were three accompanying elements that could justify the selective retaining of existing structures worthy of preservation, namely conservation, rehabilitation and rebuilding (Choe, 1969: 164–166). Hence, amidst the dynamics of new developments, a small proportion of traditional buildings, notably shophouses, were conserved as an integral component of the Concept Plan using the adaptive reuse approach.

TABLE 1.2: EMPLOYMENT DISTRIBUTION TRENDS OF THE CENTRAL AREA BY SECTOR, 1974–1989

Sector	1974		1980		1989	
	Number	Share (%)	Number	Share (%)	Number	Share (%)
Financial & Business Services	40,150	76	67,850	77	106,910	67
Transport, Storage & Communications	48,350	75	36,410	41	39,610	41
Community, Social & Personal Services	17,860	34	16,100	24	20,430	20
Commercial [a]	72,090	55	92,170	46	97,660	37
Share of Total Singapore Employment	178,450	22	212,530	20	264,610	18

Source: Adjusted from Dale (1999), Table 5.1, p. 166.
Note: [a] Wholesale, retail, restaurants and hotels

TABLE 1.3: THE CENTRAL AREA'S SHARE OF OFFICE SPACE IN SINGAPORE, 1979–1992

Sector	1979		1982		1986 [a]		1992	
	Floor Space (1000 m^2)	Share (%)	Floor Space (1000 m^2)	Share (%)	Floor Space (1000 m^2)	Share (%)	Floor Space (1000 m^2)	Share (%)
Private Sector	1,032.7	90.8	1,272.9	90.4	1,762.4	76.6	2,371.0	90.5
Public Sector	327.0	92.3	353.3	96.3	457.9	81.1	328.0	94.1
Both Sectors	1,359.7	91.0	1,626.2	91.6	2,220.3	77.5	2,699.0	90.5

Source: Adjusted from Dale (1999), Table 5.4, p. 169.
Note: [a] Affected by the recession during the period 1984–1986, when office construction declined significantly in the Central Area.

Conservation

Though recognised as an indispensable element in the Concept Plan of 1971, conservation measures only became effective after the early 1980s, statutorily institutionalised in 1989 with a Conservation Master Plan for action (URA, 1993.). Extensive redevelopment undertaken over the last three decades has raised the material quality of life but certain features of the "good old days" have been permanently lost in the Central Area, such as the thriving and dynamic open-air nightlife of the 1950s and 1960s.

Loss has been compensated by other gains such as cleaner streets and drains and more hygienic living and recreational space. But what has been lost, such as the local street culture, old established communities and traditional life-styles, is not recoverable (Dale, 1999; *Straits Times*, 26 November 1998). The current conservation of a limited number of pre-war buildings constitutes a social compromise to make up for the loss of a cultural and distinctive Asian identity and character as a result of large-scale renewal and a fast-changing landscape in the downtown area. With great effort being made towards revenue generation, and the fact that buildings to be preserved should qualify as architectural monuments of importance, the result was that fewer structures were evaluated as being worthy of preservation. Practically, rehabilitation had been undertaken as most of the properties were privately owned and the government had held a position that maintenance or rehabilitation was at the owners' expense. Nonetheless, rehabilitation was merely a transitional measure if buildings were earmarked for renewal and would sooner or later be demolished (Dale, 1999: 125).

Learning from this experience, conservation has now been perceived as an integral component of urban planning in providing "a sense of history, a memory of place, an identity and a soul to the city" (URA, 1993b: 6). Greater effort, however, is needed to make the new and the old compatible in the physical landscape, while minimising opportunity costs in the prime Central Area. Hitherto led by an economic priority model, conservation of historic sites is planned as a potential growth sector. These sites or monuments are retained not for their cultural or historic assets but primarily as tourist attractions. Accordingly, as expressed by Dale (1999: 246), conservation areas have been transformed into a built form of consumption, in support of the business demands of the tourism industry.

The conservation of entire historic districts such as the ethnic enclaves of Chinatown, Little India and Kampung Glam, and the Emerald Hill areas, Singapore River and the Heritage Links in 1989, which cover 4% of the size of the Central Area or 260 hectares in total, are symbolic of such efforts. Action plans have been incorporated in the Central Area Development Guide Plan (DGP)[11] to search for and restore the traditional traits in potential sites. Conserved structures are predominantly traditional two- or three-storey shophouses and selected institutional buildings with unique architecture for enriching local historical and cultural heritage (URA, 1991a; MND, 1989; Keung, 1998; Boey, 1998). Conservation guidelines were revised in 1996 to give owners more leeway and flexibility in readapting old buildings to new uses, and innovative restoration was encouraged to help create more localised characters in conserved sites.

Towards the end of the 1980s, the 1971 Concept Plan was due for revision. Drastic revision was anticipated and much needed as the Singapore economy was recovering comfortably from the 1985–1986 recession and was prepared for a new phase of industrial restructuring towards the knowledge economy and attaining the status of a developed nation (see Economic Planning Committee, 1991).

Concept Plan Revision

Following the Master Plan update in 1985, the Ministry of National Development in 1987 moved on to revise the island-wide Concept Plan in a substantive and comprehensive manner. Much attention was focused on the Central Area where commercial developments consisting of offices, shops and hotels were highly concentrated and growing steadily since 1970 following large-scale land acquisition, slum or squatter clearance and land reclamation.[12]

Rapid changes in the redistribution of the population, and economic and technological development such as the provision of a public transit system (MRT) and highways island-wide have called for changes in planning concepts and strategies in the provision of commercial and office space, and their locations. For example, appropriate facilities have to be provided at a shorter distance to consumers who live in the new towns. In the hierarchy of services, it was conceived that the Central Area should overwhelmingly maintain its position at the top of the hierarchy. Decentralisation of services to the outside of the Central Area would be concentrated at the designated regional, sub-regional and fringe centres and other MRT station sites (Commerce Sub-Committee, 1988). Where state-owned vacant sites were available, their release for private commercial development would follow the conceived strategies, and market demand.

In September 1989, the URA merged with the MND's Planning Department and Research and Statistics Unit to become the new Urban Redevelopment Authority, a statutory board and the national planning and conservation authority. The new authority assumed in a more effective way the comprehensive and integrated planning responsibilities for the whole island. Its role was to enhance Singapore's image as a world city and, in particular, revise the 1971 Concept Plan comprehensively with the following objectives (MND, 1989: 14–15):

a) Increase the island's land stock through reclamation;
b) Provide a greater variety of housing to meet greater expectations of the population;
c) Decentralise commercial activities to regional centres;
d) Provide more housing, especially quality housing in the Central Area;
e) Provide more amenities and schools in residential areas; and

f) Upgrade parks, green space and waterfront bodies to enhance the quality of recreational areas.

The Concept Plan revision, being strategic and conceptual in character, was accompanied by Development Guide Plans as a local planning tool which provides details on large-scale plans to guide urban development. Each of the 55 DGPs defined for the island will have clear indications as to its land use and intensity controls according to the principles laid down in the Concept Plan, such as an optimal mix of land uses, a balanced variety of housing, communal and recreational facilities, an efficient transport network at the local level and commercial activities in a hierarchical order based on the national decentralisation policy (Prasad, 1998: 17).

In 1991, the revised Concept Plan was approved by the Singapore Cabinet. Since then, this advanced stage of urban development has been infused with environmental and economic sustainability ideas in an attempt to make the CBD one of Asia's dynamic and key financial hubs as well as an attractive place for quality living.

PHASE 4: POST-REVISED CONCEPT PLAN, AFTER 1991

By the 1990s, Singapore as a city was ranked fourth in terms of the size of the foreign exchange market after London, New York and Tokyo, and was one of the key international financial centres handling over US$500 billion annually (Lee, 2000: 19). However, rising operating costs, land limitations and the need to build its own multinational corporations in order to enhance corporate competition in the international marketplace have all exerted pressure on Singapore to move towards a new stage of development. This is characterised by a regionalisation drive to export investment capital and management expertise to selected countries in Asia (Economic Planning Committee, 1991). Back home, a greater emphasis has been placed on strengthening Singapore's position as a regional, if not global, financial hub for international business and corporate headquarters in preparation for the knowledge economy (URA, 1976/77; 2001; Wong, 2001).

A high-quality and gracious living environment is needed to support the new globalisation challenge where attracting internationally sought-after talent and capital will be a crucial factor for sustained success. In line with this pursuit, the Urban Redevelopment Authority is committed to ensure an adequate supply of commercial space in the key business areas, especially the new downtown core (Tan, 1999: 145).

The New Downtown Core

For an island city-state of only 682 square kilometres in 2001, the geographic dispersal of its CBD activities will be restricted to the outlying new towns. Further spill-over to neighbouring Malaysia and Indonesia is less probable, given Singapore's current strong linkages with the developed West and the nature of its export-led development strategy which is reliant on the whole world as its marketplace rather than its neighbouring countries.

The new downtown core will comprise the existing Golden Shoe and the new reclaimed land of Marina South covering an additional area of 360 hectares. In the revised Concept Plan, the development of Marina South has been planned in three stages, Years 2000, 2010, and Year X,[13] with a greater land area being put to productive use at each stage (Figure 1.6). The three key objectives are to: (a) meet future needs for commercial space; (b) create a vibrant hub for entertainment and cultural activities, functionally linked with the existing CBD; and (c) accommodate a sizeable number of quality apartment blocks in support of a lively and dynamic nightlife. In design, the commercial cum residential environment will be accessible by mass transit integrated with a more pedestrian-friendly atmosphere, ample open space and a thin green belt along the coastline (URA, 1992b: 7–8; 1996/97: 15).

By Year X, when Singapore's resident population reaches four million,[14] the new downtown core (Golden Shoe plus Marina South) will supply a total commercial floor area of 6.1 million square metres, up from the present 2.1 million square metres. Of the 6.1 million square metres, 2.8 million square metres will come from Marina South where 26,000 quality apartment units will also be built. In the words of the ambitious URA, ambitious statement, the new downtown core will be "a truly integrated working, living and recreational area with an efficient transportation network and all-weather pedestrian linkages" (URA, 1996b). This ambitious plan has called for a re-examination of whether there will be a need for a high concentration of commercial activities in the twenty-first century, at an age of accelerated use of information and telecommunications technology.

Singapore's New CBD in Search of a Global City

With globalisation and widespread use of information technology being intensified, Singapore as a potential global city in general and a business core in particular is expected to experience greater competition at two levels. The first is the international or inter-city level, where it has to compete with other key centres in the Asia-Pacific such as Hong Kong, Taipei, Shanghai, Beijing and Sydney as a financial hub. Global competition between cities today is largely based on market dominance in the form of financial transactions, commodity exchanges and highly specialised services (Jensen-Butler and van Weesep, 1997).

The second level of competition is the intra-city competition between Singapore's Central Area and its self-contained outlying new towns. The issue is whether the Central Area can maintain its lead in the future against decentralising and deterritorialising forces attributable to the increasing use of ICT in the global city network which tends to drain its resources in favour of the outlying sub-centres. In the last three decades, higher-level retail services such as large department stores, which used to be concentrated in the Raffles Place/High Street area from the 1840s, have since moved out of the Central Area towards the Orchard Road tourist zone and into the new regional and sub-regional centres at Jurong, Bishan, Pasir Ris, Woodlands and Tampines, each of which has a shopping mall to serve the decentralised population centres.

There have been recent attempts to revitalise the quiet after-office environment in the Shenton Way/Raffles Place area of the CBD. For instance, the growing vibrancy brought about by the expansion of the arts/culture scene and the planned quality housing zones in Marina South are reflective of gentrification efforts to make the city centre more lively at night (see URA, 2001). There is no certainty as to how Singapore's city core will actually grow in the future, even though the CBD has been structurally planned in the long term. It is generally believed that, on the basis of time-space convergence, major advancements in transport infrastructure and ICT in business, institutional and household contacts will favour greater dispersal and working from home (see Wong, 1996; Short and Kim, 1999).

Despite the dispersal of economic activities, increasing global integration has favoured world cities of great dominance. Cities equipped with efficient conventional infrastructure would still enjoy a rightful competitive edge. According to Sassen (1998: 134), these cities would "function as command points in the organization of the world economy; as key locations and marketplace for the leading industries...and as sites for the production of innovations in those industries". Logically, the centrality index of individual cities corresponds with the effectiveness of the agglomeration of their economies as well as the dynamics of specialised functions in the latest financial and corporate services. Sassen (1998; 1999) further asserts that the more globalised the economy becomes, the greater the agglomeration effects that the central positions would produce in global cities.

This new form of centralisation of top-level management and activities would act as a new central place conducting globally integrated operations. The centrality of a globally influential Central Area will be underlain by a spatial dimension characterised by a strong embeddedness of information flow and a highly interactive hub of business and non-business activities. This implies that most of these high-level activities would occur in the CBD, whose role is likely to continue to be important.

In summary, the CBD is likely to remain as a key nodal point for face-to-face business interactions, particularly for decision-making, energy conservation and as a lively core area if the young middle class is attracted to live there. Indeed, four decades of rapid urban transformation have not changed the central-place functions of Singapore's Central Area, despite its reconfigurations over time and in size (Figure 1.7). The most significant change was the planned expansion into Marina South and Marina East in a series of land reclamations during the late 1960s and 1970s. But the form of centrality enjoyed by the conventional CBD is likely to be reshaped by the impact of digital highways linking major cities as nodal points. These points will be well-connected in the form of cross-national urban systems in the realm of a wired regional or global village (see EDB, 1998; Economic Planning Committee, 1991). Their intensity of linkage will correspond with the extent of interdependency in global trade or other selected exchanges (Brunn, 1992; Knox, 1994). Each urban system is expected to remain hierarchical, and individual cities' positions in the system will be dictated by their organisation, financial power, ability to provide very specialised goods and services, and attractiveness to key multinational corporations for establishing headquarters, and to international organisations for convening conferences, exhibitions, etc.

Finally, quite unique to Singapore, the city-state is a territorialised institution, offering many operational possibilities in specialised services, as the headquarters for a large number of MNCs and as a wired centre in the Asia-Pacific. It has been able to accumulate and make functionable the latest management skills and applied ICT technology to serve the global economy and to serve as an effective command point (see Todd, 1995). Accordingly, John Friedmann (1995) qualified Singapore was already a "control centre" in Southeast Asia in the mid-1990s, a second-level world city characterised by multinational articulations equivalent to Frankfurt in Germany.

Singapore's CBD stands out visibly as a centre of economic power from which it operates and asserts its influence on the neighbouring regions. As a global city in transition, the city-state must demonstrate its ability to attract and control multinational corporations, acting as deterritorialising institutions and knowing no borders, in a defined and specified territory. Failing to do this means that the global-city status will be at stake. Again, the features of an advanced knowledge-based economy reliant on intensified ICT applications are deterritorialised in nature. Its operations are less restricted by national borders and it functions best on the basis of connectivity and trade interest, and is not hindered by physical distance.

CONCLUDING REMARKS

Physical development in the Central Area of Singapore over the last four decades has been demonstrated by the radical transformation of a financial heartland, operated through the modernisation efforts of a newly independent city-state. From a dualistic and congested downtown core filled with dilapidated housing inherited from the colonial administration, the Central Area has transformed itself into an efficient modern financial district comparable to that in any global city.

Two forces have been responsible for making such a transformation in both physical and mental states possible. The internal factor is attributable to the replacement elites who were committed to an effective governance that has brought about generally improved material living standards. Their pro-business and pro-capitalist operations had been met with a positive response from influential MNCs sited in the renewed

CBD which employed Singapore as a regional command centre. At the expense of cultural heritage and traditional life-styles, the transformation has been a process of social change underlain by a strong political will and a consistent application of land-use planning and implementation. The evolution has also been a process of diffusion of Western urban planning ideas introduced by the United Nations experts with the support of their local counterparts' commitment and hard work. The change has been guided by a series of plans, the most significant of which was the 1971 Concept Plan. Sustained economic growth in the 1970s and the 1980s generated new aspirations for better material comfort (more cars, better and larger housing units and improved quality of life, etc.), and this called for a comprehensive revision of the Concept Plan in the late 1980s. The 1991 and 2001 revised Concept Plans have linked the enhancement of quality of life directly with economic growth, associated increasingly with the globalising marketplace into which Singapore has been strongly integrated.

Globalisation and intensified use of information and communications technology, however, have created a demand for new CBD patterns and specialised services. It is widely believed that the CBD is likely to stay as a central place for business interactions and specialised goods and services, despite the decentralising functions exerted by advanced technology. More importantly for Singapore, the CBD is a representation of economic power upon which it relies for its continued prosperity and ascent to the status of global city.

ENDNOTES

1. Professor in the Department of City Planning, Massachusetts Institute of Technology, Boston.
2. The first floor of shophouses was used for business. Many shopowners and their family members and helpers lived in the upper levels.
3. Roof material made of coconut or palm leaves. It was a cheap and locally available material commonly used in traditional Malay settlements.
4. Under the 1947 Rent Control Act, landlords were not allowed to collect rentals higher than the 1939 level, and repossessions by landlords were highly restricted.
5. By definition of the 1950s, areas lying between the Central Area and the predominantly agricultural zones were broadly classified as suburbs. These suburbs were largely occupied by private property residential areas made up of terrace houses, semi-detached houses and bungalows at the fringes of the Central Area (Bukit Timah, Bedok, Mountbatten Roads). They were inhabited by middle- and high-income groups.

6   Britain's post-war Abercrombie's regional strategy had had spill-over effects on its colonies. The strategy led to the passing of a comprehensive system of control in the Town and Country Planning Act in 1947, which favoured population dispersal through slum clearance and the creation of self-contained new towns outside the city area (Gibson and Landstaff, 1982: 26–27). In Singapore, the building of new towns in outlying zones by the HDB in the early 1960s was practically a dispersal of the over-congested population from the Central Area accompanied by comprehensive urban renewal programmes.

7   Under the new Planning Ordinance, a Chief Planner was appointed as the chief land-use controller and implementer of land-use policies, as laid down in the Master Plan. He also chaired the monthly-held Master Plan Committee meetings relating to state land allocations, with the involvement of representatives from other relevant government departments and statutory boards.

8   Singapore had initially requested the assistance of the United Nations Technical Assistance Administration in 1961. This led to the Lorange Report (cited in URA, 1989) named after Emile Lorange who came to Singapore for six months in early 1962. Lorange recommended that the government should embark on an urban renewal programme (Choe, 1969: 162). The second United Nations team led by Charles Abrams, Susumu Kobe and Otto Koenigsberger arrived in 1963 to follow up on the earlier proposal.

9   In 1976, under the URA's new norm of open-space provision, the standard was increased from 0.3 hectare per 1,000 people to 0.6 hectare per 1,000 people.

10 The ratio of floor area to land area. For example, the plot ratio of the Golden Shoe area ranges from 5 to 10 (highest in the island), which means that the total floor area is allowed to be five to ten times that of the land parcel proposed for development.

11 The Concept Plan is a broad-based and indicative long-term land-use document. The plan scale is very small and does not provide details. Guided by the Concept Plan, Development Guide Plans are prepared using local planning methods, indicating detailed land-use plans designed for implementation at the local level. There are a total of 55 DGP plans throughout the city-state. On completion in 1998, they became the Master Plan of Singapore. However, some flexibility is allowed even for approved DGP plans, subject to justifiable rationale and policy change. All DGP plans are master plans *per se* and are updated once every five years.

12 In 1982, for instance, the Central Area provided 53% of the total commercial floor space (8.8 million square metres), and 71%, 37% and 56% of the island's office, shopping and hotel floor space respectively.

13 Year X is an unknown year when the resident population reaches the ultimate optimal capacity of 4 million. The current resident population (citizens and permanent residence holders) is 3.8 million.

14 In 2000, the target population size was revised upward by the government to 5.5 million.

CHAPTER 2

Infrastructure as a Modernising Agent: The Transition from Physical Infrastructure to Infostructure

> Knowledge is critical for development, because everything we do depends on knowledge. Simply to live, we must transform the resources we have into the things we need, and that takes knowledge...we must do more than simply transform *more* resources, for resources are scarce. We must use those resources in ways that generate ever-higher returns to our efforts and investments. That, too, takes knowledge, and in ever-greater proportion to our resources.
> World Bank (1999), *World Development Report 1998/99*, p. 16.

INTRODUCTION

Infrastructure development is an indispensable ingredient of urban land-use development in the modernisation process of a nation. Modern cities and urban systems are heavily dependent on infrastructure networks in order for their economic social systems to function effectively (Graham and Marvin, 1996). An efficient infrastructure facilitates delivery of information, goods and services, supports economic growth and assists in achieving social objectives such as raising living standards and educational levels. Whilst growth and living standards are interdependent, infrastructure has a medium- to long-term goal and its needs and focus vary according to changing circumstances. Infrastructure in the last few decades, however, has gradually modified its content and emphasis as the post-industrial economy shifts towards the services. Singapore is exemplary of this change as its economic base moves from low-skill industries to high-value industries, and now towards a knowledge-based economy in the twenty-first century.

This chapter examines why physical infrastructure is perceived as a modernising agent for social and economic progress, and its associations with the national economy of Singapore since the 1960s. Further analysis is made on the extended meaning of infrastructure when, after the 1980s, Information Technology (IT) replaced physical infrastructure as the leader of advanced infrastructure following rapid global informatisation, where information and knowledge have become a new commodity and a key product of the production process (Castells, 1996). Whilst modern physical infrastructure takes up a substantial amount of land and its use preferably requires land-use planning, knowledge-based infrastructure (infostructure) places emphasis on the internal functioning and processing of data, information and knowledge that lead to the production of value products. Discussion is much centred on information and communications technology development, seen as the future powerhouse supporting Singapore's plan to transform itself into a regional trade, financial and knowledge-based information hub. It is this strategy of advanced global integration upon which Singapore, as a semi-peripheral economy, counts for its continued growth and prosperity in a core-dominating world market system. The chapter also looks at whether IT has any effects on spatial development in a rigidly planned Singapore.

Scope of Infrastructure[1]

The definition of infrastructure varies from place to place. In defining infrastructure for the European Union, Convery (1998) gives it a broad context encompassing both hardware (concrete and visible) and software (infostructure) components. Convery's definition for hardware infrastructure has extended from the conventional public-run economic-related facilities to cover social infrastructure (schools, universities, hospitals, prisons, etc.) and cultural and recreational infrastructure (public and private buildings, parks and open spaces, housing), which may be private properties. For software infrastructure, he includes not only telecommunications and information technology in daily use, but research infrastructure designed to safeguard the environment and help sustain pleasant urban living. Hence, for Convery, infrastructure means typically the "physical constructs which have been provided by human endeavour and which underpin the economic and social life of a community. They comprise investments which have a relatively long life, and which are a shared endowment from the past".

In terms of physical infrastructure, Kessides (1996: 213) defines it as "the long-lived engineered structures, equipment, and facilities, and the services they provide, that are used in both economic production and by households. [It] comprises public utilities (electric power, piped gas and heating, telecommunications, water supply, liquid and solid waste disposal), public works (major dam and canal works for irrigation, as well as roads), and other transport sectors (railways, urban transport, ports and waterways, and airports)". Here, infrastructure is given a narrower sense. It covers infostructure and Kessides' definition of physical infrastructure is restricted to urban use in which it is invested, managed and upgraded by the public authorities or government-assisted firms aiming for greater system efficiency, improved human capital, governance and performance at the macro-economic level. Infostructure comprises facilities as well as services provided or facilitated by the government, semi-government or privately owned enterprises which are communications and information technology-oriented, and largely knowledge-based.

Linkage of Infrastructure to Economic Growth

Like any tangible material, infrastructure represents values and beliefs. Infrastructure need not necessarily bring about the well-being of a society. It may lead to mutually reinforcing (e.g., agglomeration economies), but also damaging (e.g., diseconomies of scale), activities (Convery, 1998: 4). It has been widely recognised that infrastructure contributes to economic development, though quantification of this contribution has remained an unresolved and debatable issue, and that returns on infrastructure investment are much dependent on public policy towards private investments, and on the efficiency and timing of investment. Connected to this, it can be observed that infrastructure in developed countries is generally far more adequate than in developing countries.

At the level of firms, there are two ways that infrastructure serves their production process, namely: (a) as intermediate inputs identical to external economies of scale in lowering the unit cost of service provided but at a higher level of production; and (b) enhancement of the productivity of labour and capital by reducing commuting time, improving information flow and facilitating interaction and exchange in the private sector. All these enhance international competitiveness, offer better marketing opportunities and reduce transaction cost as a whole (Mody and Reinfeld, 1997; Kessides, 1996: 213–217).

Infrastructure investment produces distributional effects and growth effects. Distributional effects may contribute little to the producing area as its benefits in generating individual income, regional or sectoral output could be absorbed by regions or areas outside the producing area's administrative boundary, based on which the effectiveness is usually accredited. Growth effects are the aggregate of benefits accumulated from the rise in economic output, productivity, employment and economic welfare (improved transport facilities, for example). Studies in the United States have shown that a reduction in public infrastructure investment would lead to a decline in the national output growth and productivity growth rates (Binder and Smith, 1997). A couple of other empirical studies also show identical findings. Research conducted by Groote, Jacobs and Sturm (1998) on the effects of transport on output in the Netherlands during the period 1853 to 1913 was based on data-oriented econometric techniques. They asserted that there was corresponding growth in the Dutch gross domestic product by examining the induced effects through a reduction in costs of transport and communications, expenditure and income effects and changes in the spatial setting of the national economy. Both forward and backward effects were found to be positive. Lewis' (1998) study was conducted on the contrasting developing country of Kenya. The provision of improved roads and water supplies has been shown to stimulate income rises through a series of multiplier effects, and better quality of services.

International organisations such as the World Bank, whose objective is centred on macro-policy matters, believe that infrastructure, besides generating economic growth, contributes towards poverty alleviation and environmental sustainability (World Bank, 1994a). Environmental sustainability is assumed to be a consequential contribution arising from economic growth as the poor enjoy clean sanitary, non-polluting sources of power, more secured disposal of waste and improved transport facilities. According to the World Bank estimate, developing countries in the early 1990s spent US$200 billion or 20% of their total investment annually on new infrastructure (World Bank, 1994a: 1). Despite such outlays, due to poor efficiency and wastage and poor maintenance, one billion inhabitants still had no access to clean water, and almost two billion lacked adequate sanitation. A shortage of telecommunication and transport networks and electricity was also commonplace. In the city-state of Singapore, spectacular economic growth has been registered in the last four decades, and it is widely recognised that the contribution by a reliable and public-managed infrastructure has been substantial.

INFRASTRUCTURE AND MODERNISATION

The interpretation of modernisation varies in nature and follows the social and political need of the changing juncture of historical moments. Often, it is through mobilising the aspirations of certain identified social groups by a politically organised institution or party that social change towards progress or better living standards is justified and induced. Progress and development are modernist concepts that have been strongly associated with economic growth, anti-traditional behaviours and social rationality in human history (Knippenberg and Schuurman, 1996). Diffusion of Western-based modernisation ideals through the colonies or territories subjected to their influence can be traced as far back as the sixteenth century following the European expansion. However, the diffusion through colonisation until the middle of the twentieth century was largely restricted to legal, social and cultural systems introduced at a very formal public administrative level, while local traditional norms were left to run their own course (Brookfield, 1975; Bristow, 2000). In colonies where economic exploitation was feasible, a basic communications system, such as ports, roads, railways, and telegraphs, was put in place to support the operations of traders, merchants, manufacturers and financiers in a world system of markets. Through colonisation, an inevitable by-product inherited by colonised territories was, at least partly, an accustomed culture based on borrowing and imitation. Borrowed ideas often were engraved unconsciously but firmly in the minds of the inheritors, in particular, in those of the local thinking elites. During the immediate post-World War Two era, the diffusion of modernisation impulses took a sharp turn in content, aims and initiative in decolonising territories preparing for national independence and seeking planning assistance from international agencies, notably the World Bank and United Nations (Ward, 2002: 223–225). The impact was tremendous as reflected in the strategies guiding their development path.

For most leaders of newly independent nations conscious of the general progress of the populace, modernisation theory had then a practical value for action and policy implementation to justify political mandate and commitments. Though the broad post-war concept of modernisation covered political, social, educational, environmental and health aspects, local leaders' key course of action was to transform their dependent territories from an agriculture- or commodity-based economy to an industrial one, thus placing themselves on the path of "catching up" with their European metropolis. This imitation process as constructed in the 1950s and early 1960s originated from a structural-functionalist concern of Western economists and other social scientists focused on how traditional societies could be modernised, transformed and made more productive. Putting it bluntly, the primary goal of the newly independent states was economic growth so as to counter the prevailing high risk of unemployment and underemployment, by applying pragmatic and workable macro-economic policies (Preston, 1996; Leys, 1996; Huff, 1994). With substantive support from the United States, the vision of modernisation, as part of the world capitalist system's goal for the expansion of markets and influence, "gained worldwide near-hegemonic adherence" (Knippenberg and Schuurman, 1996: 60), and acted quite effectively as a deterrent against Soviet communist influence in developing countries from the 1950s to the 1980s.

Given the great diversity in ways to pursue modernisation, implementation of its substance therefore provides great flexibility, and much room for local adaptation. Fully committed to building a developmentalist state when Singapore achieved self-government in 1959 (Low, 1998), Singapore followed the recommendations of the World Bank team that visited the city-state in 1955 and identified the manufacturing industry as the leading economic sector. The positive relationship between industrialisation and modernisation was the study theme of many influential authors of development in the 1950s (e.g., Lewis, 1955; Hirschman, 1958; Myrdal, 1957; Koenigsberger *et al.*, 1971). Goh Keng Swee (1995a), the chief economist of Singapore's self-governing cabinet, made it clear that cities were modernisers and he recalled in 1971 the rationale of the manufacturing option:

> [I]t was the progress of manufacturing activities in the West and its near absence in the East that explained the disparity in wealth.

The expansion of industry was expected to introduce new technology, new social attitudes, raise the levels of the existing skills, provide employment for the large numbers of unemployed or underemployed citizens. In short, industry would modernise and enrich...[and it] would not only generate economic growth but also help to bring about a rapid transformation of social attitudes to those more consistent with needs of modernising societies.
(*Ibid.*: 7)

By 1959, Singapore was already in a good position for industrialisation. It had inherited a relatively well-structured and maintained infrastructure and a bureaucratic system. Endowed with an important seaport, and a military and administrative centre falling within the network route in the old British empire's Far East where a heavily invested infrastructure and related services were required, it enjoyed a privileged status in the colonial hierarchy and system of production (see King, 1990). In 1956, as a large port in Southeast Asia, it had six dry docks. In 1955, an international airport was completed at Paya Lebar. In 1957, the Singapore Industrial Promotion Board was set up and a year later, it introduced pioneer and expansion bills to provide tax incentives to encourage industrial growth (Huff, 1994: 289–290). In 1961, a more action-oriented and instrumental Economic Development Board (EDB) was created to replace the Singapore Industrial Promotion Board and it became responsible for an industrialisation programme which, until 1965, was based on import-substitution, using Malaysia as a common market for Singapore's manufactured products.

The EDB's role shifted swiftly towards export-oriented industrialisation after the loss of a hinterland when Singapore was forced to leave the Federation of Malaysia in 1965. The unplanned emergence of an independent Singapore obliged its leaders to contemplate how a small and urbanised state could survive economically. Rajaratnam, in 1967, recognised the genuine difficulties faced by the import-substitution industrialisation model in terms of market outlet (Rajaratnam, 1985: 218–223). It was following this policy shift that the PAP government's expenditure philosophy became more concerned with Singapore's international competitiveness that was closely associated with the infrastructure provided by the government to attract foreign investments and its efficiency. Efficiency was pinpointed, in particular, by educational training, continuing education, widespread use of technology, and retraining of the workforce in more updated skills (Low, 1998: 88–97). Thus, industrialisation was rationalised on the premise that it would make best use of the two resources available—human and land resources.

Consequently, the EDB's operations were primarily two-fold. First, it had to actively court multinational companies to set up plants in Singapore. This would help create jobs, bringing in high technologies in large-scale operations and securing a global network of markets, a historic juncture noted by the premier Lee Kuan Yew as a critical turning point (Lee, 2000: 67–69). Second, an aggressive development of land for industrial facilities, especially at Jurong and in the new towns, was launched.

PHYSICAL INFRASTRUCTURE DEVELOPMENT IN SINGAPORE

Guided by an economic-priority principle (see Wong, 1998), Singapore's development path since the 1960s was conceived by United Nations advisers such as Charles Abrams, Susumu Kobe, Otto Koenigsberger and Albert Wensimius. As a dynamic society ready for transformations and changes, an action programme was needed for its growth. Infrastructure was a key component (Abrams, Kobe and Koenigsberger, 1963). For more than three decades, there has been a strong continuity in the investment in, and implementation of, this infrastructure-oriented policy whilst the economic base was broadened and deepened. From a labour-intensive industrial structure in the 1960s, Singapore has moved on with the globalisation age towards the promotion of more skill-intensive and technology-intensive industries and service-oriented jobs. Correspondingly, the focus of infrastructural investment has moved from physical infrastructure to infostructure after the 1980s.

As analysed earlier, the physical infrastructure provision has two implications for Singapore. First, it has served to attract multinational corporation investments, essential for export-led growth and for exploring the market potential of Singapore products, taking advantage of their well-established distribution networks worldwide. Second, infrastructure's demands for land allocations are disproportionally high because of Singapore's multiple status as a global city, city-state and nation-state (e.g., defence). Consequently, land space occupied by telecommunications, utilities, roads, public transit, ports, airports and their related facilities has exceeded the total land space for housing. The priority given to infrastructure has been reflected characteristically by a three-fold rise in land allocations in the last 30 years (Perry, Kong and Yeoh, 1997). A few key components of physical infrastructure are briefly discussed next.

Transport and Communications Infrastructure

Seaport

Strategically located at the southern tip of the island, the deep-water seaport of Singapore was the lifeline of the Singapore economy during the colonial days, and its present-day contribution has remained substantial (Figure 2.1). Indeed, the port has been expanding since the 1960s to cope with increasing demand, as the nation and the neighbouring hinterlands grow.

Well-supported by its facilities, the Singapore port now serves 400 shipping lines linked to 740 ports worldwide, especially in transhipment handling. The major port operator, PSA Corporation, has four terminals covering 339 hectares and handled a throughput of 16.5 million TEUs (Twenty-foot Equivalent Units) in 2002 (PSA, 2002). Pasir Panjang Terminal is currently being developed into a "new generation" mega container terminal to serve newer ships carrying 18 rows of containers across (Port Technology, 2003). PSA Corporation operates its various terminals as one integrated facility supported by three adjacent distriparks or cargo-distribution-centre complexes with extensive warehousing facilities. PSA Corporation also has interests in ports worldwide—in Europe, Africa, and Asia—thus facilitating Singapore's global reach.

Seeing the need to maintain the leading position of the port to support national growth and to strengthen trade links with major world economies, the Maritime and Port Authority of Singapore (MPA) was formed in 1996 by merging the Marine Department with the National Maritime Board, the regulatory departments of the former Port of Singapore Authority. The MPA's mission is to protect Singapore's strategic maritime interests and to promote Singapore as a major port and maritime centre (MPA website: http://www.mpa.gov.sg, retrieved on 15 June 2003).

Additionally, Jurong Port, managed by the Jurong Town Corporation (JTC) in the western sector, handles bulk and industrial cargoes, including cement and steel products. As one of Southeast Asia's leading industrial deep-water ports, it has 23 berths—21 on the mainland and two offshore at Pulau Damar Laut. In 1996, it handled 13.3 million tonnes of cargo and a large amount of crude oil (JTC, 1997). Awarded a full port licence in January 2001, Jurong Port is currently undertaking an expansion plan to equip itself with two new container-vessel berths and raise its container handling capacity to 1.4 million TEUs by the middle of 2004 (Jurong Port website: http://www.jp.com.sg/news, retrieved on 20 February 2003).

Currently, Singapore faces strong competition from ports being developed in the region, especially Malaysia. Singapore's competitiveness in terms of being a fast and efficient port and shipping hub with numerous connections is being eroded due to the lower fees and charges offered by ports in neighbouring countries, especially Malaysia. In 2001, the Danish container line, Maersk Sealand, relocated from Singapore to the Port of Tanjung Pelepas in Johor, Malaysia. This was followed by the announcement in 2002 that the Taiwanese Evergreen Marine Corporation would be relocating its regional transit hub to Tanjung Pelepas (*Agence France Presse*, 3 April 2002). The need to regain cost competitiveness led PSA Corporation to retrench 496 employees in February 2003 (PSA Corporation, 2003).

Airport
From a very modest airport at Kallang built in the late 1930s for single-propeller aircraft, the airport shifted to Paya Lebar in the 1960s. Subsequently in the 1970s, the dramatic rise in air traffic called for the development of the much bigger Changi Airport on reclaimed land at the eastern tip of the island. For the last ten years, Changi Airport has won international acclaim for its excellent services. In 2000, the airport handled 28.6 million passengers, a rise of 83% from 1990, and 1.68 million tonnes of air cargo (Department of Statistics, 2001: 158–159). From its current two runways, the airport will eventually expand to include four runways to accommodate a projected 70 million passengers in probably the next 30 years.

Road Construction
Like most capital cities that have experienced great infrastructure development, roads in Singapore have gone through a qualitative and quantitative change. Figure 2.1 shows that in 1958, the road network was sparse and highly concentrated in the Central Area close to the seaport. The pace of urbanisation has been rapid since the early 1960s, following the programme of the new PAP government to redevelop the slum areas in the Central Area by relocating the bulk of the "surplus" population to

high-rise housing in new towns at the outlying zones. By 1975, the most significant extension was to the Jurong industrial area in the west—a priority industrial development scheme—to support the transport of goods and to facilitate the commuting of workers (Figure 2.2). Much of the island, however, had not yet been developed for public housing. By the 1990s, some 25 new towns had been built island-wide in a span of less than 40 years, and they are now well-linked in a radial pattern converging towards the Central Area, the traditional downtown core (Figure 2.3).

Since the mid-1970s, the overall land transport strategy in Singapore has aimed at: (a) implementing a policy of restrictive management of private car ownership and usage; (b) upgrading and encouraging the use of public transport; and (c) raising road capacity. As shown in Table 2.1, the change in road supply is more drastic in high-order roads with greater carrying capacity. Whilst the rise in density of the local road network is small, the expansion of arterial roads has been impressive. The expressway (a six-lane carriageway in both directions) was a new phenomenon in the early 1980s. In 2000, its total length reached 150 kilometres, stretching from the Johor Causeway in the north to East Coast Parkway near the downtown core, and from the Jurong industrial area in the west to Changi International Airport in the east.

TABLE 2.1: PUBLIC ROADS IN SINGAPORE, 1961–2000

Year	Expressway	Major Arterials	Collector Roads	Local Roads	Total (km)
1961[1]	-	133	68	692	893
1965	-	138	68	888	1,094
1970	-	240	113	1,585	1,938
1975	-	257	122	1,788	2,167
1980	-	352	157	1,847	2,356
1985	73	435	202	1,935	2,645
1990	104	529	260	1,989	2,882
1995	132	567	326	1,947	2,972
2000	150	571	375	2,004	3,100

Source: Department of Statistics, *Yearbook of Statistics* (various years).
Note: [1] The public roads of 1960 or earlier were categorised differently, incomparable with those after 1961.

Before 1995, it was the Public Works Department of the Ministry of National Development that was responsible for the planning, design, construction and management of public facilities such as roads, bridges, airports, schools, hospitals, etc. (MND, 1988: 21). Land transport policy was, however, formulated by the Ministry of Communications. To overcome the cross-ministerial problems that might arise from time to time, a centrally managed statutory board, the Land Transport Authority (LTA), was set up in the Ministry of Communications in 1995 to coordinate planning, development and maintenance of the road networks. The new authority has integrated the separate functions of different agencies and infused its strong policy objective to promote a "congestion-free" city. Since 1996, its key missions have been outlined as follows (LTA, 1998: 3):

a) To deliver an efficient and effective land transport network that is integrated, efficient, cost-effective and sustainable to meet the nation's need;
b) To plan, develop and manage Singapore's land transport system to support a quality environment while making optimal use of the transport resources and safeguarding the well-being of the travelling public; and
c) To develop and implement policies to encourage commuters to choose the most appropriate transportation mode.

Besides road networks, the LTA also develops and manages other public transport services such as the city rail network, known as the mass rapid transit, as well as buses and taxis. In March 1998, there were about 3,000 buses, 69% of which were air-conditioned, and 16,900 taxis in service (LTA, 1998: 16). The bus service is the most important mode of transport, accounting for about 3 million passenger-trips or one-third of Singapore's daily commuting travels in both public and private transport. The key role of bus routes is to supplement the rail mass rapid transit service, but they serve shorter travel needs, and quite frequently provide feeder services for passengers to shift to the rail transport for longer-distance travel.

Rail Mass Rapid Transit (MRT)
The decision to build a three-line rail MRT system in the early 1980s was a challenging endeavour. It was the most costly option

recommended by a specialist group engaged to study the public transport issue in Singapore. The report indicated that developing a high-performance express bus system should be adequate to cater to travel needs, and a three-line rail MRT might only be required in the distant future (Ministry of Communications, 1980). Since the start of its service in 1987, the MRT has gained popularity among public-housing dwellers for its comfort, reliability and speed compared to the bus system. Passengers use the MRT generally for longer commuting distances (an average of 12.6 kilometres per trip). In 2000, the MRT served some 1.1 million passenger-trips on an average weekday, a sharp rise from 765,300 in 1995.

The total current heavy track distance covered by the MRT is 83 kilometres, serving 48 stations island-wide. To cater to zones with a small number of users, light and medium tracks will also be provided. By the year 2004, an additional 85 stations are expected to come into service, and this will include new lines to Changi Airport, the North-East, Sengkang, the Marina area adjacent to the Central Area and Punggol (Singapore MRT, 1997/98). To facilitate the movements of international travellers, the MRT was extended to Changi Airport in the early 2000s (see Figure 2.3).

Other Public Utilities

Sanitary conditions were deplorable in the slums of the Central Area in the immediate post-war colonial period, as noted by a Housing Committee study (Housing Committee, 1948). From the 1960s, slums had been cleared and the great majority of the inhabitants resettled in the new towns. In the 1980s, when 85% of Singaporeans were already living in public housing apartments where standard sanitary facilities and clean water were provided, the overall situation showed a significant improvement. Table 2.2 shows the access to safe drinking water and sanitation in Singapore in relation to urban populations in other Southeast Asian nations. While conditions in Malaysia are much closer to those of Singapore, cities in other countries, except Myanmar, have also shown improvements over the period 1980–1996.

TABLE 2.2: ACCESS OF URBAN POPULATION TO DRINKING WATER AND SANITATION—SINGAPORE AND OTHER SELECTED EAST ASIAN ECONOMIES, 1980–1996

Country	Access to Safe Drinking Water		Access to Sanitation	
	1980 (%)	1990–96' (%)	1980 (%)	1990–96 (%)
Indonesia	35	78	30	73
Laos	21	40	11	70
Malaysia	90	100	n.a.	100
Myanmar	38	36	38	42
Philippines	65	91	81	88
Thailand	65	94	64	98
Singapore	100	100	80	100

Source: Compiled from World Bank (1994), pp. 146–148, and World Bank (2000), Tables 3.5 and 3.10. The data refers to the most recent year available in this period.
Note: n.a. = Data not available

Water

Singapore does not produce enough water for the consumption of its population due to its small land area. Since the 1920s, water has been imported from the neighbouring Malaysian state of Johor. At present, about 60% of the water supply comes from Johor (Yap, 1995: 65), and protracted negotiations have been underway since the 1980s to increase the amount of water that may be sold to Singapore under agreements signed in 1961 and 1962. In 1960, there were three impounding reservoirs in Singapore, four at Pontian and Gunong Pulai, and water intakes along the Tebrau, Scudai and Johor Rivers. Sources of supply in terms of reservoirs rose over time in both Johor and Singapore. By 2000, the total supply system was furnished by 19 raw-water reservoirs (including those in Johor), nine treatment works, 14 storage reservoirs and 5,060 kilometres of pipelines island-wide.

Consumption of water has increased substantially over the last three decades. The volume consumed rose from 150.3 million cubic metres in 1968, to 256.8 million cubic metres in 1980, and 506.1 million cubic metres in 2000,[1] a rate of increase that was much higher than that of the population growth. The rise in usage by the commercial and industrial sectors is most dramatic, from 18.9% of the total consumption to 29.6% and 35.9% in the respective years (PUB, 1967; 1989; 2000). Various means have been used to reduce the demand for water, including stricter standards and more stringent capacity limits for water fittings, public education campaigns, a water conservation tax, tax rebates and grants for water conservation measures, and regular water audits for commercial and industrial users. On the supply side, the government has explored, since the 1960s, alternatives to rainfall collection. It has since developed the Sungei Lunggui catchment in Malaysia by building an impounding reservoir with a capacity of 770 million cubic metres to regulate the flow of the Johor River. The construction at Singapore's expense helps to justify the city-state's right to draw the maximum of 250 million gallons of raw water per day under the 1962 agreement. In Singapore, water catchment areas have been progressively extended so that over 40% of the island's land area is used for rainwater collection (Figure 2.4). Water reuse has been actively encouraged. The government is also building desalination plants, and is actively pursuing water reclamation from sewage using ultra filtration and reverse osmosis technology to produce "Newater". Presently, "Newater" is fed indirectly into the water system by pumping it into local reservoirs, and makes up about 2% of the water supply. Nevertheless, water security remains a sensitive issue in the relationship between Singapore and Malaysia. While it is technically possible for Singapore to achieve self-sufficiency in its water supply, the current state of technology allows this only at a prohibitive cost.

Power
In the early 1960s, electricity was generated at the main power station in Pasir Panjang near the seaport, and at another in the Jurong Industrial Estate. The 1970s saw the installation of Senoko power station in the north at Woodlands and in the 1980s, Seraya power station was commissioned on Jurong Island. Like water, consumption of electricity rose quickly from 1,240 million kilowatt-hours in 1967 to 6,660 million kilowatt-hours in 1980 and 27,080 million kilowatt-hours in 1999. Power cables are installed underground in order to save land space for other services.

A plan for Common Services Tunnels, an underground tunnel system for utility services such as water pipes and power and telecommunication cables linked to buildings, has been proposed in the new downtown area of Marina South adjacent to the existing Central Area. The tunnels will also accommodate chilled-water pipes for air-conditioning and pneumatic refuse conveyance systems (URA, 1998). This is a new 20-kilometre physical communication network, which will be able to substantially save surface land space in the future financial district. According to the plan, this network will enhance service reliability, functionally reduce traffic disruptions due to maintenance, and serve as an aesthetic way to beautify the cityscape.

Sewerage System
In 1972, Singapore completed installation of a comprehensive sewerage system. It ensures that all waste water from industrial, housing and commercial premises is discharged into the sewers. Today, the whole population is served by modern sanitation facilities. Industries discharging biodegradable pollutants beyond the allowable limits may choose to discharge the effluent directly into the sewers after treatment, or pay a tariff to the Public Utilities Board (PUB) which will treat the discharge at its sewage treatment plants. Under the jurisdiction of the Ministry of the Environment, the PUB's measures to control water pollution consist of (Ministry of the Environment, 1998):

a) The provision of sewerage infrastructure and a solid management system to prevent pollution at source;
b) Setting rules and regulations for industries to pre-treat their trade effluent to prescribed standards prior to discharge into the sewerage system; and
c) Forbidding industries which use or store substantial amounts of chemicals to be sited inside any water catchment areas.

The PUB now operates six sewage treatment plants and 145 pumping installations. There is one industrial water works, and a network of 2,730 kilometres of sewers throughout the island of 670 square kilometres (see Figure 2.5).

Construction of a massive Deep Tunnel Sewerage System (DTSS) began in 1997. When completed, nearly 80 kilometres of tunnels will convey sewage by gravity to two water reclamation plants in the Tuas area and Changi East. Phase I, costing S$3.8 billion, includes the 48 kilometres of North Tunnel and the Changi East Water Reclamation Plant, and is scheduled for completion and commissioning in 2008. When this is completed, sewage from existing water reclamation plants will be diverted into the North Tunnel. Singapore presently discharges waste water into the narrow Straits of Johor, about one kilometre off the coast at a depth of ten metres. With the DTSS, waste water will be discharged five kilometres out to the sea in the Straits of Singapore at a depth of 35 metres, where stronger currents should ensure that coastal water quality remains unaffected. Phase II, costing S$3.6 billion, has been scheduled to begin in 2008 and will be completed by 2015. During this phase, the 30-kilometre South Tunnel and the Jurong Island Water Reclamation Plant will be constructed. It is expected that by 2045, all existing sewage treatment plants and pumping stations will be decommissioned and the 290 hectares of land presently occupied by these will be released for other developments (PUB website: http://www.pub.gov.sg/sw_future.html, retrieved on 16 June 2003; *Asian Infrastructure Monthly*, 2000; Ministry of the Environment, 2001).

Having discussed the evolution of the physical infrastructure which facilitates basic economic growth, the focus is now shifted to the advanced infrastructure essential for maintaining high growth rates for a more mature economy, which is characterised presently in Singapore by a relatively high cost of production. From the mid-1970s, following the oil crisis, world economic development took a sharp turn from Fordism to a flexible specialised production system,[2] which relies heavily on knowledge-intensive or advanced infrastructure. The formation of the latter is a long process. According to Mody and Reinfeld (1997: 131–132), it is "more demand-oriented and consists of innovative applications designed to meet [an] array of specific user needs". It brings about high value-added benefits and more effective time management, involving an extensive global network and operations, as well as a reliance on the heavy use of information technology. These latter elements are increasingly seen as being more important than labour cost, manpower availability and market distance in determining the success of firms.

TOWARDS INFOSTRUCTURE: THE KNOWLEDGE-BASED ECONOMY

As stated above, infrastructural support has been a crucial element to the Singapore government in attracting international investment to support its export-led growth strategy in the last 30 years. Since the 1980s, however, the information revolution has nullified Singapore's geographical advantages, though the strategically located seaport and airport have remained important. The rules of this new global economic game have shifted to the quality of information access, and information support services and skills to bolster the productivity gains of Singapore's workforce and to maintain its competitive edge (Wong, 1996). Since the 1990s, knowledge disseminated by the increased use of IT and training and retraining of Singapore's workforce to meet new demands have been perceived as a new source of growth in Singapore's increasingly service-oriented economy focused on high-tech operations, trade links and financial services.

Indeed, future financial transactions are expected to be less dependent on national regulatory systems and regulations, and a deregulatory mode of planning is gaining momentum (Newman and Thornley, 1996: 9). With a dramatically rising usage of the Internet, global capital and business dealings will occupy a key role in high-value financial services in the new millennium, in which Singapore, well-aware of the high cost of industrial goods manufactured on its soil as compared to its Southeast Asian neighbours, hopes to make itself a financial and a high-tech hub in the Asia-Pacific region. Capturing such high-level functions would help ensure a better position for the nation in an increasingly competitive global economic hierarchy in a polarising world (Castells, 1999a; Sassen, 1998).

Unless Singapore maintains its current lead in the region, it will fall to the lower echelon of the hierarchy. Singapore's choice of using the latest information technology to support its world trade activities is obvious. As a small, newly industrialising economy, it has only a limited domestic market of 3.8 million people. It also lacks its own MNCs to influence global technological development. Achieving a worldwide IT application implies that economies of scale, and hence a feasible return on costly IT investments, could be realised. A strengthened world trade linkage would enhance Singapore's integration into the global financial and high-tech networks where it aims to build itself as a hub in the East Asian sector, and to bring in the latest technology through large MNC investors who would use the city-state as their regional headquarters.

Today, the relationship between knowledge and development captures great research interest in a fast-moving globalisation process where the share and value of high-tech industries in world trade has risen proportionally. The World Bank estimates that over half of the

GDPs of the major high-income OECD[3] countries are built on the production and distribution of knowledge. Different from factors of production such as supplies of labour, land and natural resources, this growth-related knowledge is a dynamic comparative advantage which depends more on the quality and training of the workforce in acquiring, absorbing and communicating knowledge (World Bank, 1999: 23–24). This trend shows that there will be a dramatic impact on the future quality of the workforce engaged in the production sectors and the means by which knowledge (specialised or general knowledge used in the production and distribution of goods and services) is received and disseminated.

Singapore's IT Plans and Implementation

In 1981, the National Computer Board (NCB) was created to coordinate computer education and training aimed at providing industries with appropriate IT manpower. Another task was to encourage global IT vendors to market their software products through Singapore, hence offering the city-state an opportunity to develop its software industry. In 1986, NCB launched its first National Information Technology Plan to develop a strong export-oriented IT sector. Developed further from its 1981 programme, this was an action-oriented plan incorporating seven objectives, such as manpower training, cultivation of IT culture, promotion of IT as a communications infrastructure, encouraging the widespread application of IT, fostering the growth and technological innovation of IT, enhancement of local IT development to international competitive levels and, finally, building a strong community of public and private organisations in IT development (Wong, 1997). Associated with this plan was a communications infrastructure, TradeNet, a nation-wide electronic data interchange system, designed for computer-to-computer exchange of business documents required for international trade. It is a system that integrates import, export and transhipment[4] documentation processing procedures for both air and sea cargoes (NCB, 1987).

In 1991, the NCB crystallised its plan to link businesses in Singapore with the world, especially with those developed IT centres in the West, including Japan. In establishing such a global network, the aim was to market high value-added products from Singapore, designed and manufactured for on-time delivery and at minimal costs. In 1996, a five-year National Science and Technology Plan 2000 costing S$4.0 billion[5] was initiated to carry out the restructuring and upgrading of Singapore's industry and business clusters (EDB, 1997).

The pro-IT policies have encouraged IT-related MNCs to produce and export hardware and software. From 1982 to 1994, for example, the total volume of IT sales (domestic and export) rose by 19 times (Wong, 1997: Table 3). IT usage in firms has also reflected a positive trend.[6] The latest IT focus is demonstrated by the vision of Industry 21, designed to advance Singapore further to become a global hub of knowledge-driven industries. It is a self-enhancement model stressing four key inputs such as vibrancy, robustness, globality and knowledge. Local companies are encouraged to collaborate and eventually catch up with world-class firms as well as to absorb, adapt and apply new knowledge and skills, whilst the workforce should upgrade itself and adopt a lifelong-learning mindset. Vibrancy means that local entrepreneurs will have to be creative and be more prepared to take risks (http://www.sedb.com.sg/industry21). The government-linked companies would be given support to establish Singapore MNCs. Singapore is one of the newly industrialising economies which has been strongly integrated into the world-dominating Triad regional groupings (North America, Western Europe and Japan) and it would like to see greater ICT innovations. Such innovations and improvements would help increase local MNCs' range of options to undertake new organisational forms, to closely follow the international production systems, and to enhance the capability to penetrate potential global or regional markets (Charles, 1996). ICTs also have a delocalising effect in that they bring about a more effective separation of capital from labour, thus they can act in favour of land-scarce Singapore's investments overseas using local land resources and labour.

Spatial Integration of ICTs and Research Institutions

In spatial terms, development of ICTs has been incorporated in Singapore's long-term land-use plan, the revised Concept Plan of 1991 (URA, 1991a). Apparently, technological changes, including ICT development, have an "antipolistic" inclination to lower the need for concentration because they render a greater freedom of locational choice; in fact, corporate decision-making can take place in any part of the world. Many researchers, however, argue that ICTs have both centralising and decentralising effects in population and economic activity distribution (Kellerman, 1993: 97; Graham and Marvin, 1996: 284). Decentralisation is facilitated as less urbanised zones enjoy lower land cost than the core area, and less congestion. More importantly, ICTs generate new demands for infrastructure investments and other related activities and opportunities.

Within a city itself, though perceived as a "virtual" network system, ICT networks are believed to follow closely the "hard" network of energy, water flows, transport of goods and people and other resources. Improvements in ICTs promote logically the interactions between ICTs and the physical infrastructure networks. The rationale is that the management and decision-making processes of both need to match with each other based on real demand and supply and flow of network operations so that an improved functioning of the city can be achieved (Graham and Marvin, 1996). This presumption is highly relevant for the unique situation in Singapore where intra-urban and inter-urban processes of urban growth do not take place naturally in the city-state.

First, the intra-urban forces in Singapore are subject to strong domestic planning policy control. This small island-state has no direct hinterland. Since the adoption of a Concept Plan in 1971, the city-state has become a rigidly and effectively planned city where industrial lands and business parks designed for high technology are spatially designated and their land prices are determined by open tender. Indeed, the stringently implemented Concept Plan in the last 30 years has indicated that the distribution of physical infrastructure, especially road networks and public transit lines, predetermines the distribution patterns of the ICTs. The IT2000 Report launched by the National Computer Board in 1992 aimed to transform Singapore into an "intelligent island" by the first decade of the twenty-first century (NCB, 1992). Following the premise of Singapore's IT2000 Masterplan, Singapore One has been established by the joint efforts of the Infocomm Development Authority, A*STAR, the Economic Development Board and the Media Development Authority. Equipped with broadband service, its primary aim is to deliver, to the greatest possible extent, a new level of interactive multimedia applications and services to homes, businesses and schools throughout Singapore. By early 2003, the broadband infrastructure covered over 99% of the island, with network access via ADSL, cable, wireless and fibre technology. Voice, data, audio and video information can be transmitted simultaneously at high speed from one terminal to another island-wide (Singapore One, 2003).

Figure 2.6 shows the long-term land-use plan (Plan Year X) for Singapore projected by the Urban Redevelopment Authority, the national planning authority. The plan indicates that there will be a strong integration of the physical infrastructure with the infostructure. The island-wide road network is largely a grid pattern, supplemented by ring-shaped MRT lines converging at the Central Business District in the Central Area. Within the ring-shaped MRT lines are the Central Catchment Areas under strict conservation with reservoirs for the local water supply. Aligning its plan with this long-term land-use planning, the NCB's vision is to integrate its activities, as well as those of the industries, business parks and institutions such as the Information Technology Institute, Institute of Systems Science, National University of Singapore, Nanyang Technological University, Singapore Telecom and the Ministry of Defence. Throughout the island, these institutions form two technology corridors, one in the north and another more important one in the south.

Second, Singapore's current development status is situated somewhere between the developed core and its surrounding developing countries (Malaysia, Indonesia, Thailand Cambodia and Vietnam). There is a substantial development gap between these countries and Singapore. With most of its manufactured products being exported to the developed world and a strong association with the developed economies, Singapore's urban development is influenced primarily by globalisation effects as part of the global urban system established in the form of functional hierarchies. As such, any decentralisation of economic activities originating from Singapore to the rest of Southeast Asia or elsewhere depends essentially on the offer of potential investment destinations (location, labour cost and appropriate skills, and other incentives). The next millennium will also see the expansion of the airport and the seaport facilities to meet the challenges of the increasingly competitive global trade in which Singapore aims to be a key player in the Asia-Pacific.

CONCLUDING REMARKS

Infrastructure has been widely recognised by post-war developmentalist states as a modernising agent and a precondition for economic take-off. It supports and facilitates the government administration, private business operations and daily activities of the general public. In Singapore, it has also served in the last three decades to attract MNCs whose leading technology, global marketing networks and competitive products have bolstered the city-state's export-led economy. Since the 1980s, the knowledge-based IT system has breathed new life into the classical infrastructure framework to enrich its content and form a virtual advanced infrastructure.

The shift from physical infrastructure to knowledge-oriented infostructure has reflected the essence in managing two scarce resources in Singapore: human resources and land resources. While the former have been reinforced by lifelong learning and policy support in knowledge-based training, the latter have been consolidated by the establishment of a new statutory board in June 2001—the Singapore Land Authority.[7] With its primary mission to optimise land resources, the Authority's dual objective is to "create, maximize and extract value along the economic, social, community, recreational and aesthetic fronts" as well as to "promote a pro-growth and pro-enterprise culture whilst balancing the social and community interest" (SLA, 2002: 21). Nevertheless, the shift in the nature of infrastructure has not altered the pursuit of the "economic priority model" for a new wealth facilitator to sustain growth in a highly globalised world where national boundaries can no longer easily control the flow of capital, services and knowledge. Aiming to advance from a semi-peripheral, newly industrialising economy to the heartland of the developed world, Singapore strives to maintain its competitive edge, and "global competition" has become its persistently used catchphrase. In an attempt to establish itself as a financial and high-tech hub in the Asia-Pacific and to build up its own MNCs in ICTs, the Singapore government liberalised the state-monopolised telecommunications market in April 2000, allowing foreign firms to compete freely with the government-linked Singapore Telecommunications Corporation (SingTel).[8] This is likely to be followed by a liberalisation of the financial sector since the city-state also aims to become one of the global financial hubs in the near future. It is obvious that challenges in the days ahead will be tremendous.

Can Singapore's strong state-initiated ICT drive serve as a lesson for other developing nations to improve their national economic performance? Singapore's case may be unique in certain aspects, and its transferability is uncertain and is subject to local situations. First, the "economic priority model" has worked in Singapore to win electoral support by sufficiently satisfying the people's aspirations for improved material living standards. This model has long been infused into the political culture of the ruling political party, and is used as an electoral mandate. Hitherto, other social and political concerns have played second fiddle to these materialistic aspirations. For many developing nations, economic growth, albeit important as a development strategy, is only one of the areas of concern in maintaining political control and power. At times, it may not even be classified as a priority area to be allocated with adequate resources. Second, the city-state's highly profit-seeking government-linked companies are difficult to find in many developing countries, where efficiency is not only generally lower, but political pressure to use national resources for equity distribution and welfare redistribution may also be much greater, thus affecting state companies' effective functioning as an infrastructure "incubator". Third, over 30 years of reserve build-up and supported by budget surpluses, Singapore has the capacity to introduce high-cost infostructure whereas such capacity is unlikely to be available in many developing countries, particularly those having a large rural sector to subsidise.

ENDNOTES
1. Part of the purified water is resold to Johor. In 2000, for example, about 10% or 50.6 million cubic metres was sold to Johor.
2. Whilst Fordism involves mass production to minimise unit cost through work process repetition by a largely semi-skilled workforce, the flexible specialised production system is a combination of craft and mass production, ensuring quality production of goods with emphasis on workers' individual skills.
3. Organisation for Economic Cooperation and Development, which comprises developed countries in Western Europe, North America, Oceania and Japan.
4. Transhipment does not involve unloading of cargoes onshore and it constituted about 80% of the total sea cargo load in the year 2000.
5. As of June 2003, 1 US dollar was equivalent to 1.74 Singapore dollars.
6. A preliminary survey of 2,000 firms by the Singapore government in the late 1990s showed that the growth potential of electronic commerce in the city-state was good, despite a low starting point. Of the 2,000 firms

surveyed, about three-quarters possessed corporate Internet access and more than one-third owned corporate websites. The survey also reflected that, in 1997, revenue generated by electronic commerce support services accounted for S$144 million and surged by 85% to S$359 million in 1998. An average of 11% of growth has been projected for the IT industry during the period 1998–2003 (*Straits Times*, 7 July 1999: 52).

7   The Singapore Land Authority was formed by the amalgamation of four departments within the Ministry of Law, namely the Land Office, the Singapore Land Registry, the Land Survey Department and the Land Systems Support Unit. It has become the main custodian of all state lands, and is involved in formulating policies to facilitate the allocation of various land uses, and in the acquisition of land for public purposes (SLA, 2002).

8   According to a report by the *Straits Times* dated 25 January 2000, SingTel undertook to negotiate with a British firm, Cable & Wireless Hong Kong Telecommunications, on a merger to form the second-largest phone company in Asia with a total capital of S$100 billion. The attempt ended in failure, but such a merger aimed to upgrade SingTel to a world-class operator.

CHAPTER 3

Industrialisation, Multinationals and Land-Use Development

> JTC Corporation will be the world-class industrial developer and a key driving force in advancing Singapore's economic prosperity...To remain relevant and competitive in this new world economic order, we at JTC recognise the need to expand on our developmental role. It is no longer enough to provide first-class infrastructure and services. We need new ways of doing things—to innovate, experiment and create value for our customers.
> **JTC Corporation vision and Chairman's statements,**
> JTC (2002), *Annual Report 2001/2002*, pp. 15–16

INTRODUCTION

Among the other sectors that have made identical or substantial contributions to Singapore's growth (e.g., banking and retail services, transportation, tourism, development of arts/culture and research activities), industrialisation efforts are a key driving force leading to tremendous land-use modernisation and change. For many, industrial landscape modernisation may be perceived as largely dependent on the manufacturing multinationals that were attracted to the city-state by multiple incentives and political stability (see Huff, 1994; Deyo, 1981; Heyzer, 1983). Manufacturing capital influx intensified following the 1974 oil crisis that sent MNCs overseas in search of cheaper production centres and market expansion in developing countries.

In a world of increasing interdependency, dependency, however, is a flexible concept that can be interpreted as a beneficent relationship by one nation but assessed in a resentful light by another (Drakakis-Smith, 1996: 215). Dependency is indeed a relative term whose interpretation is fundamentally associated with whether the end could justify the means. If the development process has led to a sharp rise in material living standards that warrants sustained political governance, using multinational corporations equipped with high technology and world-class management skills as a means to lead a dynamic industrialisation drive and achieve that end is conceivably justifiable[1] (see Lee, 1993: 253; Lee, 2000). From an *entrepôt* dependent on import-export of raw materials in 1960, the dependency feature of Singapore has since evolved progressively through an array of social, economic and technological changes in a more sophisticated and globalising world. In the globalising process where self-imposed isolation is tantamount to self-exile in economic gain, trade has become more interdependent yet indoctrinated with different levels of dependencies.

This outcome of industry-led performance is statistically significant over the last 40 years. In per capita terms, the city-state's gross national product in 1997 was equivalent to 14% of that of ten Southeast Asian states. The per capita GNP was US$32,940, followed closely by that of oil-rich Brunei Darussalam, but not by that of Malaysia, its closest neighbour (World Bank, 1999). Little of Singapore's accumulated material wealth has been derived from its naturally endowed resources. Rather, accumulation has been attributable to the market value of products and services accessible to world markets and the quality of infrastructure and inputs of multinational corporations, with the strong support of a local quality workforce. A progressive export- and foreign direct investment-led industrial development integrated with the advanced world economy has been largely responsible for the outcome (World Bank, 1994b).

It is necessary to reiterate here the circumstances that had compelled Singapore to head for industrialisation at the time of achieving self-government in 1959. First of all, the future of the *entrepôt* trade on which Singapore was heavily dependent had become questionable as a source of continued growth in an era where neighbouring hinterland countries (notably Malaysia and Indonesia) had achieved independence and were heading to modernise their own national ports (Bowen, 2000). Port competition implied that much commodity flow would be siphoned off Singapore towards other national ports for direct export. Even if commodity flow was maintained, continued dependence on relatively low-value agricultural and mineral exports from neighbouring countries would be tantamount to an economic suicide, as the returns would be too low to allow facility and equipment modernisation, and reinvestment.

The second circumstance was an attempt to counter the preset core-periphery trade relationship. It was unquestionably a political mandate or the legitimacy of post-war leaders emerging from colonial rule in breaking away from domination by Western colonial regimes that had imposed upon their colonies to be suppliers of raw materials and importers of manufactures from the metropolis (Stutz and de Souza, 1998: 416; Potter *et al.*, 1999; Castells, 1992). Thirdly, it was the internal mechanism and functioning of industrialisation that made the option of industrial development appealing. Specifically for the small island-state of Singapore, a limited land supply had naturally prevented the republic from using a sizeable proportion of its land for agricultural production, even at an intensive pace.

Having set the broad industrialisation background, this chapter positions itself to examine the evolution of industrial development in Singapore from 1960 to 2000. The first section presents the theoretical framework and the rationale of industrialisation as a basis for economic development, and the role of the state as an initiator and facilitator of industrial development. The second section addresses the industrialisation strategy and the circumstances for the shift from the labour-intensive model in the 1960s and 1970s to the knowledge and skill-intensive model after the mid-1980s. Finally, the spatial development of industries is presented in different periods in the last section.

INDUSTRIALISATION DRIVE AND THE ROLE OF THE STATE

The 1950s circumscribed an era of industrialisation in newly independent territories. On the economic front, industry was seen and accepted widely as capable of producing multiplier effects with its forward and backward linkages that agriculture could not. Benefiting from economies of scale and a post-war rising consumer market, industrial workers were seen to be more productive than subsistence farmers who were predominant in numbers (Knox and Agnew, 1989; Wong, 1999a; Kuznets, 1998).

The end of World War Two had brought to light the technological superiority of the Allies and an optimism that science and technology, an indispensable component of industrialisation, would provide quick solutions to the social ills, such as poverty, unemployment and deprivation of basic housing and education, plaguing the developing world. Industrialisation was regarded as something that would move "traditional" societies into the modern age where want and suffering would be a thing of the past. The success of the Marshall Plan in post-war Europe furnished confidence that investments through foreign aid, savings or foreign companies would also lead the underdeveloped Third World to economic growth and prosperity. Moreover, technology, with its ability to enhance productivity and generate products of greater value, went in favour of capital in subordinating wage claims "by reducing labour value per unit of output" (Bina and Davis, 2000: 193–194).

Thus, in the less developed economies trapped in a "vicious circle of poverty", a "big push" was deemed necessary to move the economy out of stagnation to a point of economic drive (Nurkse, 1953). The idea of the "big push" rests on the indivisibility of infrastructural capital, such as power, transport or communications, that must proceed to make investments productive. Such investments are characterised by a sizeable initial lump sum and low variable costs (Datta-Chaudhuri, 1980).

To many, industrialisation promised to increase the wealth of the nation by increasing its productivity and the markets for its products. Rostow's (1961) linear model of development, also known for its "universally applicable" five stages of development, offered developing nations the belief that to industrialise was to prepare for economic "take-off". Thus, economic development was essentially seen as a linear process where economic take-off would automatically occur when the right kind of integrated development policies ensuring a balanced development of key economic sectors were adopted (Hirschman, 1981). To arrive at this, it was widely believed that the old footprints of the industrial core countries should be followed and that the state's primary role was to be a facilitator and, if necessary, a prime mover.

Role of the State

Industrialisation to the newly elected government of Singapore in 1959 thus meant a convenient campaign compatible with modernising a "traditional" society. Further, it strategically meant a counter-offensive against high rates of unemployment, and an engine of growth (for example, see Pang and Tan, 1981). Neo-classical economic theories claimed that industrial development had great potential in job provision and in reducing poverty, and that full employment was the result of the normal operations of an economy (Radwan, 1998). Tolerating high unemployment rates, therefore, would not only have caused a loss of votes but would also represent an unsettled risk leading to social chaos instigated by the leftist-led trade unions at that time.

In a more comprehensive view, industrialisation was indeed a complex process involving labour and technological change as well as capital accumulation (Bina and Davis, 2000: 193), be it benefiting the public or private sector—a process characteristic of newly independent governments adopting strong government-led pro-capitalist development policies in the post-war era. Critical in the linkage between technology and labour is the constant pursuit of upgrading and progress for the former in order to satisfy, by means of productivity gains, the persistent demand for material improvement of the latter. Since 1959, one of the roles of the Singapore state has been to implement a strategy to control trade unionism and prevent wage claims disproportionate to productivity gains, while at the same time promoting value enhancement of its workforce through intensive educational and skills upgrading in both schools and workplaces. In the words of Bina and Davis (2000), this labour-skill transformation process, as a qualitative change in social capital with a value representation, has proceeded hand in hand with capital accumulation much tied to the dynamics of the global technological change of the capitalist world to which Singapore is strongly attached and was dependent upon for its sustained progress in the four subsequent decades. As discussed later in this chapter, it is through state capital accumulation that the modernising state of Singapore has played a crucial role in drastically transforming land use.

Since the early 1960s, central to this capital accumulation process was the establishment of the commercial government-linked companies (GLCs) that, if successful, would have enabled the state to effectively induce technological change and educational upgrading by the formation of new skills, and put in place an infrastructure highly conducive to multinational investment. Well-aware of the weaknesses of indigenous industrial entrepreneurs, and the time-consuming process that might be involved in engaging the import-export traders towards industrial undertakings, the government took the initiative of "industrialisation by invitation" (see Blomstrom and Hette, 1984), and assumed an extensive and high-level involvement in industrial development. Duplicating this European tradition of industrialisation, state involvement in industries was recognised as a "legitimate and often an indispensable function of modern government". In the political philosophy of the post-war era, creating industrial public enterprises[2] was in fact a fashion and a "moderate socialist thought" largely practised in Western Europe (Friedmann, 1954: 11–13). This thought undoubtedly had a strong influence on the young PAP political leaders constructing a socialist government whom United Nations consultants sharing identical prevailing ideas advised.

In defining Singapore's "socialist" style of state in 1969, Goh Keng Swee (1995b: 183–184), one of the key masterminds behind Singapore's industrialisation, highlighted that it had always been important for the state to own a substantial part of national wealth as a means of production, including industrial estates under the Jurong Town Corporation and public housing estates under the HDB.

In the 1950s and early 1960s, it was widely believed that the highest returns and productivity gains could be achieved by building a few large, capital-intensive manufacturing industries instead of many small ones. Small firms were supposed to be relatively unprofitable because their unit cost would be high since their production runs were limited. In contrast, large firms were able to enter into mass production, utilise the latest capital-intensive techniques of production, reduce unit production cost, and give a maximum rate of return (Mehmet, 1995: 65).

State-controlled enterprises were predominantly trade-, infrastructure- and heavy industry-oriented, for example, Neptune Orient Lines, National Iron and Steel (Natsteel), Keppel Shipyard, Jurong Shipyard, Sembawang Shipyard, Port of Singapore Authority, Public Utilities Board and Singapore Telephone Board.[3] By its accumulative portfolio, and capitalising on the rising demand in steel in the late 1960s in both domestic and international markets, Natsteel made a six-fold profit during the period 1964–1969.

In the Jurong industrial area built in the early 1960s, there were large-scale heavy industries, comprising notably a steel mill, an oil refinery and a shipyard, acting as a magnet to stimulate Singapore's economic growth (Hughes, 1993). In the process of developing the GLCs and consolidating the role of the state in enterprise management, the local companies tended to be concentrated in traditional businesses such as banking, insurance, property development, food and beverages and other labour-intensive industries and services. The majority of the local companies served the local market (Ministry of Finance, 1993: 32).

The export-oriented strategy was launched immediately after Singapore's departure from the Federation of Malaysia in 1965. In order for them to be effective in the overall development outcome, the GLC's role—given their newness and their relatively small available capital, technological build-up and marketing network—was to complement the leading global MNCs that had mastery control of technological innovations and diffusion, particularly of capital and markets of high-value commodity flows worldwide.[4] Manufacturing-based MNCs were expected to take the lead in Singapore's export-oriented industrialisation (EOI). The GLCs' growth and corporate expansion later was a natural result attributed largely to their institutional power and adaptation, as well as efficiency in both working capacity and global linkage.

The role of the state encompasses equally significantly the management of educational upgrading and assurance of a pro-business trade unionism in favour of investment activities. Education deserves a more detailed discussion in view of its spatial impact on land use.

Educational Upgrading

Like most post-colonial societies, the number of school-going children in Singapore rose tremendously after the 1960s, following the introduction of a "universal education" system supported by a substantial rise in the education budget. Moreover, workforce upgrading had been seen as a critical supporting component in achieving a self-sustaining economy, often stressed by public authorities on many occasions. In a public speech in August 1979, for instance, Goh Keng Swee, then the Education Minister, reminded the people that having drive, shrewdness and enterprise alone was no longer adequate to become successful business leaders as did the pre-war predecessors. Modern enterprises were, he said, distinctly different from the pre-war businesses in a management system that required technical skills and knowledge in order to make the right decisions. He suggested that tertiary education would be important in order to succeed in an increasingly competitive business world and secure a high-paying job (Goh, 1995b).

Again in redressing the 1986 recession, the MTI Economic Committee highlighted the importance of job training, retraining, and being internationally competitive through improving the technical proficiency of industries, management skills and business efficiency (MTI, 1986: 111). In the Strategic Economic Plan produced in 1991 in support of Singapore's undertaking of overseas ventures, it was announced that the education and training system should ensure a high degree of work competence and industry relevance. Teamwork, international orientation, work ethics and lifelong learning, among others, were also placed on the working agenda (Economic Planning Committee, 1991).

In associating the universal education system, industrial training, upgrading and research with land use, the translation of educational policies in spatial terms is reflective in the widespread distribution of schools and other educational institutions in public housing estates and other population centres. Over the last four decades, the planning of primary and secondary schools within easy reach of school-going children has been a basic criterion. By the end of the 1990s, as a result of intensive investments in education and as the economy moved on to the knowledge and skill-intensive era much in need of manpower, the proportion of the population with post-secondary and university qualifications had almost doubled from 15% in 1989 to 27% in 1999. Reflected most significantly in the improvement were the younger adults aged 25 to 39, among whom the number of university graduates rose from 6% to 18% of the cohort during this period (Department of Statistics, 1999: 61).

Having illustrated the role of the state-controlled industrial enterprises and the emphasis on education in managing industrial development, attention is now shifted to the industrialisation strategy and its implementation in Singapore, noting that the location, intensity and nature of industrial land use are fundamentally and inevitably influenced by changing strategies.

THE INDUSTRIALISATION STRATEGY AND ITS IMPLEMENTATION

Singapore's industrialisation policy was intrinsically motivated and extrinsically induced. It was formulated in the early 1960s under the strong initiative of the United Nations (UN), whose task then comprised assisting developing countries in industrialisation. At the invitation of the Singapore government, a United Nations Industrial Survey Mission, led by a Dutch economist, Albert Winsemius, visited Singapore in 1960. His study led to the release of the popularly known Winsemius Report that was to become the nation's industrialisation blueprint.

The mission observed that political uncertainty and labour unrest in the late 1950s had led to a decline in manufacturing. Between 1957 and 1960, the number of workers in manufacturing had fallen by more than 20% from 54,000 to 43,000. To reverse this trend, the report recommended that "a dynamic export industry which can compete in export markets both in quality and price" be created, and that a successful industrialisation programme could only take place with the help of foreign entrepreneurs, managers and capital (United Nations, 1961: 13–14). Concomitantly, a series of liberal investment and workforce policy measures were suggested such as quality infrastructure provision, tax reductions, provision of loans and funds for joint ventures, guarantees against nationalisation and expropriation, and accepting foreign nationals to work in Singapore in managerial posts or as technicians (*ibid*.: 66–74).

To spearhead industrial development, the UN mission proposed the establishment of a non-political body, the Economic Development Board, to formulate and implement the industrialisation policy. Its task included gathering and evaluating feedback from private businesses and trade unions, functioning as a "one-stop" agency providing all assistance needed to investors. Endorsing the establishment of the Jurong Industrial Estate and a number of smaller industrial estates throughout the island by the government, the mission made a land requirement estimate of 3,160 hectares up to 1980 (Table 3.1).

TABLE 3.1: INDUSTRIAL LAND REQUIREMENTS PROPOSED IN WINSEMIUS REPORT, 1960–1980

Use	1960	1961–65	1966–70	1971–80	Total (hectares)
Light, semi-heavy, service	243	324	729	405	1,296
Heavy	122	446	486	810	1,863
Total	365	770	1,215	1,215	3,159

Source: Lee (1973), p. 31.

The recommendations of the report were closely in line with the prevailing orthodoxy that capital accumulation was the key to economic development. Although the report did not consider import-substitution industrialisation (ISI), the strategy was adopted by the Singapore government as a pre-take-off option,[5] like other newly independent states, for a short period from 1960 to 1965.

The Import-Substitution Industrialisation

Prior to 1960, there was no tariff protection for the three broadly defined industries in Singapore, comprising namely: (a) industries linked to primary products produced in the hinterland (natural rubber, coconut, vegetable oil, timber and other tropical produce); (b) industries catering to the local consumer market (beverages, clay products, furniture); and (c) ancillary and maintenance industries servicing local demand such as engineering, printing, vehicle and ship repair, etc. (Pang and Tan, 1981: 142). The Singapore Industrial Promotion Board set up in 1957 had a very limited scope of operation and was handicapped by a lack of funds and personnel. The colonial administration had no intention to expand the scope of industrial development, and this was left to the new PAP government to handle through an import-substitution strategy.

The ISI strategy provided two apparent advantages for newly emerging nations to undertake self-expansion and "infant" industrial development. First, it facilitated the engagement of indigenous entrepreneurs from a very weak industrial base involved in the manufacturing of non-durable, and at a subsequent stage, more durable, consumer goods within a localised family-based business network, often with limited capital. This involved technically less complex goods and modern technology such as food, drinks, tobacco, and garment and textile production. Second, the local enterprises enjoyed free access to a domestic market protected by high tariffs and restrictions against imports.

With no exception, Singapore adopted the ISI strategy from 1959, following the establishment of self-government. With the formation of the Federation of Malaysia in 1963, plans were made to use Malaysia as the hinterland for Singapore's manufactured goods. Between 1960 and 1965 when the ISI prevailed, tariffs were imposed on certain products manufactured locally such as soaps, detergents and paints, etc. Quotas were also introduced during the period 1963 to 1965 to protect as many as 230 locally made industrial products (Pang and Tan, 1981). Indeed, the Jurong Industrial Estate was planned to be a major industrial hub in the hope for a long-term political union of Singapore and Malaysia[6] (see Lyle, 1958; State of Singapore, 1961).

During the 1960s and 1970s, labour-intensive industries, notably textile, garment, footwear and leather manufacturing, played an important part in job creation. In 1969, these largely foreign-invested industries, attracted by generous tax and export incentives, low operating costs and a supportive labour policy, generated almost 15% of all new employment opportunities. From the 1980s, they began to decline after the launch of the Second Industrial Revolution in 1979. The new high-wage policy went in favour of more capital-intensive fibre manufacturing, yarn texturing, weaving and knitting of fabrics, finishing of yarn and fabrics, etc. In 1990, the contracting garment industry still employed 28,000 people in 370 establishments, producing a total value of US$285 million (Douglas *et al.*, 1994). Despite a strong adherence to free trade principles, a low tariff of 5% was maintained against imports to assist the local garment industry (Lim and Associates, 1988).

The expulsion of Singapore in August 1965 from the Federation of Malaysia led by the Malay nationalists of the United Malays National Organisation probably turned out to be a blessing in disguise for the city-state's subsequent industrialisation. Having lost the hinterland market, Singapore stepped onto the path of export-oriented industrialisation just as Taiwan did in the early 1960s amidst the widespread criticism of "neo-colonialism" (Potter *et al.*, 1999), and the search for a new market in developed countries such as the United States of America, Europe and Japan was underway (Lee, 2000: 82). This bold move saved Singapore from many years of change when the shift from ISI to EOI became inevitable in the 1970s as the weaknesses of the ISI strategy were gradually exposed.[7] The failure of the ISI strategy persuaded governments of many pro-capitalist developing countries to shift to a reliance on external markets to sustain industrial growth.

The Export-Oriented Strategy

The adoption of EOI in 1965 saw a drastic shift in Singapore's policy towards a greater depth of trade liberalisation and management on the basis of an outward-looking trade policy. It symbolised equally a new phase of economic development, skipping the factor-driven stage, which was heavily dependent on supplies of local primary resources, as experienced by South Korea and Taiwan in the 1950s and early 1960s.

When wage levels and service and product quality are internationally competitive, the EOI strategy can generate export multipliers, leading to a higher level of competitiveness, and hence more rapid growth of demand and output (Cornwall and Cornwall, 1992). Singapore went directly for an MNC-led, investment-driven strategy in light of its limited natural resources and low-skilled human resources. This aggressive foreign-led industrialisation programme focused on modern technology and large-scale facilities, based on which innovation-driven MNCs were targeted. At the international and macro-level, being innovative meant firms investing in Singapore should enjoy a competitive advantage in globally linked production systems, rather than a comparative advantage offered by factor-driven industrialisation (Gwynne, 1996: 256-257; Ettlinger, 1991; Porter, 1990; Rodan, 1989). Consequently, great efforts were used to attract MNCs from the United States, Japan and Western Europe possessing high competitiveness potential and seeking a lower labour cost base in their global export operations.

From the early 1970s, companies such as General Electric, Hewlett-Packard, American Optical, Timex, Bethlehem Steel, GTE Grumman, Lockheed, Philips, Siemens, Olivetti, Beecham, Sieko, Sumitomo and Yamazaki set up operations in Singapore. Over 50% of Singapore's labour force then worked directly or indirectly for foreign MNCs (Schein, 1996: 47). Foreign direct investment (FDI) in Singapore has served multiple functions, such as being a source of capital formation and a mechanism for technology transfer, skills training and structural transformation of industries (Lloyd, 1999: 313).

At the micro-level of operations, however, this foreign-led industrialisation had to rely on low labour costs, a comparative advantage supported by the local workforce and selected labour inflows from Malaysia with relatively high labour discipline and productivity. This trend was terminated in 1979 when Singapore started its "Second Industrial Revolution", symbolising a new capital-intensive and machinery-intensive stage. This stage was a deepening of the EOI initiated at a time of tight labour markets and rising wages. A wage correction policy was launched to raise wages substantially as a means to restructure the economy towards higher value-added technology. By raising wages, it was hoped that firms relying on cheap labour would relocate, making room for high-value and more skill-intensive industries, and increasing specialisation, especially in the electronics industry. The strategy was to continue with greater emphasis on economies of scale, product quality improvement, innovation in production processes and greater use of information technology to enhance productivity. The government recognised that Singapore would be less competitive in traditional low value-added manufacturing areas and higher wages could only be justified when manufacturing was geared towards a higher level of automation and a more skilled and knowledge-based workforce.

The knowledge-intensive stage began in the early 1990s as Singapore's economy became more globally linked and outward investment in the region took shape. Innovation and sustaining the innovation process have become the main source of competitive advantage, with emphasis being placed on a highly skilled workforce and research and development endeavours. This has been made possible by a government that has accumulated more than S$80 billion[8] of reserves to finance advanced education, training and innovation programmes.

Table 3.2 shows the dramatic change in the socio-economic scenario in the past four decades. In 1960, manufacturing contributed 16.7% to the total GDP. This increased rapidly to 25% in 1970, reaching a peak in 1980 at nearly 30% with the advent of industrial restructuring. Since then, manufacturing's contribution to GDP has stabilised, reaching a plateau of around 27%, a level on par with most developed nations where services have become the main sector of employment. During the period 1960–2000, per capita GDP grew by almost ten times. A tight labour market, declining household size and higher levels of female employability supported by educational upgrading have all contributed substantially to the rise of the labour participation rate of women.

However, the high-wage strategy was affected by the worldwide recession that occurred after the second oil crisis in 1980. In parallel, the premature phasing out of labour-intensive industries also resulted in high operating costs and a recession in the mid-1980s. The recession reflected Singapore's fragile dependence on the capital and technology of MNCs whose capital flow was fluctuating (Goldblum and Wong, 2000: 116). It was the first occurrence of an economy contraction in more than 20 years. The Economic Committee, convened to examine the causes of the recession, recommended the continued upgrading of the economy, focusing on industries and services that required a highly skilled workforce and provided high returns to investors. The Committee also recommended that "excess" savings in Singapore, which had been channelled into the property and stock markets rather than into productive investments, be channelled abroad to help build an external arm of the economy (MTI, 1986).

TABLE 3.2: GDP AND MANUFACTURING GROWTH OF SINGAPORE, 1960–2000

Year	Population[a] (1,000)	Average Annual GDP Growth (%)	Per Capita GDP (at 1990 prices)	Contribution of Manufacturing to GDP (%)	Literacy Rate	Labour Force Participation Rate	
						Male	Female
1960	1,634.1	}9.1	3,606	16.7	52.3[b]	72.9[b]	18.1[b]
1970	2,074.5	}9.0	6,834	25.0	72.2	67.6	24.6
1980	2,282.1	}7.3	14,715	29.7	83.5	81.5	44.3
1990	2,705.1	}8.2	21,812	28.6	89.1	79.0	53.0
2000	3,263.2	}7.7	34,806	26.4	92.5	81.1	55.5

Source: Department of Statistics (1973; 1983; 1988; 1991; 1996; 2001)
Note: Average annual GDP growth and per capital GDP are computed, the latter on the basis of total population.
[a] Figures from 1980 refer to citizens and permanent residents only.
[b] Figures for 1957 from 1957 population census data.

In the face of diminishing returns on capital investment, the key to continued competitiveness is to shift from capital accumulation to knowledge accumulation, focusing, for example, on research and development (Peretto, 1998: 392; Castells 1999b). According to Castells and Hall (1994), changes in the value of tradable products that affect firm performance have come about through three developments in the globalising economy, namely: (a) a technological revolution through information technologies and genetic engineering; (b) a global economic structure that works in real time in worldwide space; and (c) an increasing reliance on the generation of new knowledge and access to, and the possession of, appropriate information for productivity and competitiveness.

Consequently, with concerns about high costs, land constraints and over-accumulation of savings, particularly the Central Provident Fund (CPF) savings, and the need to capitalise on overseas ventures by foreign MNCs, the establishment of an external economy by going regional in search of new business opportunities was conceived (Tan and Lee, 1999). Again, the policy as outlined in the Strategic Economic Plan published in 1991, was to prepare Singapore for overseas ventures in recognition of the limits of industrial expansion through capital accumulation. Incentives were offered to Singapore nationals who volunteered to be posted overseas in compensation for inconveniences while living abroad. Venturing overseas means that domestic land to be allocated for industrial use is restricted to a reasonable level, except for the intensification and upgrading to high-value industry clusters such as biomedical parks. A large part of the industrial expansion is expected to take place overseas in mainly Asian countries with great growth potential and a large domestic market.

Ironically, the petrochemical industry is here to stay in consideration of its high-value output over the years, contributing more than one-fifth of total manufacturing output in 2000 (Table 3.3). While there has always been an oil-refining capacity in Singapore, it was only in the mid-1980s that Singapore expanded the higher value-added petrochemical product industry. Plans for developing Singapore's capacity for ethylene production began in 1977 with the assistance of the Japanese government. The first naphtha cracker came online in 1984 and was operated by the Petrochemical Corporation of Singapore (DBS Bank, 1996). A second cracker came online in 1997, increasing Singapore's annual ethylene production capacity to over 950,000 tonnes (Monetary Authority of Singapore, 1999), representing about 35% of total ASEAN ethylene production.

Through a series of reclamations and amalgamations of nearby islands, JTC is currently planning to make Jurong Island a world-class chemicals hub. With 70 companies investing S$21 billion, Jurong Island has become the second-largest ethylene production centre and the third-largest oil refinery centre in the world (JTC, 2002). With economies of conglomeration derived by grouping petrochemical companies adjacent to each other, it is expected that companies will find the outsourcing of supporting services and functions easy and convenient.

Two other key ambitions strongly associated with Singapore's industrialisation were also outlined in the 1991 Strategic Economic Plan. The first was to upgrade Singapore to a truly global city through establishing strong networks with both neighbouring countries in the region and the world. Local companies were encouraged to invest overseas to tap as many economic benefits that globalisation could offer as possible. The second ambition was to complement the first by developing local enterprises, with the help of the EDB's Enterprise Development Division, to compete and survive in the international marketplace. Promising local companies would be assisted in becoming MNCs (Economic Planning Committee, 1991).

TABLE 3.3: OUTPUT OF PETROCHEMICAL INDUSTRIES IN COMPARISON WITH OTHER SELECTED INDUSTRIES, 1966–2000

S$ million

Industry Type*	1966	1970	1980	1990	2000
Refined Petroleum Products	263.3	1,221.8	11,520.3	11,364.5	19,610.9
Chemicals and Chemical Products	93.4	112.6	929.4	4,921.9	15,943.8
Machinery and Equipment	59.1	357.6	2,209.3	3,380.7	7,456.9
Electronic Products and Components	n.a.	n.a.	5,344.0	27,878.1	81,802.7
Total Manufacturing	1,531.4	4,627.2	32,805.8	71,453.8	158,745.7

Source: Department of Statistics, *Yearbook of Statistics* (various issues).
Note: *Classification of industries is not strictly comparable as the Singapore Standard Industrial Classification as been revised over the years.

In summary, it is recognised that three outcomes arose from the EOI in land-use planning and allocations. The first was the spatial expansion of Keppel and Jurong Ports (and their warehousing facilities nearby) and the airport (ultimately Changi Airport in the east) plus the corresponding development of its airfreight and maintenance services to match the rising demand. It is also logical to say that since the 1990s, Singapore, in order to maintain an economic lead, has started work on two fronts, using MNCs to deepen its global market penetration. Domestically, it has laid the foundation for a knowledge-based economy that functions as a central node of the regional economies. There has been an intensification in the introduction of cutting-edge manufacturing industries in Singapore, notably those involved in highly specialised products. Table 3.4 explains why the predominant role of the foreign MNCs needs to continue in

Singapore's external economy. In 1998, foreign MNCs dominated the two key industries of electronics (computer hardware, memory chips, etc.) and high-value petrochemicals in Singapore. Almost 70% of the total S$82.4 billion of equity investment in manufacturing was associated with foreign MNCs. Local manufacturing firms were more significant players in lower-value products such as machinery, transport equipment, food, paper and metal products.

TABLE 3.4: FOREIGN AND LOCAL EQUITY INVESTMENT IN SINGAPORE'S MANUFACTURING INDUSTRY, 1998

Industry	Foreign Equity (S$ million)	%	Local Equity (S$ million)	%	Foreign and Local Combined (S$ million)	Total %
Electronic products and components	27,022.6	87.0	4,049.6	13.0	31,072.2	100.0
Chemical & chemical products	16,608.4	95.1	860.9	4.9	17,469.3	100.0
Petroleum & petroleum products	3,679.1	97.5	96.2	2.5	3,775.3	100.0
Machinery	2,348.4	48.9	2,457.3	51.1	4,805.7	100.0
Transport equipment	1,488.3	22.2	5,228.3	77.8	6,716.6	100.0
Fabricated metal products	1,032.9	32.2	2,177.7	67.8	3,210.6	100.0
Instrumentation, photographic & optical goods	822.1	89.8	92.9	10.2	915.0	100.0
Paper & paper products	804.0	28.3	2,037.3	71.7	2,841.3	100.0
Rubber & plastic products	756.2	30.4	1,734.7	69.6	2,490.9	100.0
Food, beverages & tobacco	618.7	20.4	2,408.5	79.6	3,027.2	100.0
Others	2,292.0	37.8	3,765.6	62.2	6,057.6	100.0
Total	57,472.7	69.8	24,909.0	30.2	82,381.7	100.0

Source: Adapted from Department of Statistics (2000) and Ministry of Trade and Industry (2001), pp. 29–30.

On the international front, a similar trend of MNC dominance has been demonstrated in Singapore's investments abroad. As shown in Table 3.5, of the total S$173 billion invested overseas in 1998, about

S$100 billion or 57.8% was invested by wholly foreign- and majority foreign-owned firms[9] having an operations office in Singapore. This trend declined, however, in 2000 when the proportion fell to 55.2% following a significant rise in the overseas investments of wholly local-owned firms. Not surprisingly, in reflecting the features of a mature, developed economy, tertialisation and producer services of the investment in support of manufacturing have become the key investment agenda. Only 19.5% of the total direct overseas investment of Singapore investors in 1998 was in manufacturing. Of the total direct overseas investment by locally controlled companies, many of which were GLCs, about one-quarter of the total investment (S$40.9 billion) was in manufacturing. Almost half of this manufacturing activity was in the fast-growing market of China (Department of Statistics, 2000: 45, 47), where operating costs are lower and labour supply seems to be unlimited.

TABLE 3.5: SINGAPORE'S INVESTMENT ABROAD, 1998–2000

Company Type	1998		2000	
	Total (S$ million)	%	Total (S$ million)	%
Wholly local-owned	44,905.3	26.0	67,705.0	30.8
Majority local-owned	28,099.4	16.2	30,803.9	14.0
Wholly foreign-owned	85,384.0	49.3	106,109.2	48.3
Majority foreign-owned	14,748.6	8.5	15,110.8	6.9
Total	173,137.3	100.0	219,728.9	100.0

Source: Calculated from Department of Statistics (2000), pp. 23–27 and Department of Statistics (2002), pp. 25–29.

According to Lloyd (1999), East Asia as a whole has benefited from MNC investments in economic terms, despite adverse effects such as acceleration of the rural-urban exodus, and speculative activities in property and financial transactions associated with the financial crisis that broke out in 1997. Arguably, therefore, the

Singapore overseas ventures are likely to continue to be in the form of foreign MNC-led investments. The presence of Western MNCs implies that they are not only taking strategic advantage of vertical integration (lower cost, local resources and specialised local production and expertise, for example) but they are also exploiting horizontal integration, including expanding market opportunities in the Asia-Pacific. Sharing a common interest by establishing a strategic alliance with the MNCs, Singapore firms can be self-reinforcing. Linking organisationally, financially and technologically with powerful global cities such as New York, Tokyo and London helps contribute towards establishing Singapore as a global city (see Thompson, 2000). Lakshmann and his research partners (2000: 49–51) observe that the growth of New York, London and Tokyo into influential global cities has been associated with an industrial backbone and a network using industrial technologies as a key economic base. Nevertheless, their operations are largely dependent on financial and trade activities on an international scale. Positioned at the top of the global city hierarchy, their dominance has resulted from an array of factors such as a technological edge and organisational knowledge, and being effective centres in innovations, management and coordination of MNCs worldwide.

Thus, the continued dependence and weaknesses inherent within Singapore's pursuit of sustained growth following the regionalisation drive since the end of the 1980s are expected to persist until the homegrown MNCs can play a greater role (Peebles and Wilson, 1996: 240–241). How long this will take is unknown. Industrial estates in Singapore have developed in tandem with the economic policy of Singapore as well as the spatial redistribution of the country's population through the public housing programme. (This is discussed in greater detail in the chapter on public housing.) Over 90% of industrial estates (by land area) in Singapore are managed by the Jurong Town Corporation and the Housing and Development Board.[10] It is fair to suggest that the Singapore government, which has a firm control over the supply of industrial land, is equipped with a very powerful tool to translate its industrialisation policy into the intended morphology, shaping the landscape to a substantial scale. This physical transformation is dealt with in the final section.

PHYSICAL DEVELOPMENT OF INDUSTRIAL ESTATES

Planning of post-independence Singapore's industrial estates arose from modernisation as a development ideology and a values motivator championed by the economic planning agency, the EDB. The Planning Department, which was created in 1960 at the same time as the EDB, had a role that was limited to land-use allocation and development control (Dale, 1999: 106–107). Consequently, the Jurong Industrial Estate was placed directly under the jurisdiction and management of the EDB.

This section looks at the expansion of JTC industrial estates in Singapore since 1960 to illustrate the pattern of industrial development. Much in compliance with the prevailing planning principles, the growth of Singapore's industrial sector was met with new factories built to accommodate the rising demand and the fact that non-polluting industries should be situated in proximity to population centres to cut down on travel and commuting time. Hence, besides Jurong, flatted factories[11] were built in most housing estates to capitalise on the abundant pool of labour supply, and support industrial growth at the neighbourhood level. Land-extensive industries and those that required sea frontage or with high nuisance values were located in the outlying areas away from population centres. After presenting a broad survey of the distribution of JTC estates, we will look more closely at the Jurong Industrial Estate and examine the factors that led to the development of Singapore's largest industrial estate.

Industrial Estates in Singapore

Industrial development went through a general process from the sporadic and spontaneous patterns of the colonial days to a planned and rigidly regulated stage after independence. In the early 1950s, in the absence of development control, industries in Singapore were by and large randomly distributed in the midst of population centres or where land was cheap (Yuen, 1991: 49). Nearly a quarter of all industrial sites were then found in the Central Area, with another 40% located in its fringes, such as Bukit Timah, Pasir Panjang and Geylang.

Planned industrial estates did exist prior to 1959. In 1951, the Colonial Development Corporation built a ready-made industrial estate at Bukit Timah for small-scale and medium-sized industries, supplemented with services and facilities such as roads, electricity, water, sewerage and banking (United Nations, 1962b: 334). A second estate of 22.5 hectares was developed by the Singapore Improvement Trust at Alexandra. These estates were of modest size and scope, and were located in areas of relatively high population density. Subsequently, the need for industrial estates was recognised by the first Master Plan Committee, whose Industrial Resources Study Group recommended that between 500 and 1,000 hectares would need to be set aside to meet the needs of the manufacturing industry during the period between 1955 and 1972 (Colony of Singapore, 1955). Selecting Jurong for industrial use was first mooted in August 1956 when it was noticed that a hilly area adjacent to Damar Laut could be levelled to fill the coast (EDB, 1967: 100).

Jurong presented several advantages as an industrial town. It was the least encumbered area in Singapore, with a relatively low population density and inexpensive land adjacent to deep coastal waters. The 1957 census recorded about 37,000 persons (mostly engaged in agriculture and fishing) in the area, a low population density of 385 persons per square kilometre, compared with an average density of 2,500 persons per square kilometre for the whole of Singapore. Rubber and coconut plantations and market gardening covered about a third of the area, while another third was covered by mangrove forests. The topography of Jurong was characterised by low hills running in two parallel ridges from southeast to northwest with an average height of 37 metres (Figure 3.1). Jurong was incorporated into the 1958 Master Plan but the project remained dormant until 1960. Industrial land development at Jurong and other areas can be divided into four phases during the period 1960–2000.

Industrial Development, 1960–1970
In early 1960, at the suggestion of Goh Keng Swee, an industrial plan was drawn to develop 5,000 acres (2,000 hectares) with port facilities and railway connections. A Japanese Survey Team visited the site in December 1960 and recommended an enlargement to 9,000 acres (3,650 hectares), covering the coastline to be reserved for waterfront and heavy industries. Residential areas were integrated and sited behind the general and light industries adjacent to the coastline's heavy industries. In this way, the more polluting industries were kept away from the residential areas.

Jurong was originally designed around an iron and steel mill, fed by iron ore, coal and limestone from the region (EDB, 1967), with an annual capacity of 500,000 tonnes to serve Southeast Asia (Hanna, 1964: 3). Oil refining, aluminium smelting, ship breaking, sawmilling, cement works and textile manufacturing industries were also considered. To facilitate the import of raw materials and the export of finished products, a deep-water port was built.

Development at Jurong began with the levelling of hills and using the resulting material to fill nearby swamps, thus extending the coastline seaward. By 1963, work on the Jurong Port began. The same year also saw the start of production for state-owned heavy industries such as Jurong Shipyard and National Iron and Steel Plant. At the same time, the JTC developed low-cost housing for workers in close proximity to the industrial sites, though this did not prove popular for many years.

During this period, 1,720 hectares of land were allocated for industries and infrastructural facilities such as electrical sub-stations and water mains. However, the development of social amenities, greenery and the town centre did not progress as rapidly until 1970, when most of the industrial lots had been prepared. From press clippings and other sources, it was evident that life in Jurong, often described by the press as "Dullsville", was spartan. The dissatisfaction of the residents was centred on the lack of amenities such as post offices, shops, schools, and public transport between Jurong and the city centre, where workers came from. Persistent and rising levels of air pollution became common as industrial development picked up speed. The air pollution was labelled as a "bluish earth-clinging pollution" and identified as smog (*Straits Times*, 24 February 1970). The lack of amenities and transport was eventually solved as the increasing population of the Jurong industrial areas made their provision economically viable.

Outside Jurong, smaller industrial estates for light labour-intensive industries located at population centres such as Redhill, Tanglin Halt, and Kallang were also planned. Generally, factories that required large industrial sites were located away from the city, first in Jurong, and later, Sungei Kadut and Kranji, the least encumbered areas of Singapore. In areas of high population density, multi-storey flatted factories were built. During this phase, most JTC flatted factories adjoining new towns were built just outside the Central Business District (Figure 3.2).

Industrial Estates, 1970–1980

The pace of industrialisation took off notably in the 1970s, following the 1974 oil crisis that activated a global industrial shift. More industrial estates were developed in Singapore to keep up with the demand for industrial facilities. Except for petrochemical industries, the focus of industrial development during this period was less on heavy capital-intensive industries, but on those that could provide local employment.

Development in Jurong extended towards the Gul Basin in the west and towards Sungei Pandan in the east. By 1975, 5.7 square kilometres of land had been reclaimed from the sea and 15.1 square kilometres of mangrove forests cleared (Figure 3.3). Most of the hills had been cleared by this time, leaving a large area of land lying less than ten metres above sea level. The coastline, pushed forward by reclamation, was made longer by creating the Gul and Benoi Basins to allow more sites to have water frontage. On the islands, reclamation extended the shore to the edge of the reef flat. A road network, based on the grid system, was put in place to provide access to the industrial estate. Generally, more polluting industries were located away from population centres, and the land-use pattern in 1975 reflected standard practices in the design and layout of industrial towns. Air and water pollution in Jurong also diminished after more measures were introduced following the introduction of the Clean Air Act in 1972, and tough enforcement actions were taken against factories that failed to comply.

Away from Jurong, in Toa Payoh, the HDB built integrated housing estates with about 20% of the land set aside for industrial use. Approximately half of the industrial land was developed and managed by the JTC, while the HDB developed the remainder for relocation of factories and workshop complexes, usually small-scale "backyard" industries, whose sites had to be cleared for new developments (See-Toh, 1998).

Thus, new industrial sites were located at Toa Payoh, Ang Mo Kio and Ayer Rajah to take advantage of the potentially high manpower resources in the housing estates, especially the readily available female assembly-line workers. While industrial development at Jurong was substantially expanded during this period, large tracts of land were developed at Loyang, Sungei Kadut, Kranji and Woodlands. Some industrial estates were established specifically for one or two industry clusters. For Jurong, the islands south of the coast were reserved for the petrochemical industry, whereas woodworking factories were relocated at Sungei Kadut and Kranji, and aviation industries at Loyang, close to Changi Airport in the east (Figure 3.4).

Towards the end of the 1970s when the "Second Industrial Revolution" was launched, factory construction in Singapore began to shift structurally, becoming intensified and capital-intensive in response to the rising land and labour costs and the need for higher value-added and technology-intensive industries. Correspondingly, large-scale labour-intensive industries which had served their purpose of solving unemployment problems in the 1960s and early 1970s were being gradually phased out.

Industrial Development, 1980–1990

To plan for higher value-added industries, the JTC undertook a comprehensive review in 1979 and produced a ten-year Master Plan in which new estates and factory buildings would be constructed and designed in such a way that they would appear attractive to investors. Through the use of better planning techniques, a more efficient use of land was achieved. More factories were built near population centres to maximise labour participation, especially for women. Concomitantly, in its efforts to upgrade the skills of Singaporean workers, the JTC would provide land at cost for industrial training institutes, such as the German Training Institute, along with architectural and engineering design services (JTC, 1979/80). These programmes marked a qualitative change in the manufacturing sector of the Singapore economy. Such improvements in factory buildings, layout and landscaping were deemed to be necessary to attract the targeted industries required for a new phase of industrial upgrading.

Industrial estates in new towns and elsewhere, continued to expand during the 1980s, with higher-standard factories being built and older industrial estates being upgraded. Geographical coverage was extended further from the Central Business District to Tampines, Kaki Bukit, Kampong Ubi and Woodlands, leading to an expansion of flatted factory space (Figure 3.5). At the same time, the Science Park, located near the National University of Singapore and supported by the university's research environment, was maturing. As a facilitator as well as a regulator, the JTC suspended new industrial developments for several years to prevent an oversupply in the market following the economic recession of 1985/86. The JTC also reduced rents and gave rebates to its tenants and lessees.

Industrial Estates, 1990–2000

The 1990s saw the industrial policies continue to be guided by a knowledge-based economy. The review of the Concept Plan in the early 1990s had set out to establish an ultimate industrial land bank of about

13,000 hectares. In its implementation, the JTC embarked on a programme called the Industrial Land Plan for the 21st Century (IP21) to maximise the productivity of land through intensification of existing industries, decanting older industrial estates of low-value industries to make way for high-technology and high-value added industries, and developing industrial parks in other countries in the region where land and labour were more abundant and cost-competitive.

In 1991, the JTC launched the first international business park in Jurong East. Business parks are designed and promoted as sites that give industries the opportunity to collaborate and innovate. Consisting of a mix of small and large, public and private organisations, they create an atmosphere for highly transparent and close collaboration and social interaction among research-oriented high-tech firms.[12] These parks are located close to tertiary institutions in a bid to foster collaboration between the business sector and academia. Singapore has wooed talents from prestigious international research institutions such as Johns Hopkins University, INSEAD, Wharton School, MIT, Georgia Tech and the University of Chicago Graduate School of Business and encouraged them to work jointly with the local universities and research centres (EDB, 2000). Figure 3.6 shows the two technology corridors designed by the 1991 Concept Plan to facilitate such interactions, and other industrial spaces developed in tandem during the 1990s as a result of further growth. By 1998, flatted factories were developed at Woodlands as well as Loyang, while industrial workshops and land were developed at Changi, Tampines, Yio Chu Kang and Woodlands (Figure 3.7).

In Woodlands, an entire industrial estate was decanted of 563 companies occupying 18.4 hectares to make way for a wafer fabrication park (*Straits Times*, 31 October 1995; 3 January 1996). The new knowledge-intensive economy has called for heavy capital investments but a reduction in business costs in Singapore by creating industry clusters so that synergistic advantages can be realised through the sharing of facilities. Presently, there are industry clusters for the chemical, wafer fabrication, advanced display, biomedical, logistics and food sectors.

During this period, greater demand for industrial land had led to the reclamation of 20 square kilometres from the sea at Jurong, mostly through the enlargement and agglomeration of the southern islands. On the mainland, the Tuas reclamation project resulted in 6.5 square kilometres of new land, making it one of the largest reclamation projects in the world. From the early 1990s, further amalgamation of the southern islands began to form a single Jurong Island to cater to the expansion of the petrochemical industry. Along with land preparation, the transport network has been extended. Several roads have been upgraded to expressways and many traffic interchanges have been improved with flyovers. Public transport to Jurong has been improved considerably by the extension of the mass rapid transit system to Boon Lay. At the same time, Jurong Port has been expanded and there is now a second link by bridge to Peninsular Malaysia (Figure 3.8). By 2000, reclamation and amalgamation works were virtually completed in accordance with the 1991 revised Concept Plan.

To summarise, the industrial development goal in Singapore is to create a conducive environment for industrial firms to conduct operations in Singapore while optimising the use of limited land resources and labour. Factories that have little nuisance value and do not need large areas of land are located near or in population centres to take advantage of a ready supply of labour and to reduce travelling time. Polluting industries or land-intensive industries are located away from the city centre where land values are lower and at a reasonable distance from population centres. However, with urban expansion, these areas, which were once rural, are now enveloped by housing and other developments.

In terms of production output, a glance at the principal manufacturing statistics during the period 1980–2000 reflects the economic effects (Table 3.6). As the statistics show, the insignificant increase of the number of manufacturing firms is attributable to the restructuring starting from 1979. This has edged out small, less-competitive and labour-intensive firms in favour of larger and more capital- and technology-intensive ones. Correspondingly, compared with the five-fold increase in output and direct exports, the low 20% to 28% rise in manpower in different years over the 20-year period indicates the upgrading of the workforce and technology. In other words, manufacturing land-take does not need to expand at the same scale to support growth, but is far less than originally expected.

TABLE 3.6: PRINCIPAL MANUFACTURING STATISTICS, 1980–2000

Year	Establishments	Workers	Output (S$ million)	Direct Exports (S$ million)
1980	3,390	288,170	32,810	19,870
1985	3,530	254,800	38,820	24,390
1990	3,700	351,670	71,330	47,000
1995	4,040	370,280	113,360	69,010
2000	4,000	346,150	158,770	100,960

Source: Department of Statistics (1990), p. 110 and Department of Statistics (2001b), p. 96.
Note: All numbers are rounded to the nearest 10.

Future Developments

A key concern of the Singapore government is the maintenance of the country's international competitiveness. Future industrial development must therefore adapt to a fast-changing global business environment where the increased use of the Internet has changed the traditional ways of doing business. Global trade supported by new information technologies is likely to reduce the importance of direct spatial linkages. Corporate control, notably the supranational control of the influential multinational firms, over production centres, including factories, will cut across national boundaries. Industrial estates that remain in Singapore will need to adapt and be reoriented towards meeting the rising demands of highly specialised production functions (Sassen, 1999; 2000).

It is in anticipation of the new global economy that Singapore has begun in earnest the development of business parks, deemed as the core industrial set-up of the future. A total of 14 business parks have been placed in the pipeline by the 1991 revised Concept Plan (Figure 3.6). These parks are expected to nurture homegrown MNCs to face challenges in a competitive corporate world (JTC, 2001) where, according to Castells and Hall (1994), access to, and possession of, appropriate information is key to the survival of firms.

Continuing along the designated path, the 2001 Concept Plan has re-emphasised the importance of the intensification of industrial premises and closely following the prevailing high value-added industries. These encompass manufacturing and research in electronics, chemicals, pharmaceuticals, biomedical sciences and engineering. Greater flexibility for businesses is on the agenda with the introduction of a new zoning system. The system, for example, allows all uses, except pollutive ones, to be housed within one single building block. Known as a "white zone", it creates mixed-use buildings where housing, offices, shops, clean industries, research and recreational facilities will be placed under the same roof (URA, 2001). As an industrial implementation agency, the JTC will undergo further corporate restructuring in order to be more agile in its operations and management. In this aspect, the start of the new-generation iParks (Industrial Park of the 21st Century) and Science Hub at Buona Vista are two examples which are expected to integrate this mixed use (JTC, 2001).

CONCLUDING REMARKS

The key ingredient that contributed to the success of Singapore's industrialisation was the close relationship between state-initiated industrialisation backed by modernisation ideals, and the matching of profit-oriented international MNCs. This has produced an extraordinary spatial outcome of landscape change. The planning tool and implementation effectiveness underlain by this relationship has brought about a new and modern Singapore. The model is supported by strong local initiatives and motivations, and an efficient public administration and infrastructure to make it work. The Keynesian approach explains the incessant intervening and structural adjustments in micro-policy matters by the government in the implementation process, as it is believed that the free market system cannot be effectively self-regulatory. The regulatory framework put in place has also incorporated the upgrading of the education system and labour control to mitigate conflicts between employers and employees. The extensive state involvement is characteristic of a top-down approach from a committed developmental leadership which, in its drive towards modernity, has built up the GLCs to complement the operations of MNCs while strengthening themselves in the process. In promoting economic growth as a general policy, this leadership has a strong conviction in the strategic advice provided by top consultancy services from international organisations and universities.

Singapore's industrial take-off is demonstrated by the dramatic shift from its deep-rooted primary resource-based *entrepôt* trade to a manufacturing-based, export-led trade initiated after 1965. The continuity of the export-led economic base has been characterised by constant responses to global trade and technological demands "with maximum speed, a policy that would guarantee economic viability, and to treat the whole matter as an emergency" (Regnier, 1992: 52). The crux lies in a structural change from comparative advantage to competitive advantage at the global level. Yet, the Singapore industrialisation model is an outcome of a strongly Keynesian and state-led capitalist approach, supported by a pro-business strategy, a heavy dependence on Western capital and world market access, management, technology and innovations. Western corporations have found Singapore to be a useful centre that provides a lower cost of operations in terms of both the horizontal and vertical integration of the global production network, and facilitates their global market penetration. The reliance on foreign MNCs is also eminent in Singapore's overseas ventures initiated after the 1990s.

The strong local initiatives and motivations behind this export-led strategy and MNC demand are equally important. In the 1960s, industrialisation was seen as a means to solve a serious unemployment problem, as well as to provide the economic wherewithal for the government's public programme. These two objectives, reducing unemployment and providing housing, were seen as crucial in establishing political and social stability. To lead the domestic industrial drive, government-linked companies were created to fill the gap that could not be filled by the weak local industrial entrepreneurs. Moreover, without an efficient public administration, infrastructure, educational upgrading of the workforce and taming of an initially radical unionism, the extent of economic growth would have been much mitigated.

The nature of Singapore's industrial dependency has, however, modified its content in the process. While it can be identified as being dependent by having incorporated a heavy input of foreign capital in its major economic sectors, with concentrated utilisation of capital-intensive imported technologies (Drakakis-Smith, 1996: 236), it is no longer an exporter of labour-intensive manufactures and the consumption pattern of its population has resembled those of rich developed countries in many aspects. Instead, Singapore has ascended to a higher level of the technological ladder, but burdened by high operating costs, it has to seek overseas ventures to capitalise on lower costs and market opportunities elsewhere. In so doing, it imposes a dependency relationship on others in an increasingly interdependent global trade system. Building up its own MNCs to consolidate its role in the global division of labour in technology, finance and management services is the current emphasis, aimed at achieving a favourable position in the intensifying global competition. The outcome of such efforts has yet to be seen.

In retrospect, Singapore's industrial policy, which was initiated primarily for social and political stability, has been transformed into a search for the long tenure of the PAP government by justifying legitimacy with sustainable economic growth. In terms of approach, the strategy has incorporated a pro-MNC and strong developmentalist spirit in its political philosophy. The regional investment undertakings and strengthening global links must be seen only as an effective instrument towards such an end.

ENDNOTES

1. In 1997, there were almost 200 American manufacturing companies investing a total of S$19 billion in Singapore (Lee, 2000: 82).

2. Using Franklin Roosevelt's classical definition of state-owned industrial enterprises, which has great validity when applied to those in Singapore, we can define them as "corporation[s] clothed with the power of government but possessed of the flexibility and initiative of a private enterprise" (Friedmann, 1954: 20).

3. The Singapore Telephone Board became a cash-rich public-listed corporation in the early 1990s known as Singapore Telecom (SingTel). It is one of the key GLCs that is highly influential in domestic and overseas investments.

4. Indeed, key MNCs in the developed nations are responsible for three-quarters of the research and development investments, involving skills necessary for the continued innovations of new products and expensive processes normally beyond the scope of small firms. Spatially, the research and development centres are often major research-university clusters or established centres of innovation (Bina and Davis, 2000: 195; Stutz and de Souza, 1998).

5. Import-substitution industrialisation was a popular strategy adopted by developing countries, particularly in Latin America in the 1950s and early 1960s. It is an induced outcome of Prebisch's (1950) interpretation of the world economic system based on the influential core-periphery model. Prebisch's thesis on the unequal terms of trade argues that manufactured goods are traded against agricultural products

in world trade, benefiting the former at the expense of the latter. The basis of his argument is that, in the reversionary period of an economic cycle, prices of manufactures in developed countries are maintained by cutting down production. In the prosperous time of the cycle, prices are increased following wage increases of workers supported by trade unions. On the contrary, wage levels of primary product workers in developing countries would remain stagnant. Their farm produce as basic items of consumption would fall in price in the international market because of the saturated demand, as a result of rising affluence in developed countries whose consumers tend to shift towards consumer durables (Gwynne, 1996: 252).

6   A railway link to Malaysia was also built in Jurong to facilitate the import of raw materials and the export of manufactured goods to the Malaysian hinterland. This railway line was dismantled after the separation since the goods traffic by rail had not increased between Singapore and Malaysia.

7   The weaknesses of ISI employed in developing countries, particularly Brazil and Argentina, have been experienced in many aspects. First, it led to a high cost of production due to a lack of economies of scale and the easily saturated domestic market, characterised by the low purchasing power of the majority of the population. Second, industrial development became inward-looking and lacked technological dynamism and innovations. Protective measures implemented through the use of tariffs, quotas, licensing and exchange controls, provision of low-interest loans by government banks and financial institutions (Black, 1999: 94) and lack of open competition led to market failure with features identified by Schmitz (1994) as follows:

   a)   Excessive administrative regulations giving rise to bureaucratisation, corruption and discouragement of productive private investment and initiatives;

   b)   High exchange rates contributing to the reduction of the relative gains earned from agricultural exports; and

   c)   Cheap credit for the installation of machinery, leading to over-equipping of factories. Good profits are, however, maintained even at a low capacity of utilisation because of the protection of the domestic market.

   With a dependence on foreign supplies of capital goods and the above weaknesses, the fast initial industrial growth was not sustainable once the domestic market became saturated. Export expansion, however, was hindered because of the industrial inefficiency and structure.

8   "Wholly local-owned" or "wholly foreign-owned" refers to 100% of ordinary paid-up shares being owned by Singapore or foreign companies respectively. "Majority local-owned" or "majority foreign-owned" refers to more than 50% of ordinary paid-up shares being owned by Singapore or foreign companies respectively. Investments abroad include: (a) total direct investment abroad (ordinary paid-up shares of overseas subsidiaries, associates, affiliates and their reserves, and short- to long-term loans granted by the parent companies); (b) portfolio investments; and (c) other foreign assets.

9   Private industrial estates make up about 9% of the total industrial land stock. However, many of these sites are located in residential areas and will therefore be redeveloped for other uses.

10 These are ready-built factory units constructed in medium-rise to high-rise blocks. They house multiple tenants/lessees who share common properties such as car parks, loading/unloading areas and cargo lifts.

11 Each business park may be specialised in identified niche sectors of the economy. An Admissions Committee, in which the URA is represented, decides on the suitability of tenants. In some cases, the tenants may be limited to a narrow range of industries.

CHAPTER 4

From Universal Public Housing to Meeting Aspirations for Private Housing

INTRODUCTION

Housing is a basic human need. It is extensively acknowledged that the state is legitimately the authority responsible for ensuring that citizens have adequate access to decent housing. In Singapore, housing policies, perceived as a test of political skills, have evolved from the management of basic needs to the management of aspirations. They are a real test of state determination, persistence and vigour as they initially involve basic welfare provision and, at a later stage, meeting a higher level of need beyond basic considerations of comfort. Indeed, housing reflects different levels of comfort to different users and, to many, it represents a social status. Consequently, it has a social representation that motivates household mobility as an implicit part of the social upgrading process. In Singapore, after four decades of effective implementation and provision of public housing by the Housing and Development Board, housing as a basic need has largely been resolved. However, general affluence and rising numbers of the middle class have increased the demand for more private housing, which is perceived as qualitatively superior to public housing. This rising demand has been met with a response from the state that sees a necessity to facilitate access as a negotiating term for support of the government's economic priority model, a model relying on material incentives and political acceptance of a one-party system.

This chapter first introduces the rationale underlying Singapore's public housing policy since 1960, and illustrates how this provision of public housing has led to a shift in the demand of its clientele. Focus is centred on investigating why an effective public housing promotion has to be met with availability of private housing, perceived to be better in terms of quality and status despite continued state efforts to upgrade public housing quality. To substantiate the claim that the aspirations for private housing are generally a result of rising affluence, a questionnaire survey of both public and private housing owners was conducted during May and June 2002. The survey aimed to examine the perception of private housing, and whether the aspirations for private housing are logically a rejection of public housing as public consumer goods, characteristic of the post-Fordist era. Finally, the public policy response to facilitate access to private housing and the problems arising from subsequent setbacks are addressed.

PUBLIC HOUSING AS MASS-PRODUCED PUBLIC CONSUMER GOODS?

Earlier in Chapter 1, widespread shortages in decent housing and overcrowding in the Central Area were primarily associated with the pre-1959 colonial policy that paid little attention to low-cost housing. Housing provision was left primarily to the private market. Construction of working-class housing was seen as less viable as it yielded much lower returns than other investments in rubber, tin and trading. The Singapore Improvement Trust (SIT), established in 1927 more as a statutory board to deal with the lack of sanitation and "diseases which could harm the reproduction of [the] labour force", was not empowered to carry out housing projects except those for homeless people (Yeoh, 1996: 137). It was financially handicapped and had limited powers to alienate land or resettle squatters, and its operations were mainly concentrated on public sites or converted military areas (Gamer, 1972: 43–44; Tan and Pang, 1991). Consequently, most SIT developments were built in a piecemeal fashion near the Central Business District. By 1959, the SIT had managed to build only 23,000 units (Wong and Yeh, 1985), housing less than 9% of the total population.

The post-1959 era witnessed a newly elected government under the People's Action Party that assumed the responsibility to ensure "universal provision" to every citizen. On the basis of free-market principles, the state stepped in to supply public goods and services that were fundamental but inadequately supplied through the market. Such goods, including basic housing, were often those for which no payment could be extracted for their consumption, but were beneficial to society as a whole if consumed (Low, 1998: 73). Indeed, behind this responsibility for the governance of welfare, there was arguably a larger social goal that "corporatised" public housing as an instrument to bolster economic growth alongside the industrialisation and modernisation efforts of post-independence states. Since 1965, with Singapore's pro-business and export-led industrialisation strategies set in motion, public housing has, to a great extent, contributed towards lower wages, higher productivity, and political and social stability that have attracted international capital and manufacturing investment (Lim, 1987: 185; Chang, 1994).

Public Housing Since 1960

Established as a statutory board in 1960, the HDB was equipped in 1967 with the new Land Acquisition Act, making it the most powerful landowner and the sole agent for promoting public housing homeownership. In its subsequent operations and practices of forced acquisition, it had largely accomplished three major objectives: planning efficiency, fiscal and social equity (wealth redistribution) and the provision of services. The social equity argument has been made on the basis that any enhanced land values or economic gain through redevelopment or improvement of services should be at the disposal of the state in favour of set social and communal objectives (Kivell, 1993; Wong, 2001). This practice of forced acquisitions—with preset prices of compensation which were lower than the market rate—throughout the first two decades of land acquisition would later explain the lower-than-expected costs of provision of public housing. It substantially reduces in real terms the cost of subsidies officially computed based on market land values when flats are sold to HDB applicants, an issue to which we will later return.

In broad policy terms, the HDB's building programmes may be summarised in five major stages, each according to a specific juncture most urgently dealt with either on the basis of affordability or political imperatives (see Castells, Goh and Kwok, 1990: 225–258). Consequently, these stages, which are outlined below, should be interpreted as layers of replacement of the old by the new aimed at achieving public policy goals.

Stage 1: Low-cost and rental housing as an immediate response to the housing crisis (1960–1964)
This stage involved meeting the immediate housing shortage, sacrificing quality and other standards. Self-contained "emergency" and standard rental flats with one, two and three rooms were built primarily within a five-mile radius of the city centre, utilising whatever land was available amongst existing developments (Liu, 1973). This was a phase of urgent construction, judging from the sheer number of units that were planned over the period of four years from 1961 to 1964, where 51,000 units were required to be built. By building the units near the Central Business District on land acquired from squatters, small farmers and residents of dilapidated buildings, alternative employment opportunities did not have to be considered as most of those affected depended on Central Area activities for their livelihood (Castells, Goh and Kwok, 1990; Ministry of Finance, 1961: 120). In the large-scale clearance of slums and squatters, resettlement benefits were primarily restricted to the concrete HDB flats, built rapidly in response to demand, with electricity and water supplies being seen as significantly improving living conditions (Yeh, 1975).[1]

Infrastructural support at this initial stage of politically driven public housing development was indeed an important aspect that merits mention. To cope with the anticipated rise in the consumption of electricity by industries and new housing, two major projects were initiated by the City Electricity Department, the only power supplier then, to provide additional power at Pasir Panjang. Over the period 1961–1964, a relatively high cost of S$78.5 million was estimated, though the investment in power was planned to be revenue-generating and ultimately self-financing (Ministry of Finance, 1961: 73–75).

Water supply aroused a great concern. With a total daily output of only 60 million gallons[2] in 1961 and daily demand projected to rise to 86 million gallons by 1965, additional sources were crucial to ensure the success of the housing and industrial projects. New water works in the Johor River (upstream of Kota Tinggi) and Skudai River in neighbouring Johor were found to be promising, producing a supply of 25 million gallons daily. Local storage was also augmented by constructing two reservoirs at Telok Blangah and Jurong respectively (*ibid.*: 76–77). Generally lacking in scope and scale in 1959, the sewerage system served merely 677,600 people, less than half of the total population. Apart from the outlying rural areas, unsewered areas included the congested old Central Area, which was developed before the introduction of a sewerage system. Whilst sewerage projects were introduced selectively to old established areas, this stage also saw the extension and improvement of sewage and sludge disposal works being completed at Kim Chuan and Ulu Pandan. The Ulu Pandan Sewage Disposal Works had replaced the Alexandra Disposal Works with additional capacity and facilities to meet the rising demand of the population (*ibid.*: 124–125).

Stage 2: Homeownership through public housing (1965–1969)
The "Home Ownership for the People" scheme was introduced in 1964 and was supported by the Central Provident Fund[3] system under which workers were required to save and buy a public apartment. The HDB planned to meet the rapid rise in demand through a series of urban renewal programmes. The slums of the Central Area were gradually cleared, replaced by flats equipped with communal services. They served predominantly lower-income households living in the slums and dilapidated quarters in the Central Area and the city fringe. In line with industrialisation objectives and job creation, HDB estates were designed for both stable communal development and easy maintenance (Teh, 1973: 24). It was effectively a process of incorporating the workforce into a new life-style promising regular wages linked directly with world demand for goods and services produced in Singapore, involving productivity gains, skills needed for higher value-added activities, and technological and management innovations.

Promoting homeownership is not merely a demonstration of political impartiality, where eligibility is based on a set of rules and regulations applicable to all, but also involves the building of social capital. This capital is crucial as a stabilising agent and for cultivating a sense of nationhood (Jacob and Manzi, 1996; La Grange and Yip, 2001). In socio-economic terms, Chua (1991a) asserts that the encouragement of homeownership raises the level of commitment of the population to a social order promoted by the government to protect the capital gains acquired through a series of governmental efforts in order to improve material living standards, including property ownership.

Stage 3: Commercialisation of public housing (1970–1979)
This marked the start of the HDB as a strongly self-financing statutory board enjoying greater autonomy in performing its functions under the

Ministry of National Development. The quantum of the government's subsidy had remained quite low because income from the sale of flats, rental of residential, commercial and industrial services, and revenue from ancillary services like car parks ensured a significant return that could be ploughed back into housing production.[4] Besides, the HDB was a key supplier of its own essential materials such as sand, granite, bricks, tiles and toilet bowls, and it also operated granite and sand quarries, and a brickworks factory. To ensure marketability, the HDB became more customer-oriented by improving the designs of the flats and the new towns. In 1974, the provision of public housing expanded to include middle-income families (Housing and Urban Development Company[5]) whose incomes exceeded the ceiling for the qualification of a HDB flat, but were inadequate for private housing. In 1989, the income ceiling was removed (Tan and Pang, 1991: 24). This has contributed to both access to private housing as well as a price spiral during the upgrading push in the first half of the 1990s, which will be discussed later.

The success of the homeownership scheme led the HDB to discourage the rental of its flats, and led to the gradual shift from smaller units of two- and three-room units of the 1960s towards four- and five-room apartments (Tan and Pang, 1991: 15). Led by a large-scale industrialisation campaign, and a planned distribution of industrial estates in Jurong as well as in sites adjoining HDB estates, residential mobility was accompanied by greater commuting mobility between the home and the workplace, as transport infrastructure was improved island-wide (Wong, 1999a).

A study by the HDB's Research and Planning Department in 2000 reflected well on the persistent patterns of residential mobility in Singapore in the last four decades, classified as an upgrading process (HDB, 2000). During the period 1961–1970, of the 27,910 moves recorded, 39.8% moved from slums and other areas to one- and two-room HDB flats, with 34.7% moving to three-room flats. The period 1971–1980 saw a massive extension of the resettlement process from the Central Area to the outlying farming and *kampung*[6] areas. Among the moves, 22.6% shifted to one- and two-room HDB flats, 50% to three-room flats, and the remainder to four-room or larger flats. Progressively during 1981–1990, of the total 74,780 moves, nearly 85% settled in three-, four- or five-room flats. Table 4.1 shows the distribution of HDB flats by type during 1980–2000. It reflects a general

TABLE 4.1: CHANGE IN DISTRIBUTION OF HDB APARTMENTS BY TYPE, 1980–2000

Year	1–2-room	%	3–4-room	%	5-room	%	Executive Apartment	%	HUDC*	%	Total Units	%
1980	117,863	31.6	231,722	62.2	20,459	5.5	—	—	2,596	0.7	372,640	100.0
1985	108,671	19.7	382,014	69.2	45,097	8.2	8,266	1.5	7,719	1.4	551,767	100.0
1990	70,903	11.4	454,090	72.8	71,754	11.5	21,602	3.5	5,472	0.8	623,821	100.0
1995	61,095	8.7	477,883	68.3	111,664	16.0	44,100	6.3	5,318	0.7	700,060	100.0
2000	57,364	6.8	540,998	63.9	181,498	21.4	63,439	7.5	3,350	0.4	846,649	100.0

Source: Computed from Department of Statistics (1990), p. 157 and Department of Statistics (1995), p. 121.
Note: * Housing and Urban Development Company, responsible for supplying larger apartments to higher-income groups from 1983 to the late 1980s. Many such estates have been privatised from the mid-1990s.

inclination to upgrade to higher-end apartments, notably after the introduction of larger executive and HUDC apartments in the early 1980s. Correspondingly, the number of one- and two–room, and three- and four-room apartments has proportionally declined in the overall housing stock.

Stage 4: Public housing used as an agent of social engineering and an instrument of economic policy (1980–1985)
Having largely resolved the housing issue by the late 1970s, the PAP government began to use the HDB to foster and promote social values, internalise social control and support general economic policies (Castells, Goh and Kwok, 1990: 244–245). The greatest contribution of the HDB was to nurture a sense of community through physical design and social planning. Design was dedicated to creating opportunities for residents to use common spaces and shared facilities, such as providing longer common corridors interspaced with shorter and segmented corridors in between. In social planning, for instance, setting aside reserve sites in new towns for future community, religious and institutional use became the norm. Such centres of social or religious functions would serve to bring together residents not merely from within but also from without the new towns for social interaction (Wong and Yeh, 1985: 388–390). Social harmony was meant to concurrently serve an equally, if not more, important national goal of rapid economic growth.

As a consequence of the government's multinational-led industrialisation, HDB residents have been effectively tied into a system that requires regular income to pay off monthly housing loans and to meet higher expenses for an improved material standard of living. Consequently, they are increasingly committed to a social order. Two of the most characteristic features are ethnic mixing and family-value consolidation (Chua, 1991b).[7]

Stage 5: Politicisation of public housing (1986 to the present)
Since the mid-1980s, public housing services, including upgrading, have been linked to support for the ruling party. The introduction of the Town Council Act in 1988 further incorporated this notion by having members of parliament oversee estate management and improvements, in order to be closer to the grassroots and to be more responsive to their feedback. Accordingly, as Teo and Kong (1997) observe, upgrading has become a

public concern of Singaporeans, who expect physical improvements to their residential environments carried out by a cash-rich government in the years of affluence as an alternative to a public welfare system. The ruling party has admitted to this use of housing subsidies in the bid for absolute power as part of "real politik". The controversy concerning political ethics was dismissed by the fact that every political party would do it to gain votes (Chua, 2000: 57; Li and Elklit, 1999).

Universal Provision of Public Housing

The Singapore government's near-universal provision of public housing for the population has been effective. Table 4.2 shows that, from housing a low 9% of the population in 1960, the HDB has managed to accommodate more than 80% of the population since the mid-1980s. The proportion reached a peak of 87% in 1990, but fell back to 84% in 2000 following the rise in private housing accommodation. Figure 4.1 illustrates the geographical distribution of public housing over the last 40 years, characterised by a gradual and systematic spread from the Central Region to the rest of the island.

Public housing provision has also been interpreted as a heavily subsidised model as reflected in official accounting records. Table 4.2 indicates that, in 1995, for example, the subsidy as a percentage of expenditure was as high as one-third. A substantial proportion of the deficits or subsidies were attributable to land costs paid to the Land Office (Ministry of Law), computed on the basis of market land values and opportunity costs. In the financial year 2000/2001, for example, land cost rose as high as 40% of the total capital expenditure (HDB, 2001: 91). In actual operations, there had been a substantial transfer of land values to the Land Office through the HDB's earlier land acquisitions, where compensations were evaluated below market rate. Contributions made by the Land Office to the Consolidated Fund are subsequently reallocated to the HDB as a government grant for the financing of public housing purchases. There are other means, such as the CPF, which act as government loans to help buyers finance their mortgages and upgrading.

Another example of subsidisation is the HDB's upgrading programme, implemented since the late 1980s, where residents need to pay only a small proportion of the actual expenses. Concomitantly, due to the corporatised and autonomous nature of the HDB that allows it the freedom to sign contracts with any business party, the subsidy level for its clientele has thus been reduced. Used as an ideological and "depoliticised" instrument epitomised in highly selective state welfarism, public housing prices are controlled within an affordable range and at low profit levels that have not attracted the private sector to act as an agent of provision.

TABLE 4.2: PERFORMANCE OF THE HOUSING AND DEVELOPMENT BOARD, 1960–2000

Year	Flats under HDB Management*	% of Population Housed in Public Flats	HDB Expenditure (S$ million)	Income S$ million	Deficit (Government Subsidy) in S$ million	Subsidy as a Percentage of Expenditure
1960	21,968	9	15	13	2	8
1965	69,660	23	43	39	4	11
1970	118,544	35	72	69	4	18
1975	214,940	43	226	181	45	5
1980	348,915	73	507	467	40	13
1985	557,612	84	2,861	1,688	1,187**	41
1990	627,165	87	1,992	1,887	105	5
1995	705,771	86	2,491	1,678	813	33
2000	828,148	84	5,298	4,160	1,138	22

Source: HDB Annual Reports (various years).
Note: * Flats built during the period 1960–1968 were predominantly rental flats. After 1965, more flats were built for sale when households had CPF savings. Rental flats continued to be made available in small numbers until the present day, particularly in the Central Area and the older towns. In 2000, rental flats accounted for only 3,840 units, 82.5% of which were of the one- to two-room type (HDB, 2001: 78).
** Figures between years are not strictly comparable as the HDB revised its accounting system significantly in 1985.

The universal provision and near-monopoly, nonetheless, have produced a dilemma where the state becomes obligated to meet popular demand because the bulk of Singaporeans are dependent on the state to provide housing. Thus, the state and the population are locked into a dependent-supplier relationship that neither party can easily break away from. This has moved the population towards a state of "clientship" where citizens "cede significant degrees of control of their life in exchange for the consumption of state-provided goods and services" (Chua, 2000: 46). It may thus be argued that through the public housing programme, the state has co-opted the population into a commitment to the status quo. However, the relationship between the state and the population is one that the state needs to maintain by promising improvements in the latter's material quality of life in exchange for political support. As Singapore becomes further enmeshed in the global economy, younger, more educated and vocal Singaporeans seek the "Singapore Dream". For the government, the politicisation of the public housing issue has to be redirected towards managing Singaporeans' rising aspirations, which include private property ownership. This differentiated clientele, mostly the middle class aspiring to private housing accommodation at the higher-end of the housing market, has increased in numbers as a result of rising affluence. Their concerns captured public attention in the late 1980s. When the Singapore Concept Plan was reviewed during 1989–1990, the proportion of private housing was reformulated to rise from 15% in 1990 to 30% in the overall housing stock by 2030 (URA, 1991a). To this end, the state has been a promoter since the 1990s in order to facilitate such access.

RISING ASPIRATIONS FOR PRIVATE HOUSING

As argued above, public housing needs were largely met by a Fordist mass production system during the period 1960–1990 that supplied standardised products through improvements in the service provision and design of HDB housing estates. However, it is human nature to hanker for better quality and greater quantity in a society where seeking material improvement in living standards has been publicly encouraged as a goal and a rightful reward for hard work and political support. In Singapore society, where status can be acquired through one's academic merits or business success without inheritance and the need for a prestigious family background, conspicuous consumption is an important means of asserting status and identity. Following the rise in affluence, homeownership, therefore, has become progressively more differentiated and fragmented (see Lett, 1998: 97–98; Hamnett, 1995).

Consumption behaviours associated with the use of household goods, choice and location of housing type, neighbourhood ambience and services, as well as other personal preferences can be indicators of social status. Housing upgrading is hence part of the process of formation of social status and identity influenced by the aspirations of expanding middle-class groups after three decades of sustained economic growth. Significantly, this growth period has been influenced by Western consumption patterns, currently very much post-Fordist in nature, focusing beyond mass-produced public consumer goods.

In the consumption of a durable and costly commodity like housing, the level of affordability rises or falls with real income change. Greater aspiration for higher-end goods can only be met with effective demand, or it will remain an unfulfilled aspiration (see Hamnett, 1995). Aspirations, however, may be facilitated by policy using, for example, fiscal measures or financial instruments as a tool to boost the affordability of higher-end goods (see Chiu, 1996). Enhancement of affordability applies to both public and private housing; the difference is that the latter requires a greater magnitude of income improvement to enhance affordability. The rise in affordability and accumulated CPF savings have enhanced the probability of access. An examination of the income change of Singaporeans makes this clearer.

Income Change

Table 4.3 shows the real growth in earnings experienced by average individuals during the period 1980–1990. Inevitably and correspondingly, greater affluence has led to a change in the household expenditure pattern from basic living items to more luxurious items, including housing. Table 4.4 shows that, in 1973, 45.2% of the average household's expenditure was on food; this dropped to less than a quarter in 1998. In contrast, budgets for housing rose from a low 15.3% to 21.6% during the same period. It may be hypothesised that aspirations are influenced to an extent by one's perception of the items that one desires to possess or own. To verify the validity of this hypothesis, a questionnaire survey was conducted during the months of May and June 2002 in public and private housing sites across Singapore.

TABLE 4.3: AVERAGE MONTHLY EARNINGS OF INCOME EARNERS IN SINGAPORE, 1980–1990

Year	S$ Per Month
1980	692
1985	1,191
1990	1,528

Source: Department of Statistics (1990), p. 64.

TABLE 4.4: DISTRIBUTION OF SINGAPORE HOUSEHOLD EXPENDITURES AS A PERCENTAGE, 1973–1998

Year	Food	Clothing	Housing	Transport & Communications	Education	Health	Others	Total
1973	45.2	6.7	15.3	11.3	3.8	1.8	15.9	100.0
1978	44.7	5.6	15.6	13.0	3.8	1.7	15.6	100.0
1983	37.7	6.1	16.5	18.3	3.7	2.3	15.4	100.0
1988	36.7	5.3	17.5	15.6	4.7	2.6	17.5	100.0
1993	26.4	5.8	21.9	20.2	5.7	2.6	17.5	100.0
1998	23.7	4.1	21.6	22.8	6.9	3.3	17.6	100.0

Source: Department of Statistics (2001b), p. 57.
Note: One-person households are excluded.

Survey Method

In the empirical survey, a total of 90 HDB household heads were interviewed, with 30 households each randomly selected from three-, four- and five-room flats respectively in three new towns.[8] In addition, 60 households from private housing areas were surveyed, comprising 30 landed properties (ten each for detached, semi-detached and terraced houses) and 30 condominium units. The questionnaire was primarily designed to assess aspirations for private housing, and the rationale for moving house. Other factors, such as buying homes for investment or to satisfy the need for quality of life, which may be implicit motives, were not considered. Investigation was focused on:

a) Whether it was the dream of public housing owners to own a private house;
b) Why public housing owners wished to move (if they wanted to);
c) The types of houses that public and private housing owners wished to move to; and
d) Whether public housing owners wished to mortgage their apartments for a loan and why.

Survey Results

Open-ended questions were used to investigate if HDB owners dreamed of owning a private house. Among the 90 respondents, 35 respondents or 38.9% acknowledged that they had such a dream, predominantly for prestige, comfort or quality (Table 4.5). Of the remaining 55 respondents who did not dream of private housing accommodation, more than three-quarters said they either could not afford it or they were satisfied with their public housing accommodation. In examining in greater detail the 20 households which were satisfied with public housing accommodation, it was found that 80% of them earned a monthly household income of less than S$5,000, a sum that would have made private housing unaffordable. Moreover, more than half of them had a household head aged more than 45 years. An older person would be entitled to a shorter time period for mortgage loan repayment and therefore higher monthly instalment rates. Low affordability was the key factor preventing public housing owners from buying a private house.

Indeed, public housing owners who expressed an intention to move house chose different types of houses. The reasons for wanting to move varied from the need for more space, to wanting the prestige and comfort of private housing, and even to downgrading from large units to smaller units, the latter as a result of having children who had left to form their own nuclear families, or simply to earn some disposable cash. Half of the public and private housing respondents said they would not move out (Table 4.6). Reasons quoted included satisfaction with the existing house and location, inability to afford a larger house or old age. Among the public housing owners who wished to move out in the near future, only one-fifth were looking for private property. Almost two-thirds of three-room HDB apartment owners wishing to move aimed to upgrade to a four-room apartment. Among the private housing owners, shifting to condominiums appeared to be popular; a few wanted to downgrade to smaller houses, including public housing, for varied reasons, such as gaining disposable cash.

TABLE 4.5: RATIONALE OF PUBLIC HOUSING OWNERS FOR UPGRADING/NOT UPGRADING TO PRIVATE HOUSING

HDB Type	Why is private housing your dream?				
	Prestige	Comfort/quality	Privacy	Others	Total
3-room	2	1	2	3	8
4-room	6	4	2	1	13
5-room	7	5	2	—	14
Total	15	10	6	4	35

HDB Type	Why is private housing not your dream?				
	Unaffordable	Satisfied with current house	Inconvenience	Others	Total
3-room	11	6	2	3	22
4-room	5	9	2	1	17
5-room	7	5	—	4	16
Total	23	20	4	8	55

Source: Questionnaire Survey, May–June 2002.

Two issues concerning tenure rights were brought up in the survey. The first was the difference between public and private housing owners in that the former, being lessees, were not legally entitled to mortgage their units for a bank loan. In response, two-thirds of HDB apartment owners said they had no loan requirement, needed to keep the house as security or simply did not want to be in debt. Thus, they had no plan to

TABLE 4.6: TYPES OF HOUSING THAT PUBLIC HOUSING OWNERS WISH TO MOVE TO

HDB Type	HDB 3-room	HDB 4-room	HDB 5-room	Exec apartment[1]	Condo-minium	Terrace house	Bungalow	Others[2]	Public housing	Not moving out	Total
3-room	2	14	—	1	1	1	—	3	—	8	30
4-room	1	3	7	1	—	—	—	4	—	14	30
5-room	—	1	—	—	3	1	1	5	—	19	30
Private housing	—	—	—	—	7	1	2	14	3	33	60
Total	3	18	7	2	11	3	3	26	3	74	150

Source: Questionnaire Survey, May–June 2002.
Note: [1] Executive apartments are the best-quality HDB 5-room apartments.
[2] Including migration overseas, moving to bigger or smaller houses, or downgrading without specifying details.

mortgage their units even if they could (Table 4.7). Among the other one-third who needed mortgage loans, 42% hoped to use it for business investments, home renovation or as disposable cash.

TABLE 4.7: REASONS GIVEN BY PUBLIC HOUSING OWNERS FOR MORTGAGING/NOT MORTGAGING THEIR FLATS

HDB Type	Reasons to mortgage flat					
	Investment	Home renovation	Cash	Others	Those not wanting to mortgage	Total
3-room	2	1	3	3	21	30
4-room	4	3	1	1	21	30
5-room	6	—	1	3	20	30
Total	12	4	5	7	62	90

HDB Type	Reasons not to mortgage flat					
	No loan requirement	Keeping house as security	Not to be in debt	Others	Those wanting to mortgage	Total
3-room	11	7	1	2	9	30
4-room	12	3	4	2	9	30
5-room	16	—	2	2	10	30
Total	39	10	7	6	28	90

Source: Questionnaire Survey, May–June 2002.

The second issue was whether the 99-year lease was a cause of unhappiness. Similar responses were given by both types of housing owners. About 43% of HDB apartment owners and 48% of private property owners[9] claimed respectively that they were unhappy with the 99-year lease. A freehold tenure, available only in old private housing estates, was the most popular form of tenure for private properties.

The survey results demonstrate that there is a general aspiration among public housing owners for private housing due to factors such as prestige, quality of living, comfort and privacy. But their response reflects affordability levels in that there is a wide gap between aspiration and actual choice of housing. The former may be interpreted as being more subjective, while the latter is more objective and realistic after considering the available options, predetermined primarily by affordability levels, perception of housing quality and comfort as well as, to a certain extent, the land issue, including tenure rights.

THE LAND ISSUE, PERCEPTION OF PRIVATE HOUSING STATUS AND QUALITY

In a situation of genuine land scarcity, Singapore housing consumers have a strong interest in the status of landownership, notably freehold titles. Earlier in 1993, in a commercial survey conducted by Frank, Cheong and Baillieu (1993) on buyers' preferences concerning condominiums, it was found that slightly more than half of the respondents felt that a 99-year strata lease was unacceptable as a title. The land issue has remained a key component of end users' concern.

It is relevant to quote here the classical Weberian interpretation of Saunders (1978) in differentiating the status of homeownership between Singapore's public and private housing owners. Though both categories of owners enjoy the use and exchange values of their dwellings, the basis in the social-class upgrading process and the level of proprietary control need to be differentiated. Arguably, the HDB dwellers own their dwellings for a lease period of 99 years, but do not own the land upon which their dwellings are built, as land has remained a state asset. HDB lessees own the assets within the four walls of their units only. Any public space outside the unit is state property, which includes corridors, lifts, void decks, parks and parking space. Contrary to this, public space and facilities in private condominiums (swimming pools, greenery, gymnasiums, car parks and security services) are shared on a pro-rata basis. Private housing is generally perceived by the public as being more attractive and prestigious than HDB apartments. First, private developers and the HDB as a developer have different objectives as far as their clientele is concerned. While serving the higher-income groups, private developers conceptually offer a perceived "ideal life-style" with high aesthetic value and are supported by advertisements, whereas the HDB, as a public provider, aims to house people on the basis of affordability. As a result, aesthetic works are minimised to cut costs. This explains why, in the survey discussed above, those who desire private housing admire it for its quality and comfort.

Second, as HDB housing is a subsidised commodity, it is natural that the public provider, which also enforces social and culture-related rules and regulations, feels justified in imposing many restrictions. Besides the landownership issue, HDB apartment owners have little input in building specifications and structures.[10] Legally, private housing has longer ownership terms, though a 99-year lease has become the norm offered by the state in public land sales for private property development. In terms of management, HDB housing is managed by town councils, headed by a member of parliament directly under the surveillance of the government. In contrast, private housing management is more autonomous, consisting of a management corporation whose members are residents. As resident members of private properties such as condominiums, they also own common properties within the same estate (Tan, 1998).

Condominiums were introduced as a living concept to Singapore in 1972 to satisfy the demand of upper middle-income groups, who were not eligible for public housing but were attracted by the recreational and social amenities of the aesthetically landscaped condominium environment. This new form of high-rise living, in terms of privacy, exclusivity, open space and shared facilities, has been quickly accepted by Singaporeans and expatriates and perceived as a form of quality housing (Teo, 1984). Again, our survey found that managerial and associate professionals are the largest cohort, symptomatic of the rising Singapore middle class most enthusiastic about upgrading their housing to private condominiums. This trend, in comparison, follows the 1961–1990 phenomenon in Britain where the professional and managerial group achieved the most significant access to homeownership in the upper end of the market (Hamnett, 1995).

Indeed, the demand for private condominiums has intensified over the last ten years, as Singapore seeks to sharpen its competitive edge, enhance its global integration, and expand its regionalisation drive. In the process, a noticeable polarisation of income groups has been observed. Table 4.8 shows that a substantial 35% rise in average real household income was achieved during the period 1990–2000. The achievement was also accompanied by a fall in the number of households earning less than S$3,000 per month from 63.2% to 41.3%. However, it can be seen at the upper end that the number of households earning S$10,000 and above per month had increased from 2.8% to 10.3%, a far bigger increase than those in the lower-income groups. This polarisation calls for a closer relook at the housing policy where private housing promotion needs to be further facilitated to counter the discontent of middle-income groups.

TABLE 4.8: CHANGE IN HOUSEHOLD INCOME, 1990–2000

Monthly household income (S$)	Households (Thousand)		Percent	
	1990	2000	1990	2000
Below 1,000	105.7	116.3	16.0	12.6
1,000-1,999	179.3	128.9	27.1	14.0
2,000-2,999	133.3	136.1	20.1	14.7
3,000-3,999	86.1	121.3	13.1	13.1
4,000-4,999	54.0	95.2	8.2	10.3
5,000-5,999	33.5	75.4	5.1	8.2
6,000-6,999	21.7	57.5	3.3	6.2
7,000-7,999	13.8	42.2	2.1	4.6
8,000-8,999	9.5	32.4	1.4	3.5
9,000-9,999	6.5	23.4	1.0	2.5
10,000 & above	18.3	94.6	2.8	10.3
Total	661.7	923.3	100.0	100.0
Average Household Income	3,076	4,943 4,166 (real term)		

Source: Department of Statistics (2001a), p. 80.

Private Property Aspirations versus the Price Spiral

As stated above, in legal terms, all HDB dwellers are lessees of state property who do not enjoy private property tenure rights. Consequently, this type of residence denies lessees mortgage facilities. With growing affluence and affordability since the 1980s, the landownership issue has been added to the relatively high physical quality of private properties as an important component in the pursuit of private residential ownership that resulted in a price spiral. Most important of all, it was the government's initiative in the early 1990s in favour of housing upgrading within public housing as well as from public to private housing that sparked the price spiral. All HDB apartments were then evaluated at a drastically higher value in the resale market to make cash available for upgrading purposes. Between 1992 and the peak of the price spiral in 1996, HDB resale prices more than tripled on average (*Straits Times*, 19

FIGURE 4.2: PRIVATE PROPERTY PRICE INDEX BY TYPE, 1990–2000

Source: Department of Statistics (1995; 2001b)

May 2002: 21). As a result, substantial household wealth in assets was built up through price appreciation in a short span of time (Phang, 2001). This sharp escalation would not have been possible without the backing of a positive economic climate and performance, and the government's liberal loan policy supporting the upgrading to private housing in particular. Attracted by a strong effective demand and high projected profits, developers made inflated bids for land parcels put up for sale by the government. In business strategies, higher bids to secure a scarce commodity in the face of intense competition normally reflect an anticipation of rising prices, characterised by the limited and controlled supply of state lands in Singapore for private property development at that time. Theoretically, the state monopoly in land supply can influence prices through the controlling of the scope of land sales (see Kivell, 1993).

Under theses circumstances, amidst strong effective demand and speculative activities, purchasers were prepared to pay a high price in anticipation of rising prices. Figure 4.2 shows the rising prices of private properties in the first half of the 1990s. Prices and demand began to drop sharply after the 1996 clampdown on the overheating private property boom by the government, which saw a decline in property prices in both public and private housing. Overall, however, the prices of private properties had surged to such high levels that it lowered the purchasing power of the middle-income groups. The 1997 financial crisis and its aftermath further decreased the purchasing power of the middle-income groups. A general depression in the construction industry that would hurt the city-state economy had surfaced.

The State as a Facilitator to Support Aspirations and the Construction Industry

The property slump continued after the 1997 financial crisis and was illustrated by the poor performance of the construction industry, as reflected in Table 4.9 by negative growth after 1999. While recovery has yet to be seen, the fall in the construction industry's contribution to the gross domestic product was followed by a corresponding shrinkage in fixed capital formation of residential buildings during the period 1997–2001. The slump has affected both private and public housing market prices. For HDB resale flats, the depressed market led to a 30% price fall from the peak in 1996 to early 2002, when a corresponding fall of 10% to 15% in the prices of new flats was observed (*Straits Times*, 19

May 2002: 21). To counter this decreasing trend, the Singapore government has been searching for measures to facilitate continued access to private property and to stimulate recovery of the building sector.

Whither Private Housing?

Like public housing, private housing has spread over the past four decades from its original core areas near the city centre to other parts of the island (Figure 4.3). The infusion into public housing areas is mainly attributable to the sale of public land parcels to private developers for the construction of 99-year-lease condominiums and landed properties. Rapid urbanisation has witnessed the elimination of privately owned wooden farmhouses in the outlying zones, replaced with infrastructure such as public housing, schools, commercial complexes and other institutional buildings. Modern concrete private housing, whether in the form of landed properties of one to three storeys, or medium- to high-rise apartment blocks, has dominated the private property market.

For the public authorities, the CPF has remained as an important measure in promoting access to private housing, given its substantial funding base. Indeed, a new ruling has been passed to allow private housing buyers to use their CPF savings for the 10% down payment from 1 September 2002.[11] The move has revived the property market to some extent. Following this, private housing prices have been projected to rise by 5% to 10% in 2003 (*Straits Times*, 24 July 2002: 23). But how far the new ruling will lead the market has remained uncertain as the economic recession has been persistent and the poor stock market performance has made many hesitant to make any move. A dilemma exists in the use of the CPF in an ageing Singapore that tends to hinder the continued use of the CPF for housing upgrading in the longer term.

The CPF is a critical instrument and institution in influencing consumer behaviour. On the one hand, it is used to an extent as a social safety net to safeguard against financial insecurity in old age by disallowing members from using it arbitrarily. On the other hand, it may be used to stimulate property demand, thus enhancing asset values. In the latter case, according to a survey in 2001 conducted by a well-known consulting agency, Knight Frank, 45% of the 1,100 interviewees blamed CPF restrictions for hindering their purchase of a private property (*Straits Times*, 24 July 2002: 3). In a social system with little old-age welfare and where public assistance is only offered to those in social distress (see

Phang, 2001), one is expected to take care of oneself using retirement savings, of which CPF savings are the key source, unless one is prepared to downgrade to a smaller housing unit to obtain disposable income.

TABLE 4.9: THE CONSTRUCTION INDUSTRY SLUMP SINCE THE 1997 FINANCIAL CRISIS

Year	Gross Domestic Product at Current Prices (S$ million)	Percentage Change Over the Previous Year	Gross Fixed Capital Formation of Residential Buildings (S$ million)[1]
1997	10,662	16.1	12,835
1998	10,98	43.0	12,812
1999	10,012	−8.8	11,212
2000	9,555	−4.6	9,700
2001	9,500[2]	−0.5[2]	8,300[2]

Source: Ministry of Trade and Industry (2001), pp. 76, 80.
Note: [1] At 1990 market prices.
[2] Estimates made based on the trend for the first three quarters in 2001.

Overusing CPF savings for housing investments has recently aroused concern among decision-makers that low-income earners would have little to rely on after retirement. It has been reported that, on average, a Singapore worker will have 75% of his assets in housing when he is 50 years of age, a proportion that is much higher than that for the average American, whose house is worth 20% of his assets at retirement Yet, Singapore's aged population (60 and above) has been projected to swell to more than a quarter of the total population by 2030 (*Sunday Times*, 28 July 2002: 46). The implication is clear that the use of CPF savings to upgrade housing defeats its purpose of providing financial security after retirement. To safeguard against poverty in old age, there has been talk about reducing CPF contributions to the Ordinary Account and increasing the Special Account contribution for old-age savings.[12] Besides, the perception of condominiums providing a quality life-style is under threat in light of the scarcity of another resource—water—that is linked directly with limited land supply.

In the context of an almost fully developed city-state of only 682 square kilometres, land supply poses a serious constraint in providing an additional large number of landed residences. Furthermore, the recent revision of Singapore's target population from 4 million to 5.5 million makes it even more difficult to offer a corresponding rise in the proportion of landed properties, given its higher land-take per user. Hence, more condominiums and private apartments will have to be placed in the pipeline, instead of landed property. The share of private properties increased from 14.4% in 1980 to 18.6% in 2000, which is still far from the 30% target (Table 4.10). In light of the strongly competing land uses on the island, it is envisaged that a higher plot ratio and taller buildings are likely to be required in order to achieve a higher proportion of private properties in the form of condominiums. In the longer term, it is expected that the number of landed properties will be reduced proportionately.

TABLE 4.10: SHARE OF PRIVATE HOUSING IN SINGAPORE, 1980–2000

Year	Private Properties	%
1980	62,750	14.4
1985	83,790	13.2
1990	103,050	14.2
1995	129,110	15.6
2000	193,030	18.6

Source: Computed from Department of Statistics (1990), p. 157; Department of Statistics (1995), p. 113 and Department of Statistics (2001b), p. 114.
Note: Vacant units are excluded.

Condominium development relies on an ample supply of water to create the "ideal life-style" environment. Water has become an increasingly expensive resource in Singapore, which is largely dependent on Malaysia for its supply. Yet, as discussed earlier in Chapter 2, because of the higher cost of producing water in Singapore, the relatively low cost of Malaysian water makes it likely that Malaysia will remain the major source of Singapore's water supply in the foreseeable future. The development of "Newater" (water reclaimed from the sewage system) theoretically promises an ample supply of recycled water. To minimise the psychological aversion of consumers, the PUB has decided to pump the treated sewage water into the reservoirs to avoid it being directly consumed by households.

CONCLUDING REMARKS

Through the demolition of slums and squatter areas, and the elimination of "traditional" farms and habitats in the outlying zones over the last four decades, the universal provision of public housing in Singapore has modernised the landscape considerably. Since the 1970s, public housing development has been integrated into a wider national land-use strategy to distribute the population throughout the island. Facilitated by the CPF system and with public housing prices within an affordable range, over 85% of the population now live in public housing estates. As a monopolistic instrument of a developmental government committed to modernist nation-building, the HDB's primary functions and role have shifted over time, from meeting an immediate basic social need in the early 1960s, to paving the way for an export-driven industrialisation process strongly integrated with the global economy after 1965. Besides systematically adjusting itself to play a greater role in bolstering economic growth and social cohesion, public housing has been linked, since the late 1980s, to political support through its upgrading and service provision programme. There are varying degrees of success.

Three decades of sustained economic growth have produced not only greater affluence but also a sizeable middle class which aspires to own private residential property, perceived as a symbol of higher social status, comfort and better quality of life. Consequently, while the lower-income groups continue to be dependent on the "paternalistic" state to provide affordable housing and upgrading, middle-class groups tend to increasingly reject the Fordist mass-produced public housing as public consumer goods. In search of a more differentiated and higher-end private housing market, younger, better-educated and more vocal Singaporeans seek the "Singapore Dream", characteristic of post-Fordist consumer behaviour.

Our survey confirms that there is a general aspiration for private housing among public housing owners because of prestige, quality of living, comfort and privacy. But their actual choice of housing has reflected quite logically the levels of affordability. Aspirations will remain a dream without the support of affordability. The management of rising aspirations for private property is deemed necessary by the state as a negotiating term for the support of its economic priority model. This model effectively relies on material incentives in order to work. Housing upgrading was indeed initiated by the government in the early 1990s. However, optimism for economic growth, a liberal loan policy, speculation and a limited land supply led subsequently to a dramatic price spiral, making affordability beyond reach for many. The government clampdown on speculation in 1996 and the recession following the 1997 financial crisis have not revived the housing market to any great extent.

Besides, heavy cash and CPF investments in residential properties have made many Singaporeans "asset rich and cash poor". Similarly, much state capital has equally been allocated to subsidise public housing and upgrading. Concomitantly, however, the increasingly ageing population will have to face the foreseeable "welfare crisis" as they will have little to rely on after retirement except their own savings. Downgrading to a lower-quality house for disposable cash to spend during retirement appears to be viable only when the asset stays at a relatively high value. There are no guarantees, however.

Narrowing the gap between private and public housing can be seen as an alternative way to satisfy those dreaming of private housing. Tenure rights is an area where the HDB can improve to provide public housing owners with more opportunities to make use of their properties, such as mortgage loans, greater resident participation and decisions over the usage of common areas. In July 2002, the Minister for National Development, Mah Bow Tan, announced that his ministry would try to ease the regulations governing HDB flats to make them more like private properties. However, he added that there would not be total privatisation of HDB estates as public housing would still be needed as a safety net for those who need it (*Straits Times*, 24 July 2002: 1). In striving for private housing as a material goal, affordability will remain the fundamental condition for access.

ENDNOTES

1. Attention should be drawn to Riaz Hassan's (1977) study of low-income families who were resettled in HDB flats. Hassan points out that resettlement is especially stressful for poorer families as living in a flat incurs higher monthly expenses (rental, utilities, etc.). This leads to a pervasive sense of insecurity that becomes a serious impediment to collective social action for community organisation and development. On the other hand, economically better-off families find public housing congruent with their aspirations of a "better life" and represents, at least symbolically, a movement towards the goal of social upgrading mobility.

2. One British gallon is equivalent to about 4.5 litres.

3. The CPF was first introduced in 1955 for a small group of workers as a mandatory superannuation and social-oriented scheme where funds

contributed by both employers and employees are kept in trust by the government, with their usage primarily restricted to the purchase of HDB flats (Ho, 1973). With its membership expanded in the early 1960s, CPF funds were first allowed for the purchase of HDB housing in 1968. The funds cannot be withdrawn before reaching the retirement age unless the contributors are proved to be permanently disabled. From June 1981, usage of CPF funds was progressively extended to cover the purchase of private residential properties.

4   The greatest subsidy goes to the smaller flats, with those purchasing the largest flats effectively receiving no subsidy on the cost of their flat. Thus, the subsidy from the HDB will naturally decline as the HDB concentrates its efforts on building large flats.

5   The Housing and Urban Development Company (HUDC) was introduced in 1974 as a corporate body to cater to the needs of middle-income groups whose monthly household income levels exceeded the HDB ceiling of S$1,500 but was less than S$4,000, a sum deemed inadequate for the purchase of private housing. Designed for higher-income groups, the HUDC sites were initially separated from the HDB estates in "close proximity to entertainment and commercial centres" and in "exclusive" residential areas with designs that incorporated a "modern concept in condominium housing" (Housing & Urban Development Co. (Pte.) Ltd., 1977). But in 1980, HUDC housing was integrated within public housing estates to facilitate a better mix of diverse income groups, and in 1982, management of the HUDC was handed over to the HDB. Construction of HUDC housing was terminated in the late 1980s when larger HDB executive apartments were built to replace it. A total of about 8,000 HUDC units had been constructed. Partial privatisation of the HUDC began in 1986, initiated by the HUDC housing owners. Full privatisation of the HUDC was made possible by the enactment of the Land Titles (Strata) (Amendment) Act of 1995 that saw the transfer. from the HDB to the HUDC housing owners of the common property as tenants in common and the issue of subsidiary strata titles to individual units. All eight HUDC estates have been privatised and managed as individual corporations.

6   This literally means "village" in Malay.

7   However, as Chua (2000) has pointed out, the government is careful to preclude the possibility of housing becoming a legal entitlement of citizenship. Instead, it is posited as a "privilege" that may be withdrawn. Citizens relate to the HDB as a consumer, free to accept or decline the conditions stipulated by the landlord, which in this case is the HDB.

8   They are the Clementi, Bukit Batok and Choa Chu Kang new towns. Selected private housing estates were predominantly located in the Upper Bukit Timah area, a key private property development belt in Singapore.

9   40% of the private housing owners interviewed were from estates with a 99-year lease; these are sites sold by the government through a public tender system. Other private estates enjoy a freehold tenure.

10 Recently, the HDB's new build-to-order scheme, which allows buyers to choose the location and when they want their flats, was well-received.

11 The existing conventional scheme allows buyers to choose only the zones, but they are uncertain as to when they will be able to move in (*Straits Times*, 16 May 2001: H1).

11 Buyers have to confirm their booking by paying 20% of the price as down payment within eight weeks of signing the application form. Prior to this new ruling, the whole 20% down payment was payable by cash.

12 Currently, 70% of the CPF contribution goes to the Ordinary Account (which can be used for housing payments, purchase of shares, unit trusts, insurance and gold, and financing education), 20% to the Medical Account and 10% to the Special Account. The Medical Account has an upper limit of S$26,000. Once filled, the balance will be transferred to the Ordinary Account.

CHAPTER 5

Development of Recreational Spaces

INTRODUCTION

Traditionally, urbanisation and nature are two contrasting issues that have conflicting notions and objectives. As and when urbanisation and economic growth take place, nature is victimised and has to give way to accommodate the ever-expanding built environment. In contemporary land-use planning for cities where high-value activities are most concentrated, retaining parcels of natural environment has become an uphill task in the face of competing scarce land resources. As Hillier (1998: 78) sensibly suggests, "balancing" different values constitutes a land-use decision that affects the quality of life of the public and the quality of the natural and built environments. Such a decision is indeed[1] an ethical judgement associated with human needs and rights. Today, as a result of rapid development and change, man-made greenery in modern cities is increasingly seen as an aesthetised representation of nature that can counter the debilitating effects of pollution, congestion and an impersonal urban life as well as prevent allocation abuse by free market forces (Berrisbeita, 1999; Smith, Poulos and Kim, 2002). The functions of greenery need new interpretations in the light of change in relation to quality of life.

Accepting that greenery is essential for health and well-being, Van Herzele and Wiedemann (2003: 110–112) emphasise three basic principles upon which urban green spaces should be built. First, they have to be citizen-based, where the focus is on usage opportunities and accessibility. The second principle lies in the differentiated functional levels of green spaces. Thus, a hierarchical system of standards is required. Indeed, most planned cities, including Singapore, closely follow specific standards. Preconditions for use form the third principle, interpretable by perceptional qualities such as distance from home, safety, naturalness, historic character, spatial organisation or design, management and attractiveness. However, accessibility as defined for Holland by Van Herzele and Wiedemann in terms of proximity, walking distance and time may have little relevance for Singapore in light of the hot and humid local climate. Equity of access is another factor, which is not examined in detail in this chapter.[2]

The crux of the chapter lies with the land constraints and the dilemma faced by Singapore in fulfilling its multiple status as a city-state, global city and nation-state. In transforming itself into a high-tech industrial hub in East Asia, and safeguarding its sovereignty, a substantial part of the city-state territory has to be allocated for infrastructure and defence, making land-use planning and allocations a perplexing task in the last 30 years of rapid industrialisation and nation-building (see Wong, 1999a). A glance at the land-use change over the period 1960–1999 in Table 5.1 shows that a substantial proportion of lands classified under "others", which covered 42% of the total land area in 1999, has been reserved for defence, normally defined as "special use" in official terms. Physical infrastructure also consumes a large amount of land. Reportedly, road- and rail-related facilities have taken up as much land as public housing areas, each accounting for about 12% to 15% of the total land-take.[3]

TABLE 5.1: LAND-USE CHANGE IN SINGAPORE, 1960–1999

Year	Built-Up Area	Agriculture[1]	Forest	Marsh & Tidal Waste	Others[2]	Total (sq km)
1960	162.4	141.7	37.8	45.8	193.7	581.4
1965	177.4	131.6	35.0	35.0	202.4	581.4
1970	189.9	116.0	32.4	32.4	215.7	586.4
1975	228.4	105.9	32.4	32.4	197.7	596.8
1980	275.1	80.9	30.0	26.0	205.8	617.8
1985	298.8	47.1	28.6	18.5	227.5	620.5
1990	311.6	10.8	28.6	15.7	266.4	633.0
1995	319.3	9.3	28.6	15.7	274.6	647.5
1999[3]	324.0	9.8	28.6	15.5	282.0	659.9

Source: Department of Statistics, *Yearbook of Statistics* (various years).
Note: [1] Includes licensed farms but excludes rubber and coconut plantations.
[2] Includes inland waters, open spaces, public gardens, cemeteries, non-built-up areas in military establishments, quarries, rubber and coconut plantations.
[3] Statistical data for 2000 and thereafter is not available.

As such, the chapter explores how the largely artificial greenery in Singapore is nonetheless seen as an indispensable recreational means to enhance quality of life in a rapidly urbanised environment. It first looks at the conceptual relationship between recreation and quality of life, which is followed by a discussion of the landscape change in Singapore, focusing on high standards of greenery provision to maintain the image of a garden city. Finally, the triangular relationship between growth, equity and environmental preservation is considered and their inherent conflicts analysed in the context of sustainability in Singapore.

CONCEPTUAL RELATIONSHIP BETWEEN RECREATION AND QUALITY OF LIFE

Concepts regarding quality of life have evolved enormously over time. Linking recreation with quality of life is, however, a relatively recent one. In ancient civilisations or agriculture-based subsistence societies, natural open space was perceived as a take-for-granted endowment. Then, struggles against natural hazards were persistent while the pursuit of good harvests and more reliable supplies of basic needs were a priority objective for a better quality of life. In societies where a land-owning class was supported by slavery and therefore freed from the problems of hunger, quality of life meant something more than basic needs. Hence, for Aristotle, quality of life was epitomised by happiness, which covers good mental and health conditions where one can realise one's potential, enjoy respect from others and achieve some subjective satisfaction. As a privileged individual who had ample time for leisure, thinking and investigating what constituted happiness, Aristotle argued that sensory pleasure did not occupy time, nor was it a physical process or a movement. For him, pleasure was a mental state where "speed does not apply", and it was "more in rest than in movement" (Ostenfeld, 1994: 21–23). Aristotle's interpretation of pleasure may not apply to the quality of life for a highly urbanised society today. But his association of pleasure with static objects at rest rather than with those in movement has reflected succinctly the need to balance development and recreation, which our modern urbanised societies now rigorously pursue.

In modern urban living characterised by the rising pace of movements (long commuting distance, heavy vehicular traffic, commercial competition of firms, etc.), safeguarding or recreating natural conditions in cities has become a planning priority. Theoretically, two key factors have contributed to the need for city recreational areas.

First, it is the physiological and psychological needs of modern urbanites. Recreation helps relieve mental stress and maintain one's mental health in normal conditions or psychological stability. It potentially reduces or eliminates tension or disequilibrium of the human organism so as to achieve to some extent the need-satisfaction goals in order to live harmoniously within an urban environment (Weiskopf, 1982; Liss, 1994). This need is ever more pressing as globalisation accelerates in the present world, where market competition is characterised by short production cycles, and determined by innovations and the sophisticated division of labour.

Market competition is likely to make life more stressful. It is not uncommon to see Singapore workers, particularly those in senior positions, spending most of their hours in offices or workplaces. Nohl (1988: 75–78) asserts that highly competitive societies dominated by speed and work efficiency, and reliant on a high degree of division of labour bring mental "repression, exploitation and alienation" to individuals, who need to counteract them by retreating to a natural state of things to restore mental peace and harmony. A natural state or natural beauty provides a sharp contrast to the psychologically undesirable consequences of imposed work ethics required in disciplined societies. Urbanites under mental tension cultivate a sentimental attachment to recreational sites more readily, as they seek a change of scenery other than that of the built environment for personal independence, freedom and self-realisation. Matching this change in life-style is the general rise in material standards of living in countries adopting a free market economy which has bolstered the demand for recreation and leisure at the same time. The scope of expansion of recreational needs is supplemented further with rising aged populations, a common phenomenon as valid in Western developed nations as in Singapore.

More specifically, the open spaces in Singapore serve well to offset the monotonous character and lack of locational individuality of mass-produced high-rise public housing estates built since the 1960s to satisfy the great housing demand of the populace. These apartments have been constructed island-wide in some 25 new towns using the self-contained Corbusian concept which provides more living space, air circulation, greenery and facilities on ground levels. In the Singaporean cosmopolitan society where a stronger indigenous culture started to take root only following its independence in 1965, green spaces, as Nohl (1988: 81) argues, are found to be even more attractive to local residents, as these spaces represent a reconciliation of culture and nature, with the latter fast disappearing in the last three decades. Users of urban open spaces enjoy recreational activities and they also develop aesthetic images of their own.

The second factor involves the environment. Sustainable development has a strong environmental requirement. Not only must the natural and man-made stock of resources in cities not be jeopardised in the long run, development should also produce a user-friendly and energy-efficient city in which it is pleasant to live. City recreational areas have hence become an instrument to counter the negative impact of environmental deterioration in view of the huge emission of vehicular pollutants, and solid and liquid waste discharge. Acting as an absorber of pollutants, urban parks and open spaces help to neutralise such negative effects. While sustainable development is today at the top of the agenda to ensure long-term urban survival by preventing resource and environmental degradation, the sustainability concept must provide a basis for urban management which integrates economic growth with the natural and built environments (Haughton and Hunter, 1994; Jowsey and Kellet, 1996). Without adequate financial support, it would be impractical to expect that laws and regulations in favour of urban sustainable development could be effectively implemented (Wong, 1999b).

URBANISATION AND LAND-USE TRANSFORMATION IN SINGAPORE

In Singapore, recreational areas are broadly classified as open spaces which comprise nature reserves, public parks, school fields, playgrounds, waterbodies, open areas around housing, and other sites in temporary or permanent disuse (PRD, 1996). Agricultural lands are recreational in character, but their areas have dramatically declined in the last 40 years as a result of rapid urbanisation and industrialisation. Compared to manufacturing and services, agriculture's multiplier effects are small. The role of agriculture in promoting economic growth is seen as minimal, particularly in a small island-state like Singapore where land limitation has severely restricted the scope for farm expansion. Furthermore, meeting the fast-growing urban population's basic need for farm produce is also impractical (Khan, 1988). Based on a pragmatic consideration of urban-industrial development and economics, agriculture has been systematically reduced since the 1960s in physical areas as well as in its contribution towards the gross domestic product.

Again, Table 5.1 shows that from 1960 to 1999, agricultural lands were reduced from 142 square kilometres to less than 10 square kilometres respectively, compared against the doubling in the built-up area for industries, infrastructure and housing. Through reclamation, a total of 79 square kilometres were added to the national territory. By 1999, only about 2,000 hectares of farmlands remained, most of which were high-value agro-technology parks involved in livestock-raising, horticulture, aquaculture and fruit production. Thanks to the nature conservation policy and the need to safeguard the central catchment areas located in the centre of the island, forest areas have not been affected in the last 15 years. Whilst forest and marsh areas and tidal sites are small, the impact of high-tech farms as a source of recreation or open space is obviously quite negligible.

The decline in farmlands implies that the provision of green areas or waterbodies has to rely on artificial means, and this falls to the National Parks Board (NPB) whose primary task is to conserve a limited number of nature reserves and to create man-made greenery on the island. Discussion will now be shifted to the evolution of recreational areas in Singapore and the role of the National Parks Board, which amalgamated with the Parks and Recreation Department in 1996 to form a larger organisation.

Recreational Areas and the National Parks Board

In 1958, there were few greenery sites, other than farmlands producing food for the local population. Most greenery areas were made up of natural vegetation in the form of forest and mangrove or freshwater swamps (Figure 5.1). By 1975, part of the forest in the centre of the island was cleared. In the west, mangrove swamps in Jurong were reclaimed for industrial development launched in the early 1960s. Many planned recreational sites were also set up by the then Parks and Recreation Department to compensate for the loss of natural vegetation.

Under the current jurisdiction of the Ministry of National Development, the NPB's primary role is to maintain Singapore's image as a garden city initiated in a 1967 tree-planting campaign. The "garden city" concept was adopted from the West with a considerable degree of discretion (see Ward, 2002) by then Prime Minister Lee Kuan Yew in developing a modern urban planning strategy in Singapore. Firstly, the concept of British origin was filtered with adjustment to suit a "verticalised" high-rise public housing landscape fundamentally different from the low-rise built form of London's suburban new towns. Logically, high-rise public housing constituted a viable option in preparing for a high-density residential environment in a land-scarce city-state. Greenery was incorporated as an inseparable component in public housing estates. Secondly, the image of a garden city was perceived as an attractive quality that would soften the "concrete jungle" and as a symbol of efficiency to woo investors crucial to economic survival in the early years immediately after Singapore's independence (ESCAP Virtual Conference, 2003).

It was then widely recognised that, as the city-state underwent rapid urbanisation and growth, there was a need to "fashion a natural haven amidst the concrete, material trappings of economic progress [and] to clothe the Republic in a green mantle resplendent with the colours of nature" (Lee and Chua, 1992: 8). Hence, park development in the last three decades has evolved from purely a provision of greenery to imprint the garden-city image in the 1960s into a more people-oriented approach of the 1970s with emphasis on facilities and aesthetic design. By the 1980s, with rising consciousness of environmental compatibility, the preservation of natural habitats such as mangrove swamps and the gradual appreciation and awareness of the restoration of nature in the cityscape, such as the creation of bird sanctuaries, became key agendas. From the late 1980s, following the release of the 1987 Brundtland Report, the garden-city concept was associated with sustainable development, integrating environment with development. This association has reinforced the political legitimacy that has placed economic growth as a top development priority.

Beginning in 1992, under the Singapore Green Plan, the garden-city concept has been condensed with a more long-term objective. Six working groups were organised to study the areas of environmental education, environmental technology, resource conservation, clean technologies, environmental noise and nature conservation measures (Ministry of the Environment, 1993). One of the objectives was to make Singapore an exportable "Model Green City" by the year 2000 (ESCAP Virtual Conference, 2003). The concept continues to evolve to match Singapore's high-rise landscape. High-rise greenery in the form of roof deck gardens, sky terraces, landscaped balconies and planter boxes is seen as an innovative way of increasing the scope of Singapore's greenery in enhancing the aesthetics of buildings. To encourage high-rise greenery, the government has announced that landscaped communal spaces like roof top pavilions, sky terraces and planter boxes will not be subject to development intensity control or development charges. Balconies may be built over and above the permitted maximum development intensity that gives residents the opportunity to construct their own gardens above ground level (Goh, 2001).

In the 1990s, recreational needs were further expanded to incorporate the user-friendly concept where park users can enjoy nature by participating in outdoor activities. This is illustrated by the introduction of adventure and riverine parks to integrate nature with recreational activities. In developing new parks or redeveloping old ones, selected themes are used to guide park design. For example, Labrador Park was redeveloped in 1995 with a "historical headland" theme whereby visitors can learn about the park's historical relics associated with World War Two. The year 1995 also saw the launching of the development plan for Pulau Ubin Recreation Area, the largest nature park, to preserve much of its natural habitat (PRD, 1996). More significantly, the 1991 revised Concept Plan initiated the construction of an island-wide park connector system to facilitate jogging or cycling along tracks decorated with vegetation. The NPB's mission generally reflects its trend of park development in accommodating these changing needs, as outlined below (NPB website, 1999):

a) To provide quality parks, greenery and related services to meet the needs of the public;
b) To promote responsible conservation and awareness of natural heritage;
c) To prudently regulate Singapore's parks and greenery;
d) To actively provide excellent educational packages and share the experience and expertise with the public; and
e) To build and strengthen key partnerships in achieving the above objectives.

Besides managing and promoting national parks and nature reserves for recreation, conservation, research and educational purposes, the NPB is responsible for technical training and promoting tropical horticulture and recreational gardening. Among the 340 public parks in Singapore, the Botanic Gardens can trace its long history back to its founding in 1859. With a small reserved area of primary forest, the Botanic Gardens possess a variety of botanical and horticultural plant collections, and other facilities for recreational activities. It has been developed with a three-core concept, integrating three key value systems, namely: (a) heritage and history; (b) tourism; and (c) education and recreation.

The major sites of public parks are given in Table 5.2 and geographically shown in Figure 5.2. These public parks can be classified into coastal parks, ridge and nature parks, city parks, community and town parks, and reservoir parks as explained below (PNB, 1998).

TABLE 5.2: MAJOR GREENERY SITES IN SINGAPORE

Site	Area (ha)	Type	Managed By
Chinese Gardens	13.5	Landscaped	JTC
Japanese Gardens	13	Landscaped	JTC
Jurong Hill	n.a.	Landscaped	JTC
Jurong Park	n.a.	Landscaped	JTC
Ang Mo Kio Town Garden East	5	Landscaped	NPB
Ang Mo Kio Town Garden West	21	Landscaped	NPB
Bedok Reservoir Park	41.7	Landscaped	NPB
Bedok Town Park	14.6	Landscaped	NPB
Bishan Park	52	Landscaped	NPB
Bukit Batok Nature Park	36	Landscaped	NPB
Bukit Batok Town Park	42	Landscaped	NPB
Bukit Timah Nature Reserve	164	Natural area	NPB
Changi Beach Park	52	Landscaped	NPB
Clementi Woods Park	12	Landscaped	NPB
East Coast Park	151	Landscaped	NPB
Esplanade Park	2.4	Landscaped	NPB
Fort Canning Park	19	Landscaped	NPB
Istana Park	1.3	Landscaped	NPB
Kallang Riverside Park	16	Landscaped	NPB
Kent Ridge Park	47	Landscaped	NPB
Labrador Park	16.8	Landscaped	NPB
Lower Seletar Reservoir Park	3	Landscaped	NPB

TABLE 5.2: MAJOR GREENERY SITES IN SINGAPORE (cont'd)

Site	Area (ha)	Type	Managed By
Marina City Park	30	Landscaped	NPB
Marina Promenade	9	Landscaped	NPB
Mount Faber Park	56	Landscaped	NPB
Pasir Ris Park	71	Landscaped	NPB
Pasir Ris Town Park	14	Landscaped	NPB
Pearl's Hill City Park	9	Landscaped	NPB
Pulau Ubin	1,019	Natural area	NPB
Punggol Park	16	Landscaped	NPB
Sembawang Park	15	Landscaped	NPB
Sun Plaza Park	9.6	Landscaped	NPB
Singapore Botanic Gardens	52	Landscaped & Natural area	NPB
Sungei Buloh Nature Park	87	Natural area	NPB
Telok Blangah Hill Park	34	Landscaped	NPB
Toa Payoh Town Park	4.8	Landscaped	NPB
War Memorial Park	1.4	Landscaped	NPB
West Coast Park	50	Landscaped	NPB
Woodlands Town Park	11	Landscaped	NPB
Yishun Park	13	Landscaped	NPB
Kranji Reservoir Park	9	Landscaped	PUB
Lower Pierce Reservoir Park	6	Landscaped	PUB
MacRitchie Reservoir Park	12	Landscaped	PUB
Upper Pierce Reservoir Park	6	Landscaped	PUB
Upper Seletar Reservoir Park	16	Landscaped	PUB
Singapore Zoological Gardens	28	Landscaped	Zoo

Source: National Parks Board website: http://www.nparks.gov.sg (1 August 2003), Public Utilities Board website: http://www.pub.gov.sg (1 August 2003), Lee and Chua (1992), Singapore Zoological Gardens website: http://www.zoo.com.sg/.

Note: NPB = National Parks Board, JTC = Jurong Town Corporation, PUB = Public Utilities Board, Zoo = Singapore Zoological Gardens

Coastal parks are mostly those reclaimed from the sea. They are flat lands, originally filled with heavily compacted soil. Vegetation growth has to be facilitated by the provision of drainage, and fertile topsoil. East Coast Park, comprising 206 hectares, is the largest park in Singapore.

Typically, it is equipped with a wide range of facilities to meet the various recreational needs of the population (cycling and jogging tracks, a swimming lagoon, sandy beaches, a few recreational centres, bird sanctuaries and pockets of parkland and landscaped ponds).

Ridge and nature parks are those with natural landscapes as their main theme of expression. These parks have been developed around natural features such as ponds, lakes, hills, ridges and wooded sites. A good example is the 47-hectare Kent Ridge Park located in the southwest of the island. This park is covered with natural vegetation in the west. Making use of its undulating topography in the north, the area is preserved with a natural ambience and greenery to provide a serene atmosphere for visitors to have a good lookout on the city landscape below them.

City parks are located within and adjacent to the city area. Their size varies from a small 0.1 hectare to as large as 30 hectares. As a source of shady vegetation in the heart of the city, they provide a cool refuge during the hot months from May to September and some breathing space to pedestrians and workers. Representative of the city parks is Bras Basah Park, surrounded by busy streets in the downtown area. Its one-hectare site is a popular attraction for local old folks and other visitors.

Community and town parks measuring from 0.1 to 40 hectares are also known as neighbourhood parks. They serve the local community in new towns or housing estates. In public housing estates, town parks are provided as a norm whereas in private housing estates, they are built by developers as required by planning standards. Town parks are generally larger than community parks as they serve a larger new-town population. Bishan Park is a 43-hectare site and is one of the most popular town parks in Singapore. It is linear in configuration and measures 2.5 kilometres in length. The park also serves as a buffer between Ang Mo Kio New Town and Bishan New Town, and is easily accessible from both housing estates. Neighbourhood parks located within the public housing estates are managed and maintained by the Housing and Development Board, another statutory board under the Ministry of National Development. However, larger town parks inside public housing estates are managed by the NPB.

Reservoir parks function as reservoirs as well as recreational areas. Thick vegetation is found around the reservoirs, integrating the beauty of water with that of the greenery. Amenities are commonly provided to facilitate family outings and morning or evening exercises. The 12-hectare

MacRitchie Reservoir Park is the oldest reservoir park. Among its attractive features for users are jogging circuits along the water's edge, cross-country running trails and canoeing facilities.

Besides being a precious natural heritage, the Bukit Timah Nature Reserve is part of the Central Catchment Area. It is covered by primary rainforests and has a very rich and diversified ecosystem accommodating a large number of tropical species of flora and fauna. Other parks under the NPB's management are either secondary forests, or mostly landscaped parks based on Western aesthetic norms, decorated with trees, shrubs and a great variety of tropical flower-bearing plants.

Park Connectors

Park connectors form a mobility network, ideally known as "nature corridors", designed to linearly link major parks and nature areas with jogging and cycling tracks. They are readily accessible to residents from transport nodal points. The connectors help birds to move between nature reserves and their refuges or wetland habitats in search of food and breeding grounds. The connectors are mainly developed from drainage and foreshore road reserves that are not meant for any built structure. According to the five-year plan of the Park Connector Network, a total of 11 stretches of park connectors, 34 kilometres in length, would be in service by the end of 1998 (PRD, 1996). The planning concept hinges upon the link between the Central Catchment Area at the centre of the island and these 11 connectors ending at watercourses and their tributaries.[4]

In design, park connectors are supplemented with densely grown plants and shrubs intermingled with wild vegetation so as to attract birds and insects (Oi, 1997). Road crossing points have remained a dilemma in considering the continuity of connectors. Not only is underpass construction for a large number of road crossing points costly, the island-wide visual impact of underpasses would also be disastrous. Ironically, the use of pedestrian crossings by cyclists is still considered illegal. Some signalised at-grade crossings are being planned by the NPB and the Land Transport Authority to resolve this issue.

Waterbodies

Waterbodies comprise natural and man-made water areas such as rivers, canals, drains, reservoirs, stormwater collection ponds, ponds, streams, fountains and waterfalls incorporated in development projects as well as coastal water frontage fit for recreational use (URA, 1993a). In the 1960s, waterbodies, like many public open spaces, were widely used as a dumping ground for household and industrial waste. The government's concern was then more focused on the expansion of reservoirs to store water and cleaning of canals, drains and ditches to control contagious diseases. Attention was drawn to waterbodies in the 1970s, and a decision was made to construct island-wide monsoon drains and establish a flood control system. This was followed by the cleaning up of big watercourses such as the Singapore and Kallang Rivers to facilitate the return of aquatic life and minimise pollutant discharges.

Control of water quality, an important element in the quality of life, has been a long-standing issue, especially in the light of the rapid rise in water consumption. In the past 30 years, water for households, industries and other uses rose from 150.3 million cubic metres in 1968 to 506.1 million cubic metres in 2000 (PUB, *Annual Report*, various years). The raw sources of water supply are the impounding reservoirs, notably those in the central catchments classified as "protected areas" (MacRitchie, Old Seletar and Lower Pierce Reservoirs). Others include Kranji, Sarimbun, Murai, Poyan, Tengah, Jurong Lake and Pandan Reservoirs in the western sector, most of which were established by closing estuaries in the 1970s and early 1980s to create impoundments (Figure 2.4). The Seletar Reservoir and Bedok Reservoir were completed in 1984 and 1986 respectively as collecting ponds for stormwater from urban catchments nearby. Maintaining a high water quality has been increasingly difficult because over 40% of the highly built-up island is being used as catchment areas. This means that much run-off is collected through non-protected or partly protected areas (Appan, 1992). During the 1970s and the 1980s, a number of industries were relocated to minimise water pollution hazards to water catchments. Highly polluting pig farms were phased out in the 1980s. All water sources within the island now meet internationally accepted standards after treatment. What is worrying, however, is that there is a rising trend in the organic content of raw water collected from partly protected catchments. It is hence an important task to monitor and scrutinise the sources of pollutants in the years to come.

For urban planners, the aesthetic values of waterbodies are as important as the water quality. In 1989, a Waterbodies Design Panel was created in Singapore, which aims not only to provide aesthetically pleasing waterbodies but also to encourage developers and professionals to be more conscious of the importance in adding aesthetic values to waterbodies. This was conceptually in line with the objectives of the Concept Plan then revised to offer a better quality of life, taking into consideration the characteristics of Singapore's tropical climate and vegetation in particular. In the design of waterbodies, a more people- and nature-oriented approach is used based on the following guidelines (URA, 1993a):

a) Use a multi-disciplinary approach to involve engineers, architects, town planners and landscape designers so that a more comprehensive perspective is attainable;
b) Use natural materials such as vegetation as far as possible so as to soften and complement the concrete banks or riverside;
c) Allow easy access by the public by way of footpaths, tracks, bridges and roads; and
d) Keep the natural state of waterbodies, and maintain a permanent body of water where possible.

In parallel with the provision and maintenance of recreational areas, the Green Plan launched by the Ministry of the Environment in 1992 was a direct response to the call for an improved global environment by the Rio de Janeiro Earth Summit in the same year. The Green Plan seeks to realise the long-term vision of a sustainable model green city of Singapore (Ministry of the Environment, 1992), and to enhance the environmental awareness of the population and promote resource and nature conservation and clean technology. The desired outcome of the plan is to achieve improved public health, a quality environment and, therefore, a higher quality of life.

Vision of the 1991 Revised Concept Plan

The Green and Blue Plan is an integral part of the 1991 revised Concept Plan, a long-term blueprint underlying future leisure and recreational opportunities in Singapore. The plan integrates the two components of greenery and waterbodies in an attempt to bring people in need of recreational activities closer to water. These two components should be functionally and physically linked so that outdoor activities such as jogging, cycling, camping, hiking and rock climbing can be carried out to that effect (URA, 1991a). The revised Concept Plan envisages that, by Year X, a series of recreational activities and sites will be available (Figure 5.3). By Year X, park connectors, natural and landscaped parks, marina sports and other activities will be distributed island-wide.

To enable residents to feel close to nature, the 1991 Concept Plan aspires to improve the accessibility of the nation's 140 kilometres of coastline. A longer coastline will be created by reclaiming land in the form of small islands. For instance, a long island will be reclaimed along the current east coast from Marina East to Changi. The Concept Plan also aims to create new cultural, retail and entertainment centres where the arts, shopping, tourism and cultural events will be integrated to satisfy the leisure needs of future generations. Sports facilities, children's playgrounds and performing arts are expected to be available at the same venue where people gather and enjoy their weekends and public holidays.

Catering to a greater targeted population of 5.5 million, the 2001 revised Concept Plan aims to upgrade the physical size as well as accessibility of green spaces. The area of greenery will be increased from the present 2,500 hectares to 4,500 hectares eventually (See Figure 5.4). To further facilitate accessibility, park connectors will be used to link parks with town centres, sports complexes and residences. To attract nature lovers, the 2001 Concept Plan also intends to open up the Central Catchment Area for low-impact recreational activities such as hiking and cycling. Scenic drives along the fringes of the Central Catchment Area made up of MacRitchie, Upper Pierce and Upper Seletar Reservoirs and the Bukit Timah Nature Reserve will be made possible. Some selected lookout points at scenic spots around the reservoirs have been placed on the drawing board (URA, 2001: 21–24; *Straits Times*, 22 July 2002).

Alongside the URA's planning of recreational sites, the concept of environmental sustainability is reinforced in the Ministry of the Environment's Singapore Green Plan 2012. The enhancement of consciousness in terms of individual responsibility and civic commitment has been highlighted to help ensure a higher level of sustainability. In practice, three principles have been deployed in the selection of nature areas: richness in biodiversity, maturity of potential sites and a high degree of sustainability in the implementation stage. A more significant strategy in nature conservation is the promotion of selected sites from nature areas to nature reserves to ensure greater long-term conservation of nature sites. In 2001, Sungei Buloh Nature Park and Labrador Park were upgraded to nature reserves (Ministry of the Environment, 2002).

However, public access to some valuable flora and fauna sites characterised by fragile ecosystems would be restricted in order not to destroy the natural habitat (Ministry of National Development, 2002: 14).

RECREATIONAL PURSUITS AND THEIR IMPLICATIONS FOR SUSTAINABILITY AND QUALITY OF LIFE

The current "clean and green city" programme in Singapore is an update of the garden-city concept, incorporating ideas of sustainable development. Hitherto, success in the implementation of the programme has been largely attributable to the strong determination of the political leadership, supported by financial and other resources made available by a pro-business, export-led development policy. In Savage's (1997: 187–193) view, this success has been achieved by the government's "pragmatic environmental ideology that is hinged on possibilistic and anthropocentric human-nature relationships". Through these relationships, achievements are made by employing possible means, including human dimensions, towards an improved environmental system. The means comprise the rigorous use of engineering and planning tools (acts, zoning and development control), and skills in management, and educating and directing, by strict enforcement, the population towards the set objectives of environmental protection, nature conservation and a healthier and more user-friendly environment, on which the quality of life is based.

At the present juncture, Singapore's economic priority model, which has contributed to Singapore's economic success over the past three decades, is being challenged by rising global market competition. A small domestic market and talent pool have continued to be perceived as a restraining factor in sustaining the growth of the city-state. The pressure to accommodate a population larger than the optimal target of 4.4 million set in the 1971 Concept Plan is rising. Can a compromise be reached between the increased size of the population and the pursuit of a better quality of life through a nature-oriented environment with an ample supply of greenery and parks? Great difficulty and uncertainty are envisaged if we consider the repeated revisions of the Pulau Ubin development plan over the last decade.[5]

With the recent rise in environmental awareness and the efforts of the Nature Society of Singapore, the development priority agenda of the government is beginning to be challenged by the public. According to the Nature Society (Singapore), public awareness of nature and the need for nature conservation has contributed towards the enlightenment of policy decision-makers. In seeking better protection for all nature areas, the NSS will negotiate for workable solutions with policy-makers. Indeed, its efforts have seen a total of 21 nature areas being included under Special and Detailed Control Plans of the 2001 Concept Plan. Its next task is to seek the protection of marine areas that have been found to exhibit evidence of marine biodiversity (NSS, 2003).

The Triangular Relationship Between Growth, Environment and Equity

In the classical perspective, planning authorities are viewed as promoting city development at the expense of the natural environment and greenery. This perspective is no longer applicable in Singapore. Today, in dealing with future urban plans, land-use planners persistently face the dilemma of "man versus nature" or "jobs versus the environment". They have to reconcile three conflicting interests: growth, equity distribution and environmental protection. Though fundamentally conflicting, the three components may be made mutually beneficial in some ways. In essence, urban development cannot sustain itself if it is translated into limits of growth (see Owens, 1997). Economic growth is a priority area for planning authorities to survive in the real world of practice (Figure 5.5). It is also a fact that social equity and the environment rely on growth and hence resources generated out of it to provide more people-oriented services (for instance, easy public access to public transport and greenery), and facilities to safeguard the physical environment. Growth, therefore, has a complementary value in the triangular relationship in which all three components contribute in one way or another to the quality of life. Sustainable development should incorporate a sustainable economy, based on which social equity and environmental conservation can coexist in a state of harmony (Campbell, 1996).

FIGURE 5.5: THE TRIANGULAR RELATIONSHIP BETWEEN RECREATIONAL PROVISION, EQUITY AND QUALITY OF LIFE

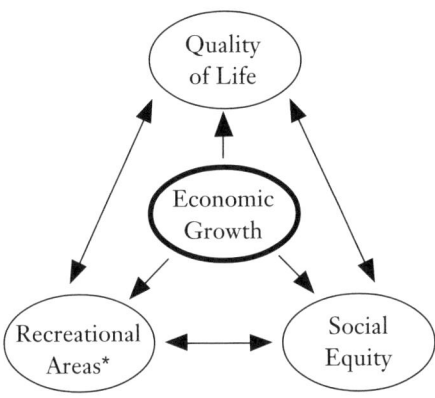

* Natural areas, parks, waterbodies, other public open spaces, etc. Golf courses are recreational sites, but have highly limited access.

Heading for Creative Conservation in an Intensively Built-Up Urban Environment?

Development necessarily results in the loss of existing landscape and, inevitably, of biodiversity if it involves construction of buildings in nature areas. By including sustainable development in the working agenda, nature conservation and park development have established "a mechanism by which damage to landscape, habitats or species can be balanced by compensating projects that create 'conservation value'"(Adams, 1996: 267).

The loss of "scarce nature capital" in a small island-state such as Singapore in fact represents a heavily felt psychological setback in light of its non-substitutability. Judging from the consequences of the loss of nature in development, artificially created natural habitats cannot be taken as the equivalent of lost habitats, especially if the ecological implications for the whole system of fauna and flora are considered. The created habitats can at best be perceived as a creative conservation effort to cater to the recreational needs of the people and a pragmatic landscape beautification endeavour, which can be highly successful as in the case of Singapore. Given that the forces of change are inevitable but may be slowed down, it is necessary for nature conservation to be exercised within the highly built environment in Singapore. The engineered landscape may be a "semi-natural and over-nurtured" product. It is nonetheless a "softener" of the concrete landscape, without which the garden city of Singapore may be transformed into a real concrete jungle that will be unbearable.

CONCLUDING REMARKS

Recreational areas have gained increasing importance in modern urban living. They play the role of nature in satisfying human physiological and psychological needs and reducing the pollution impact in cities. In the past four decades of rapid urbanisation and industrialisation, many natural areas and vegetable farms in Singapore have given way to the built environment. In replacement, large man-made recreational sites in the form of landscaped parks and waterbodies have been put in place to fulfill the functions of nature. This has been made possible by the economic growth generated and the commitment to transform the island into a garden city and, in the long term, a sustainable city-state. The dimension of sustainable development carries a new meaning in that the quality of life provided by the extensively engineered recreational landscape is a conciliation of economic growth with environment protection and social equity. Except for some exclusive golf clubs, equity is attainable as recreational sites have been rendered accessible to the general public as a whole.

Accessibility may not be an issue, but Singaporeans' use of leisure time is an issue as a result of their life-styles. Over the last 30 years, relatively rapid economic growth and rising affluence, accompanied by an ageing population, have resulted in the rise of chronic degenerative diseases (Tan, 2003). Tan's (2003) survey shows that, in 1998, only 16.8% of Singaporeans engaged in physical exercise at least three times weekly (20 minutes each time). About 55% did not exercise at all, and the great majority were those in the 30–39 and 40–49 age groups. High cholesterol and hypertension are thus common among those aged 40 and above. Work pressure and stress seem to be the key factor holding back the desire for physical exercise, whether at home or in recreational areas. As a result of a local culture that highly emphasises educational qualifications, self-improvement activities such as part-time courses and skills upgrading sessions have taken up much of Singaporeans' leisure time (Li, 1997). Another survey conducted by Ong, Lee and Tan (2003) further reinforces this point in interpreting why few volunteers are involved in community services. Their findings show that three-quarters of the interviewees could not spare the time due to work and family commitments. The opportunity cost of spending time on voluntary work discourages volunteers as they are often busy with activities linked to career upgrading.

A conclusion may be drawn from one of the earlier garden-city objectives formulated in Singapore that was meant to woo multinational investors who would perceive greenery and recreational space as a symbol of quality of life rather than as a genuine means with which to encourage workers towards a healthier life-style. Indeed, the availability of accessible and attractive greenery is integral to the quality of urban life, an important indicator of urban liveability. In both Western and local Singapore value perception, natural environments, as a source of open-space amenities and for the public good, are determinants in the choice of residential location and property values (see Geoghegen, 2002; Van Herzele and Wiedemann, 2003; Smith, Poulos and Kim, 2002). Yet, the missing link in Singapore is the widespread inability of the middle class to find time in using their recreational and natural assets meaningfully and gainfully.

A common complaint of private condominium residents who have used a substantial proportion of their savings to buy a unit is that they cannot spare the time to enjoy the facilities. Affluence has geared citizens' life-styles towards higher levels of consumption, but with less time allocated to recreational leisure. Recreational spaces such as parks, gardens and nature sites are created more for decorative purposes than for actual use and appreciation. This mismatch has called for a rethinking and contemplation at the policy level as to how the physiological needs may be balanced with material needs of the population to a more satisfactory level.

ENDNOTES

1. The exact size allocated for "special use" is unknown. But this occupies a large land area scattered island-wide, including a large part of Pulau Tekong. See Concept Plans in earlier chapters.
2. For an example of measuring equity and access to parks, consult the article published in *Political Geography*, Vol. 53, No. 3, pp. 332–346, written by Greg Lindsey, Maltie Maraj and SonCheong Kuan (2001), entitled "Access, Equity and Urban Greenways: An Exploratory Investigation".
3. A figure obtained from the URA's exhibition on land-use distribution in Singapore in 2001 and 2002.

4   These watercourses are the Pandan River, Singapore River, Kallang River, Geylang River, Siglap Canal, Bedok Canal, Tampines River, Serangoon River, Punggol River, Seletar River and Pang Sua Canal.

5   The future of Pulau Ubin, covering 1,020 hectares, which has remained largely a nature park well-known for its adventure activities, is being closely re-examined. According to the 1991 revised Concept Plan, the schedule to reclaim the island's eastern shoreline in order to house 60,000 people was set for the year 2010. With the population rising faster than the 1991 projection, the Urban Redevelopment Authority is contemplating revising its plan and developing the island ten years ahead of schedule (*Straits Times*, 14 October 1999). Nevertheless, the 2001 Concept Plan has compromised the urgency of development. The whole of Pulau Ubin has been classified as reserve land, to be used for development only when the need arises.

Conclusion

The conclusion sums up how land use has changed over time, and revisits the Singapore land-use modernisation model to see whether it is applicable to other countries. In examining the transferability of the model, we need to conceptualise this issue again against the background of Singapore's uniqueness in the global link and the changing state of developmentalism in the current circumstances, and to re-examine the land-use transformation experience of Singapore from both a macro and micro perspective.

The macro-level investigation queries the exportability of the Singapore model and its relevance to other Third World countries. At the micro-level, attention is focused on the forces that have contributed to land-use change, and how planning, re-planning and readjustment of land resources are manoeuvred according to political, economic and social needs. For instance, military land area, which occupied 10% of the total land area under the British colonial rule, has been increased to more than 10% of total land area under the jurisdiction of the Ministry of Defence. Yet, Sentosa Island, previously used as a military base, has been turned into a heavily invested tourist resort. The former Seletar civil airport is now a military air base. Pulau Tekong, an undeveloped offshore island, has been transformed into a military training ground. Also, can the rising pressure for environmental preservation from the NGO environmentalist groups be compromised? Finally, the roles of land-use planning and policy options are revisited.

SINGAPORE'S MODERNISATION EXPERIENCE AS AN EXPORTABLE MODEL?

At the macro structural level, the Singapore modernisation experience has demonstrated a leap from post-colonial Asian traditionalism and dualism to Western-based modernity. Fundamentally, the leap was made possible by a developmentalist government through reworking and reestablishing the relationship from a colonial one into a global link associated with world capitalism, persistently seeking areas of high potential business growth. Achievement is attributable to the firm and effective leadership of the ruling elites with the help of the departing colonial power and international aid agencies and experts. Using structural functionalism that serves the industrialisation model and logic of social action, the Singapore state was capable of bridging the gap between the tradition and the modern (see Preston, 1996; Frisby, 2001). In the procedural process towards modernity, the state, by its long-standing continuity of governance, has constantly identified specific points of intervention to keep the development path on track.

The persistent need of the Singapore model to adjust and adapt to changing global circumstances full of uncertainty has denied its exportability as a "model". Put straightforwardly, the Singapore "model" is a product of specific circumstances. More precisely, the modernisation model has become outmoded since the 1980s by post-modernism in the global industrial capitalist system characterised by strong market orientation, mass consumption and rising welfare control. This post-modernism is highly interdependent with the post-Fordist mode of production (Preston, 1996: 273–275). Such a consumerist life-style is expected to emerge in Singapore if global integration is successful. Under post-Fordist production, with more market-force decisions on product demands, it is anticipated that there will be less restrictive state regulations. It may be thus argued that land-use decisions in Singapore are likely to shift towards market decisions and less planned restrictions.

However, even globally well-wired post-modernist nations or cities do not rule out the importance of physical planning. If the state continues to function as a legitimate power centre, it will have to use spatial planning as a tool for social surveillance or control (Tehranian, 1995). In maintaining social, economic and political efficiency, the orderly spatial form of Singapore will serve simultaneously as a post-industrial and cyber-based modern city. This includes physical expansion and extension of infrastructure, modern urbanism and mobility of people, goods and services (see Frsiby, 2001: 20).

Furthermore, has globalisation and regionalisation brought about a crisis to developmental states that renders the Singapore "model" non-exportable? Strongly integrated into the global trade system and following very closely the globalisation trend to keep afloat and maintain its competitive edge, Singapore's state role may be perceived as being overtaken by that of the international institutions and market forces. As such, the crisis is intrinsically found within the developmental state itself, characterised by constant adjustments and alternatives. By this nature, the exportability of such a model is in doubt. Accordingly, Nederveen Pieterse (2001: 27–30) argues that, in the current global market competition, the crisis of developmentalism has demonstrated itself as a crisis of modernism, rooted predominantly in the "ecological limits to growth". Typically, the "Singapore model" is a blended product of fusing Western modernity with local traditions and characteristics. The exportability is therefore restricted to a partial or piecemeal dimension as local traditions are largely unique to recipient societies.

Being a city-state, Singapore's spatial planning since its independence has skipped the consideration of spatial equity in the context of rural-urban disparity. Uneven development, a major post-independence concern of most developing nations, has been avoided. Singapore's development has been determined more by ambitious plans set by the Concept Plan of 1970, which aimed to transform the island into a world-class city with a strong CBD and one of the command centres in the Asia-Pacific. Within the framework of an economic priority model infused with modernity and circumstantial developmentalism set by historical conditions, we have witnessed a series of land-use transformations which spread gradually from the Central Area to the rest of the island in a radial pattern.

By no means, however, can we claim that a stage of post-developmentalism has set in and developed a new agenda for Singapore's future development path. On the contrary, post-developmentalism acts strongly as an opposing force to globalisation and mass consumption that urges support of local initiatives, local grassroots groups and communal rights. It calls for simple living and efficient management of local resources, with emphasis on a balance between material pursuits and nature (Peet and Hartwick, 1999: 151–152). Quite obviously, such an ideal, advocated by certain academics who claim it is a preventive approach towards global self-destruction, is not on par with Singapore's present state of growth-oriented policy.

LAND-USE TRANSFORMATION

At the micro-level, the land use transformation has logically followed the modernist development path over the past four decades. Thus, morphology in the Central Area of Singapore has changed from a dualistic and congested downtown core filled with dilapidated housing inherited from the colonial administration into an efficient, modern financial district. Of the two forces responsible for making such a transformation, a key internal element is derived from the great commitments of the ruling elite who have created a pro-business environment. This has attracted influential MNCs, using Singapore to set up their regional headquarters in the renewed CBD. Replacing the traditional life-style, the transformation has been a process of effective application of land-use planning and implementation. Joint efforts between international experts and their local counterparts have achieved good results. Led by the 1970 Concept Plan, there has been a persistent land-surface modernisation to satisfy aspirations for modern living. More importantly, the new CBD represents the future of Singapore as a regional or global centre of economic power upon which it relies for its continued prosperity.

Infrastructure is another large consumer of land. It is a modernising agent and is an indispensable accessory to facilitate business and household movements. It has served to attract MNCs whose leading technology, global marketing networks and competitive products have been critical to international trade. The shift from physical infrastructure to knowledge-oriented infostructure has become a necessity in the management of human and land resources. Such a shift has helped to support sustained growth in a highly globalised world. Furthermore, it enhances the competitive edge, and global competition. A tremendous amount of land has been allocated to the construction of physical infrastructure such as road- and rail-related services, airports, seaports, and sanitary and drainage facilities, etc. In contrast, infostructure is far less visible than physical infrastructure but, given its virtual feature, is incorporated in the operations of, and equipment used in, various communication processes.

In the area of industrial development, the close relationship between government-owned companies and international MNCs has produced an unexpected landscape change, giving birth to a new and modern Singapore. Indeed, the Singapore model of industrialisation has combined a state-led Keynesian strategy with a heavy reliance on Western capital, which creates an advantage in terms of world market access, technology and innovations. There is an extensive top-down approach from a leadership committed to development. In summing up, Singapore's industrial policy has indeed ensured social and political stability, and helped to build a long tenure for the PAP government by justifying legitimacy with sustainable economic growth.

Housing is another important transformation that merits discussion. From slum and squatter clearance, and elimination of "traditional habitats", public housing is a prime mover in modernising the residential landscape to a great extent. More than 85% of the population now live in public housing. As a monopolistic instrument, the HDB has shifted its primary functions from meeting an immediate basic social need in the early 1960s to managing rising aspirations as a result of greater affluence and an expanding middle class. Whilst private housing is perceived as a symbol of higher social status and better quality of life, the lower-income groups have to rely on affordable public housing. Middle-class groups tend to reject public housing, where possible, as Fordist mass-produced public consumer goods.

For the state, managing the rising aspirations for private property is perceived as a negotiating term in exchange for popular support. However, optimism for economic growth, liberal loan policies, speculation and a limited land supply had resulted in a price spiral in the early 1990s, making affordability beyond reach for many. Moreover, many Singaporeans are "asset rich and cash poor" because of over-investment in residential property. Together with vast areas of public housing estates distributed island-wide, much of the state land has been converted into private residential areas through the public sale of sites.

Recreational space development has accompanied urban industrial development, with the result that recreational space is now a significant feature of modern urban living in Singapore. Rapid urbanisation and industrialisation have replaced many nature and vegetable farms with a built environment. As an alternative, man-made recreational sites in the form of landscaped parks and waterbodies have been used to fulfill the functions of nature. On the basic garden-city concept, there is a long-term commitment to build an environmentally sustainable city-state, incorporating quality of life as a key component. Recently, pressure from environmentalists and nature lovers such as the Nature Society of Singapore, a non-governmental organisation, has somewhat refrained the government from extending development plans into one of the last remaining nature islands, Pulau Ubin. Their campaign has led to a change in projected land use on Pulau Ubin. Instead of using substantial areas of Pulau Ubin for housing and industry as indicated in the 1991 revised

Concept Plan, the latest Concept Plan 2001 has designated these areas as reserve sites (see Figure 5.4).

While accessibility to recreational areas is not an issue generally, the use of leisure time by Singaporeans is affected by their choice of lifestyle. Work pressure and stress have held back many citizens from adequate physical exercise, whether at home or in recreational sites. It may be concluded that greenery and recreational space are seen as a symbol of quality of life. But a healthy life-style is not vigorously pursued because of the general inability of the population to find time to enjoy its recreational and nature assets effectively.

ROLE OF LAND-USE PLANNING

Planning impacts on land use are most characteristically reflected in urban morphology according to design and planning norms as well as affordable or fashionable building materials available at the time. In geographical terms, planning follows modernisation guidelines in the provision of structures, facilities, infrastructure and services over time. During the post-war urban renewal era, urban planners, as members of a new profession, served to protect and enhance the established commercial functions of city centres in a large number of Western cities (Ward, 1994).

In Singapore, they transformed the physical form of the Central Area, built a new CBD, and provided shop lots and food centres to accommodate the omnipresent petty traders. Whilst clearing the narrow streets of hawkers and rebuilding wider streets for vehicular traffic, they also decentralised the population, relocated industrial operators, and created new industrial zones in the Jurong Industrial Estate and flatted factories adjacent to public housing areas, and other more specialised industries in various identified sites island-wide. They were empowered by land acquisition legislation in performing tasks of renewal and comprehensive redevelopment. The population decentralisation from the Central Area had provided ample opportunities for homogenising multiple uses (industry, residential, and services) in a predominantly service-based city centre, in particular high-value banking and financial services. Renewal, however, had resulted in a less dynamic nightlife, and greater commuting distances for many. The outcome has led to recent attempts to rejuvenate and restore the Central Area in order to make it popular with younger families. The results have yet to be seen.

Stringent car ownership and usage control since the mid-1970s has indeed relieved congestion and made access to workplaces in the CBD highly dependent on public transport. Dependence has made it necessary to render mass transit to and from the downtown area since the 1980s. If traffic control is an environmental concern, the urban sustainability issue is also at stake. Urban sustainability in reality goes beyond purely environmentalism. It involves affordable housing, jobs at appropriate locations, recreational activities and a pleasant environment to live in (Ward, 1994; Silberstein and Maser, 2000). Sustainability is also associated with a choice of shorter commuting time and distance, and a more participatory role of the population concerned in its own living environment. It is therefore broadly perceived that planning vision should incorporate sustainability and social responsiveness as its central theme. This means planning together for a collective future, not on the basis of what politicians and planners think is best for the population. In so doing, the rising anti-planning sentiments, a current sign of many Western cities, can be better managed with compromise and negotiation.

Bibliography

Abrams, C., Kobe, S. and Koenigsberger, O. (1963), *Growth and Urban Renewal in Singapore*, Report prepared for the Government of Singapore (New York: United Nations Programme of Technical Assistance).

Adams, W. M. (1996), "Creative conservation, landscapes and loss", *Landscape Research*, Vol. 21, No. 3, pp. 265–276.

Agence France Presse, "Singapore port operator loses Taiwan's Evergreen to Malaysia", 3 April 2002, available at http://www.singapore-window.org/sw02/020403af.htm.

Alatas, S. H. (1969), "Modernization and national consciousness", in Ooi, J. B. and Chiang H. D. (eds.), *Modern Singapore* (Singapore: Singapore University Press), pp. 216–232.

Amin, A. and Thrift, N. (1995), "Globalisation, institutional 'thickness' and the local economy", in Healey, P., Cameron, S., Davoudi, S., Graham, S. and Madani-Pour, A. (eds.), *Managing Cities: The New Urban Context* (Chichester, UK: John Wiley), pp. 91–108.

Appan, A. (1992), "The control of water quality in Singapore", in Gupta, A. and Pitts, J. (eds.), *Physical Adjustment in a Changing Landscape: The Singapore Story* (Singapore: Singapore University Press), pp. 374–388.

Asian Infrastructure Monthly, "Deep sewage tunnel project takes off", 26 July 2000.

Bell, S. (1999), *Landscape: Pattern, Perception and Process* (London: E & FN Spon).

Bernick, M. and Cervero, R. (1996), *Transit Villages in the 21st Century* (New York: McGraw-Hill).

Berrisbeita, A. (1999), "The Amsterdam bos: The modern public park and the construction of collective experience", in Corner, J. (ed.), *Recovering Landscape* (New York: Princeton Architectural Press), pp. 186–203.

Berry, B. J. L., Conkling, E. C. and Ray, D. M. (eds.) (1997), *The Global Economy in Transition* (New Jersey: Prentice Hall).

Bhagwati, J. (1991), "Threats to the world trading regime: Protectionism, unfair trade et al.", in Koekkoek, A. and Mennes, L. B. M. (eds.), *International Trade and Global Development — Essays in Honour of Jagdish Bhagwati* (London: Routledge).

Bina, C. and Davis, C. (2000), "Globalization, technology, and skill formation in capitalism", in Baiman, R., Boushey, H. and Saunders, D. (eds.), *Political Economy and Contemporary Capitalism* (Armonk, New York: M. E. Sharpe), pp. 193–202.

Binder, D. F. and Smith, T. M. (1997), "The linkage between transportation, infrastructure investment and productivity: A U. S. federal research perspective", in Mody, A. (ed.), *Infrastructure Strategies in East Asia: The Untold Story* (Washington D.C.: World Bank), pp. 49–59.

Black, J. K. (1999), *Development in Theory and Practice: Paradigms and Paradoxes* (Boulder, Colorado: Westview Press, second edition).

Block, E. and Hottovy, T. (1988), *Future Cities and Information Technology* (Gavle, Sweden: The National Swedish Institute for Building Research).

Blomstrom, M. and Hette, B. (1984), *Development in Transition* (London: Zed Books).

Boey, Y. M. (1998), "Urban conservation in Singapore", in Yuen, B. (ed.), *Planning Singapore: From Plan to Implementation* (Singapore: Singapore Institute of Planners), pp. 133–168.

Bowen, J. T. (2000), "Singapore", in Leinbach, T. R. and Ulack, R. (eds.), *Southeast Asia: Diversity and Development* (New Jersey: Prentice Hall), pp. 379–407.

Breffett, C. and Sim, L. L. (eds.) (1993), *Proceedings: Environmental Issues in Development and Conservation* (Singapore: School of Building and Estate Management, National University of Singapore).

Breffett, C., Kong, L., Yuen, B. and Sodhi, N. (1997), *The Planning and Ecology of Park Connector Systems in Urban Areas* (Singapore: Hong Kong Bank and National University of Singapore).

Bristow, M. R. (2000), "Early town planning in British South East Asia: 1910–1939", *Planning Perspectives*, Vol. 15, No. 2, pp. 139–160.

Brookfield, H. (1975), *Interdependent Development* (London: Menthuen).

Brunn, S. D. (1992), "Cities of the future", in Brunn, S. D. and Williams, J. F. (eds.), *Cities of the World: World Regional Urban Development* (New York: HarperCollins College, second edition), pp. 478–492.

Carter, H. (1995), *The Study of Urban Geography* (London: Edward Arnold, fourth edition).

Castells, M., Goh, L. and Kwok, R. Y. W. (1990), *The Shek Kip Mei Syndrome: Economic Development and Public Housing in Hong Kong and Singapore* (London: Pion).

Castells, M. (1992), "Four Asian tigers with a dragon head: A comparative analysis of the state, economy, and society in the Asian Pacific Rim", in Appelbaum, R. P. and Henderson, J. (eds.), *State and Development in the Asian Pacific Rim* (Newbury Park: Sage), pp. 33–70.

Castells, M. (1996), *The Rise of the Network Society* (Oxford: Blackwell).

Castells, M. (1999a), *End of Millennium* (Malden, USA: Blackwell).

Castells, M. (1999b), *Information Technology, Globalization and Social Development* (Geneva: United Nations Research Institute for Social Development, DP 114).

Castells, M. and Hall, P. (1994), *Technoploes of the World: The Making of Twenty-First Century Industrial Complexes* (London: Routledge).

Chang, H. J. (1994), *The Political Economy of Industrial Policy* (New York: St. Martin's Press).

Charles, D. R. (1996), "Information technology and production systems", in Daniels, P. W. and Lever, W. F. (eds.), *The Global Economy in Transition* (Harlow, UK: Longman), pp. 83–102.

Chew, R. (1996), "Wage systems and wage reform in Singapore", in Lim, C. Y. (ed.), *Economic Policy Management in Singapore* (Singapore: Addison-Wesley), pp. 147–171.

Chief Surveyor, Singapore (1958), *Singapore 1:25,000 Topographic Map*.

Chiu, R. L. H. (1996), "Housing affordability in Shenzhen Special Economic Zone: A forerunner of China's housing reform", *Housing Studies*, Vol. 11, No. 4, pp. 561–580.

Chiu, S. W. K., Ho, K. C. and Lui, T. L. (1997), *City-States in the Global Economy: Industrial Restructuring in Hong Kong and Singapore* (Boulder, Colorado: Westview Press).

Choe, A. F. C. (1969), "Urban renewal", in Ooi, J. B. and Chiang, H. D. (eds.), *Modern Singapore* (Singapore: Singapore University Press), pp. 161–170.

Chua, B. H. (1991a), "Not depoliticized but ideologically successful: The public housing programme in Singapore", *International Journal of Urban and Regional Research*, Vol. 15, No. 1, pp. 24–41.

Chua, B. H. (1991b), "Race relations and public housing policy in Singapore", *Journal of Architectural and Planning Research*, Vol. 8, No. 4, pp. 343–354.

Chua, B. H. (1996), "Singapore—Management of a city-state in Southeast Asia", in Ruland, J. (ed.), *The Dynamics of Metropolitan Management in Southeast Asia* (Singapore: Institute of Southeast Asian Studies), pp. 207–229.

Chua, B. H. (2000), "Public housing residents as clients of the state", *Housing Studies*, Vol. 15, No. 1, pp. 45–60.

Civil Aviation Authority of Singapore [CAAS] (1998), *Annual Report 1997/98*, Singapore.

Colony of Singapore (1952), *Report on the Preliminary Island Plan* (Singapore: Diagnostic Survey Team).

Colony of Singapore (1955), *Master Plan: Reports of Study Groups and Working Parties* (Singapore: Government Printing Office).

Commerce Sub-Committee (1988), *Concept Plan Review (1988/89)*, Technical Report (Singapore: Planning Department).

Convery, F. J. (1998), *Challenges for Urban Infrastructure in the European Union* (Luxembourg: European Foundation).

Cornwall, J. and Cornwall, W. (1992), "Export-led growth: A new interpretation", in Milberg, W. (ed.), *The Megacorp and Macrodynamics: Essays in Memory of Alfred Eichner* (Armonk, New York: M. E. Sharpe), pp. 209–223.

Dale, O. J. (1999), *Urban Planning in Singapore: The Transformation of a City* (Shah Alam, Malaysia: Oxford University Press).

Datta-Chaudhuri, M. (1980), "Infrastructure and location", in Cody, J., Hughes, H. and Wall, D. (eds.), *Policies for Industrial Progress in Developing Countries* (Oxford: Oxford University Press).

DBS Bank (1996), *The Petrochemical Industry in Singapore*, ASEAN/Singapore Briefing No. 14 (Singapore: DBS Bank).

Department of Statistics (1967), *Yearbook of Statistics*, Singapore.

Department of Statistics (1973), *Yearbook of Statistics*, Singapore.

Department of Statistics (1979), *Yearbook of Statistics 1978–79*, Singapore.

Department of Statistics (1983), *Yearbook of Statistics*, Singapore.

Department of Statistics (1988), *Yearbook of Statistics*, Singapore.

Department of Statistics (1990), *Yearbook of Statistics*, Singapore.

Department of Statistics (1991), *Yearbook of Statistics*, Singapore.
Department of Statistics (1995), *Yearbook of Statistics*, Singapore.
Department of Statistics (1996), *Yearbook of Statistics*, Singapore.
Department of Statistics (1999), *Singapore 1999: Statistical Highlights*, Singapore.
Department of Statistics (2000), *Singapore's Investment Abroad, 1997–1998*, Singapore.
Department of Statistics (2001a), *Census of Population 2000*, Advance Data Release, Singapore.
Department of Statistics (2001b), *Singapore 2001: Yearbook of Statistics*, Singapore.
Department of Statistics (2002), *Singapore's Investment Abroad, 1999–2000*, Singapore.
Deyo, F. C. (1981), *Dependent Development and Industrial Order* (New York: Praeger).
Douglas, S. U., Douglas, S. A. and Finn, T. J. (1994), "The garment industry in Singapore: Clothes for the emperor", in Bonacich, E., Cheng, L., Chinchilla, N., Hamilton, N. and Ong, P. (eds.), *Global Production: The Apparel Industry in the Pacific Rim* (Philadelphia: Temple University Press), pp. 197–213.
Drakakis-Smith, D. (1996), "Less developed economies and dependence", in Daniels, P. W. and Lever, W. F. (eds.), *The Global Economy in Transition* (Harlow, UK: Longman), pp. 215–238.
Drysdale, J. (1984), *Singapore: Struggle for Success* (Singapore: Times Books International).
Economic Development Board [EDB] (1967), *Development of Jurong New Town, 1960–1967* (Singapore: EDB). [Prepared by H. Fryer, Chief Surveyor and Planner of the EDB.]
Economic Development Board [EDB] (1997), *Yearbook 1996/97*, Singapore.
Economic Development Board [EDB] (1998), *Yearbook 1997/98*, Singapore.
Economic Development Board [EDB] (2000), "University of Chicago opens Asian Campus", *Singapore Investment News*, October 2000, Singapore.
Economic Development Board [EDB] (2002), *Yearbook 2001/02*, Singapore.
Economic Planning Committee (1991), *The Strategic Economic Plan: Towards a Developed Nation* (Singapore: Singapore National Printers).
ESCAP Virtual Conference (2003), "Garden City to Model Green City", available at http://www.unescap.org/opad/vc/conference/ex_sg_14gem.htm, retrieved in August 2003.
Ettlinger, N. (1991), "The roots of competitive advantage in California and Japan", *Annals of the Association of American Geographers*, Vol. 81, No. 3, pp. 391–407.
Far Eastern Economic Review (1999), *Asia 1999 Yearbook—A Review of the Events of 1998*.
Fonseca, R. (1975), "Planning and land-use in Singapore", Working Paper, Department of Sociology, University of Singapore.
Frank, K., Cheong, H. C. and Baillieu, T. (1993), *A Survey of Buyers' Preferences—Condominiums in Singapore* (Singapore: KFCB).

Friedmann, J. (1995), "Where we stand: A decade of world-city research", in Knox, P. L. and Taylor, P. J. (eds.), *World-Cities in a World System* (Cambridge: Cambridge University Press), pp. 21–47.

Friedmann, W. (1954), "A theory of public industrial enterprise", in Hanson, A. H. (ed.), *Public Enterprise: A Study of Its Organisation and Management in Various Countries* (Brussels: International Institute of Administrative Sciences), pp. 11–23.

Frisby, D. (2001), *Cityscape of Modernity: Critical Explorations* (Oxford: Blackwell).

Gamer, R. E. (1972), *The Politics of Urban Development in Singapore* (Singapore: Oxford University Press).

Garner, B. (1967), "Models of urban geography and settlement location", in Chorley, R. J. and Haggett, P. (eds.), *Socio-Economic Models in Geography* (London: Methuen), pp. 303–360.

Geoffrey, M. and Perera, A. (1995), *Singapore: The Global City-State* (Folkestone, Kent: China Library).

Geoghegen, J. (2002), "The value of open space in residential land use", *Land Use Policy*, Vol. 19, No. 1, pp. 91–98.

Gibson, M. S. and Landstaff, M. J. (1982), *An Introduction to Urban Renewal* (London: Hutchinson).

Goh, C. T. (2001), "Perspective: Landscaping and Innovation", available at http://www.mfa.gov.sg/experience/oct2001/perspective.htm, retrieved in August 2003.

Goh, K. S. (1973), "Economic development and modernisation in South-East Asia", in Evers, H. D. (ed.), *Modernisation in South-East Asia* (Singapore: Oxford University Press), pp. 81–93.

Goh, K. S. (1976), "A socialist economy that works", in Nair, D. V. C. (ed.), *Socialism that Works: The Singapore Way* (Singapore: Federal Publications), pp. 77–85.

Goh, K. S. (1995a), *The Economics of Modernization* (Singapore: Federal Publications).

Goh, K. S. (1995b), *Wealth of East Asian Nations* (Singapore: Federal Publications), arranged and edited by Linda Low.

Goldblum, C. (1998), "De la ville à la mégapole: essor ou déclin des villes au XXème siècle?" in Burdése, J. C., Roussel, M. J., Spector, T. and Theys, J. (eds.), *Singapour, Modèle de la Métropolisation Plannifiée en Asie du Sud-Est* (Paris: Ministère de l'Equipement, des Transports et du Logement), pp. 69–81.

Goldblum, C. and Wong, T. C. (2000), "Growth, crisis, and spatial change: A study of haphazard urbanisation in Jakarta, Indonesia", *Land Use Policy*, Vol. 17, No. 1, pp. 29–37.

Gore, C. (1984), *Regions in Question: Space, Development Theory and Regional Policy* (London: Methuen).

Gould, P. G. (1970), "Tanzania 1920–63: The spatial impress of the modernisation process", *World Politics*, Vol. 22, No. 2, pp. 149–170.

Graham, S. and Marvin, S. (1996), *Telecommunications and the City: Electronic Spaces, Urban Places* (London: Routledge).

Groote, P., Jacobs, J. and Sturm, J. E. (1998), "Output effects of transport infrastructure: The Netherlands, 1853–1913", *Tijdchrift voor Economische en Social Geografie*, Vol. 90, No. 2, pp. 97–109.

Gwynne, R. N. (1996), "Trade and developing countries", in Daniels, P. W. and Lever, W. F. (eds.), *The Global Economy in Transition* (Harlow, UK: Longman), pp. 239–262.

Hamnett, C. (1995), "Home-ownership and the middle classes", in Butler, T. and Savage, M. (eds.), *Social Change and the Middle Classes* (London: UCL Press), pp. 257–274.

Hanna, W. A. (1964), *Go ahead at Goh's Folly: Singapore's Gamble with Industrial Expansion* (New York: American University Field Staff).

Hassan, R. (1977), *Families in Flats: A Study of Low Income Families in Public Housing* (Singapore: Singapore University Press).

Haughton, G. and Hunter, C. (1994), "Managing sustainable urban development", in Williams, C. and Haughton, G. (eds.), *Perspectives Towards Sustainable Environmental Development* (Ashgate, USA: Avebury), pp. 111–129.

Havinden, M. and Meredith, D. (1993), *Colonialism and Development: Britain and its Tropical Colonies, 1850–1960* (London: Routledge).

Heyzer, N. (1983), "International production and social change: An analysis of the state, employment and trade unions in Singapore", in Ong, J. H., Tong, C. K. and Tan, E. S. (eds.), *Understanding Singapore Society* (Singapore: Times Academic Press), pp. 374–395.

Hillier, J. (1998), "Paradise proclaimed? Towards a theoretical understanding of representations of nature in land use planning decision-making", *Ethics, Place and Environment*, Vol. 1, No. 1, pp. 77–91.

Hirschman, A. (1958), *The Strategy of Economic Development* (New Haven, USA: Yale University Press).

Hirschman, A. (1981), "The rise and decline of development economics", in *Essays in Trespassing: Economics to Politics and Beyond* (Cambridge: Cambridge University Press), reprinted in Kanth, R. (ed.) (1994), *Paradigms in Economic Development: Classic Perspectives, Critiques, and Reflections* (New York: M. E. Sharpe), pp. 191–209.

Ho, C. C. (1973), "Singapore's public housing experience", in Bielenstein, D. (ed.), *One World Only: Prospects and Feasibilities of Low-Cost Housing Activities in Asia* (Tokyo: Friedrich Ebert Stiftung).

Housing and Development Board [HDB] (1963), *Annual Report 1960* (Singapore: Government Printing Office).

Housing and Development Board [HDB] (2000), *social Aspects of Public Housing in Singapore: Kinship Ties and Neighbourly Relations*, Singapore.

Housing and Development Board [HDB] (2001), *Annual Report 2000/2001*, Singapore.

Housing and Urban Development Co. (Pte.) Ltd. [HUDC] (1977), *Middle Income Housing*, Singapore.

Housing Committee (1948), *Report of the Housing Committee Singapore, 1947* (Singapore: Government Printing Office).

Huff, W. G. (1994), *The Economic Growth of Singapore: Trade and Development in the Twentieth Century* (Cambridge: Cambridge University Press).

Hughes, H. (1993), "An external view", in Low, L., Toh, M. H., Soon, T. W., Tan, K. Y. and Hughes, H. (eds.), *Challenge and Response: Thirty Years of the Economic Development Board* (Singapore: Times Academic Press), pp. 1–25.

Jacob, K. and Manzi, T. (1996), "Discourse and policy change: The significance of language for housing research", *Housing Studies*, Vol. 11, No. 4, pp. 543–560.

Johnston, R. J. and Gregory, D. (1981), *The Dictionary of Human Geography* (Oxford: Blackwell).

Jensen-Butler, C. and van Weesep, J. (1997). "Perspective: Competition, urban planning and urban policy", in Jensen-Butler, C. (ed.), *European Cities in Competition* (Avebury: Aldershot), pp. 494–508.

Jowsey, E. and Kellet, J. (1996), "Sustainability and methodologies of environmental assessment for cities", in Pugh, C. (ed.), *Sustainability, the Environment and Urbanization* (London: Earthscan), pp. 197–227.

Jurong Town Corporation [JTC] (1997), *Changing in Step with our Customers— The Year in Review 1996/97*, Singapore.

Jurong Town Corporation [JTC], *Annual Reports*, various issues.

Kaye, B. (1960), *Upper Nankin Street, Singapore: A Sociological Study of Chinese Households Living in a Densely Populated Area* (Singapore: University of Malaya Press).

Kellerman, A. (1993), *The Telecommunications and Geography* (London: Belhaven).

Kessides, C. (1996), "A review of infrastructure's impact on economic development", in Batten, D. F. and Karlsson, C. (eds.), *Infrastructure and the Complexity of Economic Development* (Berlin: Springer), pp. 213–230.

Keung, J. (1998), "Planning for sustainable urban development", in Yuen, B. (ed.), *Planning Singapore: From Plan to Implementation* (Singapore: Singapore Institute of Planners), pp. 11–16.

Khan, H. (1988), "Role of agriculture in a city-state economy: The case of Singapore", *ASEAN Economic Bulletin*, Vol. 5, No. 2, pp. 178–182.

King, A. D. (1990), *Global Cities: Post-Imperialism and the Internationalization of London* (London: Routledge).

Kivell, P. (1993), *Land and the City: Patterns and Processes of Urban Change* (London: Routledge).

Knippenberg, L. and Schuurman, F. (1996), "Stripped: A critical phenomenology of progress and development", in Kohlerg, G., Gore, C., Reich, U. P. and Ziesemer, T. (eds.), *Questioning Development: Essays on the Theory, Policies and Practice of Development Interventions* (Marburg: Metropolis-Verlag), pp. 45–70.

Knox, P. and Agnew, J. (1989), *The Geography of the World Economy* (London: Edward Arnold).

Knox, P. L. (1994), *Urbanization: An Introduction to Urban Geography* (New Jersey: Prentice Hall).

Koekkoek, A. and Mennes, L. B. M. (eds.) (1991), *International Trade and Global Development—Essays in Honour of Jagdish Bhagwati* (London: Routledge).

Koenigsberger, O. et al. (1971), *Infrastructure Problems of the Cities of Developing Countries*, International Urbanization Survey (New York: The Ford Foundation).

Koh, T. T. B. (1967), "The law of compulsory land acquisition in Singapore", *The Malayan Law Journal*, August 1967 Reports, pp. 53–98.

Kuznets, S. (1998), "Economic growth and income inequality", in Seligson, M. A. and Passe-Smith, J. T. (eds.), *Development and Underdevelopment: The Political Economy of Global Inequality* (Boulder: Lynne Rienner, second edition), pp. 43–55.

La Grange, A. and Yip, N. M. (2001), "Social belonging, social capital and the promotion of home ownership: A case study of Hong Kong", *Housing Studies*, Vol. 16, No. 3, pp. 291–310.

Lakshmann, T. R., Andersson, D. E., Chatterjee, L. and Sasaki, K. (2000), "The global cities: New York, London and Tokyo", in Andersson A. E. and Andersson, D. E. (eds.), *Gateways to the Global Economy* (Cheltenham, UK: Edward Elgar), pp. 49–80.

Land Transport Authority [LTA] (1997), *Annual Report 1997*, Singapore.

Land Transport Authority [LTA] (1998), *Annual Report 1998*, Singapore.

Lee, K. Y. (1993), *Selected Speeches of Lee Kuan Yew in His 40 Years of Political Career* (Singapore: Lianhe Zaobao, Chinese version).

Lee, K. Y. (2000), *From Third World to First—The Singapore Story: 1965–2000* (Singapore: Times Media Private Limited).

Lee, S. K. and Chua, S. E. (1992), *More than a Garden City* (Singapore: Parks and Recreation Department).

Lee, S. A. (1973), *Industrialization in Singapore* (Melbourne: Longman).

Lee, T. Y. (1997), "Infrastructure geared to international economic activity: Singapore", in Mody, A. (ed.), *Infrastructure Strategies in East Asia: The Untold Story* (Washington D.C.: World Bank), pp. 69–80.

Lett, D. P. (1998), *In Pursuit of Status: The Making of South Korea's "New" Urban Middle Class* (Cambridge, USA: Harvard University Asia Center).

Lewis, B. D. (1998), "The impact of public infrastructure on municipal economic development: Empirical results from Kenya", *Review of Urban & Regional Development Studies*, Vol. 10, No. 2, pp. 142–156.

Lewis, W. A. (1955), *A Theory of Economic Growth* (London: Allen and Unwin).

Leys, C. (1996), *The Rise and Fall of Development Theory* (Nairobi: East African Educational Publishers; Bloomington: Indiana University Press).

Li, J. S. and Elklit, J. (1999), "The Singaore general election 1997: Campaigning strategy, results, and analysis", *Electoral Studies*, Vol. 18, pp. 199–216.

Li, W. K. (1997), "The effects of hedonism and intellectualism on leisure time consumption", conference paper presented at the special session, "Culture and consumption: Luxury and Leisure in Asia", ACR Conference 1997, organised by the Association of Consumer Research, Deriver, Colorado..

Lim, C. Y. and Associates (1988), *Policy Options for the Singapore Economy* (Singapore: McGraw-Hill).

Lim, L. (1987), "Social Welfare", in Sandhu, K. S. and Wheatley, P. (eds.), *The Management of Success: Moulding of Modern Singapore* (Singapore: ISEAS), pp. 171–197.

Liss, P. E. (1994), "On need and quality of life", in Nordenfelt, L. (ed.), *Concepts and Measurement of Quality of Life in Health Care* (Dordrecht: Kluwer), pp. 63–78.

Liu, T. K. (1973), "Reflections on problems and prospects in the second decade of Singapore's public housing", in Chua, P. C. (ed.), *Planning in Singapore: Selected Aspects and Issues* (Singapore: Chopmen), pp. 22–31.

Lloyd, P. J. (1999), "The role of foreign investment in the success of Asian industrialization", in Lloyd, P. J. (ed.), *International Trade Opening and the Formation of the Global Economy: Selected Essays of P. J. Lloyd* (Cheltenham, UK: Edward Elgar), pp. 312–338.

Low, L., Toh, M. H., Soon, T. W., Tan, K. Y. and Hughes, H. (1993), *Challenges and Response: Thirty Years of the Economic Development Board* (Singapore: Times Academic Press).

Low, L. (1998), *The Political Economy of a City State: Government-Made Singapore* (Singapore: Oxford University Press).

Lozano, E. E. (1988), "Visual needs in urban environments and physical planning", in Nasar, J. L. (ed.), *Environmental Aesthetics: Theory, Research and Applications* (Cambridge: Cambridge University Press), pp. 395–421.

Lyle, F. J. (1958), *An Industrial Development Programme* (Singapore: Government Printers).

Mackintosh, M. (1992), "Questioning the state", in Wuyts, M., Mackintosh, M. and Hewitt, T. (eds.), *Development Policy and Public Action* (Oxford: Oxford University Press), pp. 61–89.

McGee, T. G. (1967), *The Southeast Asian City* (London: G. Bell and Sons).

Mehmet, O. (1995), *Westernizing the Third World: The Eurocentricity of Economic Development Theories* (London: Routledge).

Ministry of Communications (1980), *Singapore's Transport and Urban Development Options: Final Report of the MRT Review Team*, Singapore.

Ministry of Defence (1975), *Singapore Topographic Map, 1:25,000*, Singapore.

Ministry of Defence (1998), *Singapore Topographic Map, 1:25,000*, Singapore.

Ministry of Finance (1961), *State of Singapore: Development Plan 1961–1964*, Singapore.

Ministry of Finance (1993), *Final Report of the Committee to Promote Enterprise Overseas* (Singapore: SNP Publishers).

Ministry of National Development [MND] (1963), *Annual Report for 1960 and 1961* (Singapore: Planning Department).

Ministry of National Development [MND] (1968/69), *Annual Report* (Singapore: Planning Department).

Ministry of National Development [MND] (1970), *Annual Report* (Singapore: Planning Department).

Ministry of National Development [MND] (1983), *Annual Report*, Singapore.

Ministry of National Development [MND] (1988), *Annual Report*, Singapore.

Ministry of National Development [MND] (1989), *Annual Report*, Singapore.

Ministry of National Development [MND] (2002), *Parks and Waterbodies Plan and Identity Plan*, Singapore.

Ministry of the Environment [ENV] (1992), *The Singapore Green Plan: Towards a Model Green City*, Singapore.

Ministry of the Environment [ENV] (1993), *The Singapore Green Plan: Action Programmes*, Singapore.

Ministry of the Environment [ENV] (1998), *Annual Report*, Singapore.

Ministry of the Environment [ENV] (2001), Press Release 17/2001, dated 22 January 2001.

Ministry of the Environment [ENV] (2002), *The Singapore Green Plan 2012*, Singapore.

Ministry of Trade and Industry [MTI] (1986), *The Singapore Economy: New Directions*, Report of the Economic Committee, Singapore.

Ministry of Trade and Industry [MTI] (2001), *Economic Survey of Singapore— Third Quarter 2001*, Singapore.

Ministry of Transport (1963), *Traffic in Towns: A Study of the Long-Term Problems in Urban Areas*, Report of the Steering Committee and Working Group Appointed by the Ministry of Transport, HMSO, London.

Mody, A. and Reinfeld, W. (1997), "Advanced infrastructure for time management: The competitive edge in East Asia", in Mody, A. (ed.), *Infrastructure Strategies in East Asia: The Untold Story* (Washington D.C.: World Bank), pp.131–146.

Monetary Authority of Singapore (1999), *The Petrochemical Industry of Singapore*, Occasional Paper No. 14, June 1999.

Murphy R. E., Vance, J. E. and Epstein, B. J. (1955), "Internal structure of the CBD", *Economic Geography*, Vol. 31, pp. 21–46.

Myrdal, G. (1957), *Economic Theory and Underdeveloped Regions* (London: Duckworth).

National Computer Board [NCB] (1983), *Annual Report, 1982/83*, Singapore.

National Computer Board [NCB] (1987), *Annual Report, 1986/87*, Singapore.

National Computer Board [NCB] (1992), *A Vision of an Intelligent Island: IT2000 Report*, Singapore.

National Computer Board [NCB] (1994), *Annual Report, 1993/94*, Singapore.

National Parks Board website, http://www.nparks.gov.sg, October 1999.

Nature Society (Singapore) [NSS] (2003), Minutes of the 49th AGM of the Nature Society (Singapore) held on 30 May 2003, available at http://www.nss.org.sg, retrieved in August 2003.

Nedverveen Pieterse, J. (2001), *Development Theory: Deconstruction/Reconstructions* (London: Sage).

Newman, P. and Thornley, A. (1996), *Urban Planning in Europe: International Competition, National Systems and Planning Projects* (London: Routledge).

Nohl, W. (1988), "Open space in cities: In search of a new aesthetic", in Nasar, J. L. (ed.), *Environmental Aesthetics: Theory, Research and Applications* (Cambridge: Cambridge University Press), pp. 74–83.

Nurkse, R. (1953), *Problems of Capital Formation in Underdeveloped Countries* (Oxford: Blackwell).

Oc, T. and Tiesdell, S. (1997), "The death and life of city centres", in Oc, T. and Tiesdell, S. (eds.), *Safer City Centres: Reviving the Public Realm* (London: Paul Chapman), pp. 1–20.

Oi, K. H. (1997), "Park connectors", in Yuen, B. (ed.), *Planning Singapore: From Plan to Implementation* (Singapore: Singapore Institute of Planners), pp. 31–41.

Ong, E. H., Lee, P. and Tan, G. (2003), "What is the Economic Value of Community Service in Singapore?" available at http://www.thecore.nus.edu.sg/sep/students/comserv/p4.htm, retrieved on 9 August 2003.

Ostenfeld, E. (1994), "Aristotle on the good life and quality of life", in Nordenfelt, L. (ed.), *Concepts and Measurement of Quality of Life in Health Care* (Dordrecht: Kluwer), pp. 19–34.

Owens, S. (1997), "'Giant in the Path'—Planning, Sustainability and Environmental Values", *Town Planning Review*, Vol. 68, No. 3, pp. 293–303.

Pang, E. F. and Tan, A. (1981), "Employment and export-led industrialisation: The experience of Singapore", in Amjad, R. (ed.), *The Development of Labour Intensive Industry in ASEAN Countries* (Geneva: Asian Employment Programme, International Labour Organisation), pp. 141–171.

Parks and Recreation Department [PRD] (1996), *Annual Report, 1995/96*, Singapore.

Peebles, G. and Wilson, P. (1996), *The Singapore Economy* (Cheltenham, UK: Edward Elgar).

Peet, R. and Hartwick, E. (1999), *Theories of Development* (New York: The Guilford Press).

Peretto, P. F. (1998), "Industrial development, technological change, and long-run growth", *Journal of Development Economics*, Vol. 59, pp. 387–417.

Perry, M., Kong, L. and Yeoh, B. (1997), *Singapore: A Developmental City-State* (Chichester: John Wiley).

Phang, S. Y. (2001), "Housing policy, wealth formation and the Singapore economy", *Housing Studies*, Vol. 16, No. 4, pp. 443–459.

Port of Singapore Authority [PSA] (2002), *Annual Report*, Singapore.

Port Technology (2003), "Pasir Panjang Terminal (PPT) and Service Facility, Singapore", available at http://www.port-technology.com/projects/pasir/, retrieved on 15 June 2003.

Porter, M. E. (1990), "The competitive advantage of nations", *Harvard Business Review*, No. 2 (March–April), pp. 73–93.

Potter, R. B., Binns, T., Elliot, J. A. and Smith, D. (1999), *Geographies of Development* (Harlow, UK: Longman).

Prasad, S. (1998), "The making of the new Singapore Master Plan", in Yuen, B. (ed.), *Planning Singapore: From Plan to Implementation* (Singapore: Singapore Institute of Planners), pp. 17–23.

Prebisch, R. (1950), *The Economic Development of Latin America and its Principal Problems* (New York: United Nations Economic Council for Latin America).

Preston, P. W. (1996), *Development Theory: An Introduction* (Oxford: Blackwell).

PSA Corporation (2003), Press Statement, available at "http://www.psa.com.sg/news/nr030222.htm" http://www.psa.com.sg/news/nr030222.htm, retrieved on 22 February 2003.

Public Utilities Board [PUB] (1967), *Annual Report 1966*, Singapore.

Public Utilities Board [PUB] (1989), *Annual Report 1988*, Singapore.

Public Utilities Board [PUB] (1994), *Annual Report 1993*, Singapore.
Public Utilities Board [PUB] (1996), *Annual Report 1995*, Singapore.
Public Utilities Board [PUB] (1998), *Annual Report 1997*, Singapore.
Public Utilities Board [PUB] (2000), *Annual Report 2000*, Singapore.
Radwan, S. (1998), "Employment and development", in Sapsford, D. and Chan, J. R. (eds.), *Development Economics and Policy* (Houndmills, UK: Macmillan), pp. 485–502.
Rajaratnam, S. (1985), *The Prophetic and the Political: Selected Speeches and Writings of S. Rajaratnam* (Singapore: Graham Brash), edited by Chang, H. C. and Obaid ul Haq.
Regnièr, P. (1992), *Singapore: City-State in South-East Asia* (Kuala Lumpur: S. Abdul Majeed).
Rodan, G. (1989), *The Political Economy of Singapore's Industrialization: National State and International Capital* (London: Macmillan).
Rosenstein-Rodan, P. N. (1961), "Problems of industrialization of Eastern and South-eastern Europe", *Economic Journal* (June–September 1943), pp. 202–211, reprinted in Okun, B. and Richardson, R. W. (eds.), *Studies in Economic Development* (New York: Holt, Rinehart & Winston), pp. 124–132.
Rostow, W. W. (1961), "The stages of economic growth", *Economic History Review* (August 1959), pp. 1–15, reprinted (with omissions) in Okun, B. and Richardson, R. W. (eds.), *Studies in Economic Development* (New York: Holt, Rinehart & Winston), pp. 183–199.
Ruigrok, W. and van Tulder, R. (1995), *The Logic of International Restructuring* (London: Routledge).
Sassen, S. (1995), "Urban impacts of economic globalisation", in Brotchie, J., Batty, M., Blakely, E., Hall, P. and Newton, P. (eds.), *Cities in Competition: Productive and Sustainable Cities for the 21st Century* (Melbourne: Longman), pp. 36–57.
Sassen, S. (1998), "The topoi of e-space: Global cities and global value chains", *Built Environment*, Vol. 24, Nos. 2/3, pp. 134–141.
Sassen, S. (1999), "Globalisation and telecommunications: Impacts on the future of urban centrality", in Ooi, G. L. (ed.), *Model Cities: Urban Best Practices* (Singapore: Urban Redevelopment Authority and Institute of Policy Studies), pp. 134–143.
Sassen, S. (2000), *Cities in a World Economy* (Thousand Oaks, California: Pine Forge Press, second edition).
Saunders, P. (1978), "Domestic property and social class", *International Journal of Urban and Regional Research*, Vol. 3, pp. 233–251.
Savage, V. (1997), "Singapore's garden city: Translating environmental possibilism", in Ooi, G. L. and Kwok, K. (eds.), *City and the State: Singapore's Built Environment Revisited* (Singapore: Institute of Policy Studies and Oxford University Press), pp. 187–202.
Schein, E. H. (1996), *Strategic Pragmatism: The Culture of Singapore's Economic Development Board* (Singapore: Toppan).
Schmitz, H. (1994), "Industrialization strategies in less developed countries: Some lessons of historical experience", *Journal of Development Studies*, Vol. 21, pp. 1–21.

See-Toh, K. C. (1998), "Planning industrial estates in Singapore", in Yuen, B. (ed.), *Planning Singapore: From Plan to Implementation* (Singapore: Singapore Institute of Planners).

Short, R. S. and Kim, Y. H. (1999), *Globalization and the City* (Harlow, UK: Longman).

Silberstein, J. and Maser, C. (2000), *Land-Use Planning for Sustainable Development* (Boca Raton, UK: Lewis Publishers).

Sim, D. (1982), *Change in the City Centre* (Aldershot, UK: Gower).

Singapore Improvement Trust [SIT] (1958), *The Working of the Singapore Improvement Trust, 1958* (Singapore: The Malaya Publishing House).

Singapore Land Authority [SLA] (2002), *Annual Report, 2001/2002*, Singapore.

Singapore MRT (1997/98), *Annual Report*, Singapore.

Singapore One website, http://www.singaporeone.com.sg, 30 June 2003.

Smith, D. (1996), *Third World Cities in Global Perspective: The Political Economy of Uneven Urbanization* (Boulder, Colorado: Westview Press).

Smith, K., Joncas, K., Parrish, B., Dane, S. G. and Glisson, L. S. (eds.) (1991), *Revitalizing Downtown* (Washington D.C.: National Main Street Center, National Trust for Historic Preservation).

Smith, V. K., Poulos, C. and Kim, H. (2002), "Treating open space as an urban amenity", *Resource and Energy Economics*, Vol. 24, pp. 107–129.

State of Singapore (1961), *Development Plan, 1961–1964* (Singapore: Ministry of Finance).

Straits Times (The), "That cloud over Jurong—it's really smog", 24 February 1970.

Straits Times (The), "Woodlands companies to relocate by 1997", 31 October 1995.

Straits Times (The), "JTC outlines compensation package", 3 January 1996.

Straits Times (The), 26 November 1998.

Straits Times (The), 14 October 1999.

Straits Times (The), 26 February 2000.

Straits Times (The), 16 May 2001, p. H1.

Straits Times (The), "SingTel's Optus bid faces delay", 15 June 2001, p. A16.

Straits Times (The), 19 May 2002, p. 21.

Straits Times (The), 22 July 2002.

Straits Times (The), 24 July 2002, p. 23.

Straits Times (The), 28 July 2002, p. 46.

Stutz, F. P. and de Souza, A. R. (1998), *The World Economy: Resources, Location, Trade, and Development* (New Jersey: Prentice Hall, third edition).

Survey Department (1958), *Singapore Topographic Map*, Singapore.

Tan, A. H. H. and Pang, S. Y. (1991), *The Singapore Experience in Public Housing* (Singapore: Times Academic Press).

Tan, B. Y. (2003), "Highlights of the 1998 National Health Survey", available at http://www.singstat.gov.sg/ssn/feat/1Q2000/pg3-8/pdf, retrieved on 9 August 2003.

Tan, J. H. (1972), *Urbanization Planning and National Development Planning in Singapore*, SEDAG Papers on Problems of Development in Southeast Asia (New York: The Asia Society).

Tan, K. G. and Lee, W. K. (1999), "Beyond regionalization, basis for sustainable growth and potential sources of expansion", in Low, L. (ed.), *Singapore Towards a Developed Status* (Singapore: Centre for Advanced Studies, National University of Singapore), pp. 87–121.

Tan, K. S. (1999), "Planning Singapore as a global business hub for the 21st century", in Ooi, G. L. (ed.), *Model Cities: Urban Best Practices* (Singapore: Urban Redevelopment Authority and Institute of Policy Studies), pp. 144–152.

Tan, S. Y. (1998), *Private Ownership of Public Housing in Singapore* (Singapore: Times Academic Press).

Taylor, N. (1998), *Urban Planning Theories Since 1945* (London: Sage).

Teh, C. W. (1973), "Housing for the people—A challenge to modern society", *SIP Journal*, Vol. 3, No. 1, pp. 20–28.

Tehranian, K. K. (1995), *Modernity, Space and Power: The American City in Discourse and Practice* (New Jersey: Hampton Press).

Teo, S. E. (1984), "Condominium development in Singapore—Residents' view on condominium living", paper presented at the High-Rise High Density Living-SPC Convention, organised by the Singapore Professional Centre in 1983, pp. 197–202.

Teo, S. E. and Kong, L. (1997), "Public housing in Singapore: Interpreting 'quality' in the 1990s", *Urban Studies*, Vol. 34, No. 3, pp. 441–452.

Teo, S. E. and Savage, V. (1991), "Singapore landscape: A historical overview of housing image", in Chew, E. C. T. and Lee, E. (eds.), *A History of Singapore* (Singapore: Oxford University Press), pp. 312–338.

Thompson, E. R. (2000), "Hong Kong as a regional strategic hub for manufacturing internationals", in Andersson, A. E. and Andersson, D. E. (eds.), *Gateways to the Global Economy* (Cheltenham, UK: Edward Elgar), pp. 169–189.

Todd, G. (1995), "'Going global' in the semi-periphery: World cities as political projects—The case of Toronto", in Knox, P. L. and Taylor, P. J. (eds.), *World-Cities in a World System* (Cambridge: Cambridge University Press), pp. 192–212.

UN ECAFE [United Nations Economic Commission for Asia and the Far East] (1955), "Economic Development and Planning in Asia and the Far East", *Economic Bulletin for Asia and the Far East*, Vol. VI, No. 5.

United Nations (1961), *A Proposed Industrialization Programme for the State of Singapore* (New York: United Nations).

United Nations (1962a), *Industrial Estates in Asia and the Far East* (New York: United Nations).

United Nations (1962b), *Report of the Ad Hoc Group of Experts on Housing and Urban Development* (New York: Development of Economic and Social Affairs).

Urban Redevelopment Authority [URA] (1976/77), *Annual Report*, Singapore.

Urban Redevelopment Authority [URA] (1982/83), *Annual Report*, Singapore.

Urban Redevelopment Authority [URA] (1983/84), *Annual Report*, Singapore.

Urban Redevelopment Authority [URA] (1985/86), *Annual Report—New Directions in the Redevelopment of Our City*, Singapore.

Urban Redevelopment Authority [URA] (1989), *The Golden Shoe: Building Singapore's Financial District*, Singapore. [Written by Chua, Beng-Huat.]

Urban Redevelopment Authority [URA] (1991a), *Living the Next Lap: Towards a Tropical City of Excellence*, Singapore.

Urban Redevelopment Authority [URA] (1991b), *A Future with a Past: Saving Our Heritage*, Singapore.

Urban Redevelopment Authority [URA] (1992a), *Downtown Core & Portview: Development Guide Plans*, Singapore.

Urban Redevelopment Authority [URA] (1992b), *Skyline*, No. 18, September/October.

Urban Redevelopment Authority [URA] (1993a), *Aesthetic Treatment of Waterbodies in Singapore*, Singapore.

Urban Redevelopment Authority [URA] (1993b), *Skyline*, No. 21, March/April.

Urban Redevelopment Authority [URA] (1996/97), *Annual Report—Planning for the 21st Century*, Singapore.

Urban Redevelopment Authority [URA] (1996a), *Skyline*, No. 39, March/April.

Urban Redevelopment Authority [URA] (1996b), *Skyline*, No. 42, September/October, Singapore.

Urban Redevelopment Authority [URA] (1998), *Annual Report 1997/98*, Singapore.

Urban Redevelopment Authority [URA] (1999), *Stock and Occupancy, 4th Quarter 1999*, URA Real Estate Statistics Series (Singapore: URA).

Urban Redevelopment Authority [URA] (2001), *The Concept Plan 2001*, Singapore.

Van Herzele, A. and Wiedemann, T. (2003), "A monitoring tool for the provision of accessible and attractive urban green spaces", *Landscape and UrbanPlanning*, Vol. 63, pp. 109-126.

Wallace, I. (1992), *The Global Economic System* (London: Routledge).

Ward, S. (1994), *Planning and Urban Change* (London: Paul Chapman).

Ward, S. (2002), *Planning the Twentieth-Century City* (Chichester, UK: John Wiley).

Wei, J., Ong, S. K., Chua, K. C. and Tan, K. A. (1999), "Planning and management of civil engineering infrastructure projects for public housing in Singapore", paper presented at the Dr. Tan Swan Beng Memorial Symposium, Excellence in Infrastructural Engineering, 18–19 March 1999.

Weiskopf, D. C. (1982), *Recreation and Leisure: Improving the Quality of Life* (Boston: Allyn & Bacon, second edition).

Whitehand, J. W. R. (1983), "Land-use structure, built-form and agents of change", in Davis, R. L. and Champion, A. G. (eds.), *The Future of the City Centre* (London: Academic Press), pp. 41–59.

Wong, A. K. and Yeh, S. H. K. (eds.) (1985), *Housing a Nation: 25 Years of Public Housing in Singapore* (Singapore: Maruzen Asia).

Wong, P. K. (1997), "Implementing the NII vision: Singapore's experience and future challenges", in Kahin, B. and Wilson, E. J. (eds.), *National Information Infrastructure Initiatives: Vision and Policy Design* (Cambridge, Mass.: The MIT Press), pp. 24–60.

Wong, T. C. (1996), "Information technology and its spatial impact on Singapore", *Review of Urban and Regional Development Studies*, Vol. 8, No. 1, pp. 33–45.

Wong, T. C. (1998), "Land transport policy and land-use planning in Singapore", *Australian Planner*, Vol. 35, No. 1, pp. 44–48.

Wong, T. C. (1999a), "The transition from physical infrastructure to infostructure: Infrastructure as a modernising agent in Singapore", *GeoJournal*, Vol. 49, No. 3, pp. 279–288.

Wong, T. C. (1999b), "Urbanisation and sustainability of Southeast Asian cities", in Wong, T. C. and Singh, M. (eds.), *Development and Challenge: Southeast Asia in the New Millennium* (Singapore: Times Academic Press), pp. 143–170.

Wong, T. C. (2001), "The transformation of Singapore's central area: From slums to a global business hub?" *Planning Practice & Research*, Vol. 16, No. 2, pp. 155–170.

World Bank (1994a), *World Development Report: Infrastructure for Development* (New York: Oxford University Press).

World Bank (1994b), *East Asia's Trade and Investment: Regional and Global Gains from Liberalization* (Washington D.C.: World Bank).

World Bank (1998), *Annual Report 1998* (Washington D.C.: World Bank).

World Bank (1999), *World Development Report 1998/99* (New York: Oxford University Press).

Yap, A. L. H. (1995), "Water for Singapore: Management of a resource in a subregional economic zone", unpublished honours thesis, Department of Geography, National University of Singapore.

Yeh, S. H. K. (1975), "Housing conditions and housing needs", in Yeh, S. H. K. (ed.), *Public Housing in Singapore A Multi-Disciplinary Study* (Singapore: Housing and Development Board).

Yeoh, B. S. A. (1996), *Contesting Singapore: Power Relations and the Urban Built Environment in Colonial Singapore* (Kuala Lumpur: Oxford University Press).

Yeung, Y. M. (1973), *National Development and Urban Transformation in Singapore*, Department of Geography Research Paper No. 149 (Chicago: University of Chicago).

Yuen, B. (1991), "Planning and development of industrial estates in Singapore", *Third World Planning Review*, Vol. 13, No. 1, pp. 47–68.

Index

A

Accumulated material wealth, 60
Agricultural lands, from 1960 to 1999, 125

B

Bedok Reservoir, 132
Bishan Park, 130
Botanic Gardens, 127-128
Broadband infrastructure, 55
Bukit Timah Nature Reserve, 131, 134

C

Car ownership, 147
Central Area, 8, 11, 95-96
    attempts to restore, 146
    buffer zone guidelines, 22
    building land use study, 22
    Concept Plan, 20
    for homogenising multiple uses, 146
    intensification of commercial and business activities, 16
    office space and employment: 1971-1990, 22-23
    planning to modernise, 10
    population in 1980, 20
    pre-World War II, 11
    redevelopment in the 1960s, 16
    redevelopment of 1971-1990, 20-27
    relocation of population from, 22
    transformation, 30
    transformed, 21, 31-32, 146-147
    urban renewal of, 15-19
    See also Conservation of historic sites
Central Business District,
    access via automobiles, 147
    to continue its importance, 30
    in the future, 29
    and housing, 94
    infrastructure and infostructure, 55
    and multinational headquarters, 144
    to stay as a central place, 32
Centralisation, of management and activities, 30
Central place, importance of, 9
Changi Airport, 43, 46, 74
Change, 8-9
    process and agents of, 10
    urban, 17

China, 76
City parks, 130
Coastal parks, 129
Colonisation, 38
Common Services Tunnels, 48-49
Community and town parks, 130
Concept Plan of 1970, 143-144
Concept Plan of 1971, 20-27, 32, 54, 135-136
   post-revised, 27-28
   revision of 26-27
Concept Plan of 1991, 83-85, 133-134, 146
   incorporation of the ICT development, 53-54
   objectives of revised, 28
   revised, 32
Concept Plan of 2001, 85, 134-135, 146
   revised, 32
Conservation Master Plan of 1989, 24-25
Conservation, 24-25
   of historic sites in the Central Area, 25
   See also Rehabilitation of structures
Control Premises (Special Provision) Act of 1969, 18
CPF, 116-117

D

Decentralization, 26
   in less urbanized zones, 54
Deep Tunnel Sewerage System, 49
Dependency, 59-60
Development,
   and conservation, 137
   type of Singapore's, 135
   an island-wide Master Plan, 14-15
   See also Knowledge and development
Downtown core, 9-10, 28-31
   in the 1940s, 14
   slums, 11, 13

E

East Coast Park, 129-130
Economic Development Board (EDB) of 1961, 40, 67
   Enterprise Development Division, 73
   Jurong Industrial Estate since 1960, 78
   planning for the industrial estates, 78-88
Economic growth, 59
   and manufacturing landtake, 84
   for planning authorities, 136
   three decades of sustained, 116
   and the use of the "economic priority model", 57

and urbanisation, 120, 124
Economic priority model, 135-136
Economy,
    based on knowledge and IT,
        34-36
    British colonial, 11
    growth and infrastructure,
        36-38
    world and slums, 11
Educational upgrading, 65-66, 71
Electricity, 94
    See Power
Environmental sustainability, 37
Ethylene production, 73
Export-oriented industrialisation
    (EOI), 65-69
    three outcomes in landuse
        planning and allocation, 74
Export-oriented strategy, 64-65,
    69-70

F
Factories,
    built near housing, 78
    end of 1970s, 81
    on islands south of the coast,
        81
    1980-1990, 82
Financial structure, 9
Financial transactions, in the
    future, 51
Food supply, under the island
    Master Plan, 14

Forced acquisitions, 93
Foreign direct investment (FDI),
    70

G
Garden-city concept, 126-127, 145
    update of, 135
GLCs
    See also government-linked
        companies and overseas
        investment, 76
Globalisation, 9, 27
    intensifying, 29-30
    and needs of urbanites, 123
    v. regionalisation, 142
    results of, 32
Golden Shoe, 21, 28
Government-linked companies
    (GLCs), 63-65
    to complement the MNCs,
        86-87
    and overseas investments, 73
Greenery concept, 20-21
Green Plan of 1992, 133
Greenery,
    to enhance quality of life, 122
    for health and well-being,
        120
    place of, in city development,
        136
    in public housing estates, 126
    and sustainable development,
        135-136

H
High-density living, 12-13
Housing, 26-27, 145
   built up area for, from 1960 to 1999, 125
   built by JTC, 80
   choose private housing? 113-117
   commercialization of public housing from 1970 to 1979, 95
   in the early 1960s, 10
   homeownership through public housing from 1965-1969, 95
   Housing and Development Board, 108-110
   low-cost and rental housing from 1960-1964, 94
   percent for public, 121
   perception of private housing status and quality, 108
   politicisation of public housing from 1986 to the present, 98-99
   post-1959 era, 92
   pre-1959 colonial policy, 92
   private property aspirations versus the price spiral, 110
   public, 77
   public as mass-produced consumed goods, 92-101
   public policy since 1960, 91, 93
   public used as an agent of social engineering and an instrument of economic policy from 1980-1985, 98
   public, in the 1980s, 46
   public under Housing and Development Board, 64
   replacement of low-density, 16
   rising of aspirations for private, 101
   role of the state, 91, 100, 112
   under colonial rule, 13
   universal provision of public, 99
   "verticalised" high-rise public, 126
   of working class, 8
   of World War II in Central Area, 12
   See also Housing and Development Board; Singapore Improvement Trust 1950s Master Plan, 13-15; Slums
Housing and Development Board, 15, 91-98, 145
   has accommodated 80% of the population, 99
   built from 1970-1980, 81
   expansion of, results of, 22

first Five-Year Plan, 17
industrial estates managed by, 77
manages neighborhood parks, 130
primary functions and role of, 116-117
public housing and state ownership, 64
tenure rights, 117
type of housing, 108-110
Urban Renewal Department, 20

I
Industrialisation,
    model of, 144-145
ICT, 29
    goals regarding, 56
    networks, within a city, 54
    and Singapore, 31
    state-initiated, 57
Import-ssubstitution industrialisation (ISI), 67-69
Independence,
    eve of, 8
    post, 8-9
Industrial development, 11
    of the colonial days, 78
    from 1960-1970, 79-80
    from 1970-1980, 80-82
    from 1980-1990, 82
    from 1990-2000, 82-84
    in the future, 85
    goal in Singapore, 84
    and the UN, 66-67
Industrial estates,
    physical development of, 78
    in Singapore, 78-88
Industrialisation, 40, 59
    export-oriented, 40-41
    goal of, in the 1960s, 87
    knowledge and skill-intensive model, 61
    labour-intensive model, 61
    in 1959, 60, 62
    1960-2000, 60-88
    program of 1961-1965, 40
    Singapore model, 86
    Singapore's success, 86
    strategy, 66-77
    See also Housing
Industrial Land Plan for the 21st Century, 85
Industrial policy, 145
Industrial policy,
    justified the PAP government, 88
Industries,
    built-up areas for, from 1960 to 1999, 125
    from 1970-1980, 82
Industry,
    as a major employer, 14

Information and communications technology, 10
Infostructure, 34-36, 41, 50-53
    Singapore's ability to introduce high-cost 57
Infrastructure,
    airport, 43
    amount for physical, 121
    built-up areas, from 1960-1999, 125
    the housing crisis, 1960-1964, 94
    physical, 144
    roads, 43-44
    seaport, 42-43
Infrastructure,
    contribution of, 38
    and demand for land space, 41-42
    in developed v. developing countries, 36
    development of, 34-35
    and economic growth, 36-38
    to infostructure, 56, 144
    investment, 37
    and modernisation of 1959, 40
    modernizing and economic catalyst, 56
    in the 1990s, 37
    physcial, 36, 41-46, 50
    scope, 35
    serves producing firms, 36-37
    transport and communications, 42-46
Internet, 51
Information technology,
    application in the future, 51-53
    to become global hub of, 53
    fostering growth of Singapore, 52
    providing manpower for, 52
    2000 Report, 54

J

Jurong,
    development of industrial areas, 80-88
    Industrial Estate, 146
    islands south of the coast developed, 81
    physical development, 81
    Port, 42-43
    reclamation from the sea at, 83-84
    selection and advantages of, 79
    Town Corporation, 64, 73, 77, 80-83, 86

K

Kent Ridge Park, 130
Key industries, 75
Knowledge
    -based economy, 79, 82
    and development, 51-53

L

Land
- Acquisition Act of 1967, 93
- acquisition, and urban change, 17-18
- Building Use Survey, 21
- development for industrial facilities, 41
- office, 99
- reclamation, 21, 26-27
- Transport Authority, 44-45
- use, 32-34, 60, 63, 141
- *See also* Common Services Tunnels

Land-use planning,
- and farm expansion, 124
- values decision, 120-121

Land-use strategy, 116

Locational patterns of land use, 10

M

MacRitchie Reservoir Park, 130-131, 134

Manufacturing,
- activities, 39-40
- industries, 74
- investments, 76
- local, 75
- number of firms, 1980-2000, 84

Maritime and Port Authority of Singapore (MPA), 42

Market competition, makes life more stressful, 123

Master Plan of 1958, 18-19

Master Plan of 1979, 82

Materialistic aspirations. *See* Economic growth

Military land area, 141

Modernisation,
- experience, 141
- guidelines follow planning, 146-147
- and infrastructure, 38
- physical development of industrial estates, from 1960-2000, 78-88
- process, 34-35
- role of industry, 40
- *See also* Housing

Multinational corporations, 31
- building up its own, 88
- demand, 87
- foreigners' role, 74-75, 77
- headquartered in the Central Business District, 144
- investments benefitted East Asia, 76
- local companies becoming, 74
- in the 1970s, 70
- in the 1980s, 71
- presence of Western, 77
- reliance on foreign in overseas ventures, 87

in Singapore, 56
Singapore's success and international, 86

N
National Computer Board, 52
National Parks Board (NPB), 125-131
National Science and Technology Plan 2000, 53
Nature reserves, 134-135
Nature Society of Singapore, 135-136, 145
New towns, 44
1948 Housing Committee report, 12
1969 Control Premises (Special Provision) Act, 21
99-Year Lease, 107-108, 113

O
Overseas ventures, 76

P
PAP government, 145
Park Connector Network, 131
Planning,
"anti" sentiments, 147
spatial, since independence, 143
Pulau Tekong, 141
Pulau Ubin, 145
People's Action Party (PAP), 92, 98
Petrochemical industries, 73-75
from 1970-1980, 81, 84
Physical land-use planning, 13
Pilot projects, 17-18
Planning Department of the MND, 15, 78
Planning directions, 8
Plan of Operation of 1967, 19
Port, built at Jurong, 80
Power, 48-49
Preliminary Island Plan, 14
PSA Corporation, 42-43
Public Utilities Board, 49-50

R
Rail Mass Rapid Transit (MRT), 45
Recreational,
sites, 134-135, 138-139
spaces, 122-127, 138-139
spatial development, 145
Redevelopment, 21
of the Central Area, 24
Regime, of post-independence, 8-9
Rehabilitation of structures, in the Central Area, 24-25
Rent Control Act of 1947, 12, 18
Reservoir parks, 130, 134
Ridge and nature parks, 130
Ring Concept Plan, 19-20
Road construction, 43-44
Rostow's linear model of development, 62

S

Seaport, 40. 42-43
    and river estuary as an economic base, 13
"Second Industrial Revolution", 70-71,81
Seletar,
    civil airport, 141
    reservoir, 132
Sentosa Island, 141
Sewage,
    disposal works, 94-95
    system, 49-50
Singapore,
    colonial period, 8
    Concept Plan, 101
    developmental approach, 8
    economic growth, 38, 41
    government, 15
    Green Plan of 1992, 126
    Improvement Trust (SIT), 13-15, 79, 92
    Industrial Promotion Board, 68
    Land Authority, 56
    modern, 10
    in the 1990s, 27-28
    the new downtown core, 28-29
    in the 1990s, 31
    One, 54-55
    as a potential global city, 29
    pre-World War II, 11
    Telecommunications Corporation (SingTel), 56
    towards and knowledge-based economy, 34-35
    uniqueness of, 31
SingTel. *See* Singapore Telecommunications Corporation, 56
Slums, 11, 16-17, 94-95, 116
    and rural-urban migration, 19
    sanitary conditions, in the post-war colonial period, 46
"Socialist" style of state, in 1969, 64-65
Socioeconomic changes, 71
Spillover to neighboring nations, 28
State-controlled enterprises, 64-65
Strategic Economic Plan of 1991, 65-66, 72-73

T

Tall buildings,
    under the island Master Plan, 14-15
Technology linked with labour, 63
Tiong Bahru Estate, housing, 13
Town Council Act of 1988, 98
TradeNet, 52
Transport, to Jurong, 84

U

University graduates, 66
Urban development,
  influenced by, 55
  large-scale plans, 27
Urbanisation,
  and land use transformation, 124-125
  and nature, 120
  and pleasure, 122, 138
Urban Redevelopment Authority, 26-28
  land-use plan, 55
Urban renewal, 11
  Department, 17-18
  early: 1960-1970, 15-16
  ending affect of the 1947 Rent Control Act, 18
  included, 17
  market-critical, 11
  physical transformation, 11
  retaining of existing structures, 23
Urban sustainability, 147

W

Water, 94-115
  bodies, 131-132
  discharges of waste, 50
  supply, 47-48
Winsemius Report, 66
Workers in manufacturing, 1950 to 1960, 67
Working class, housing of, 8, 13
World trade, in the future, 51

FIGURE 1.1: POPULATION DISTRIBUTION IN 1947

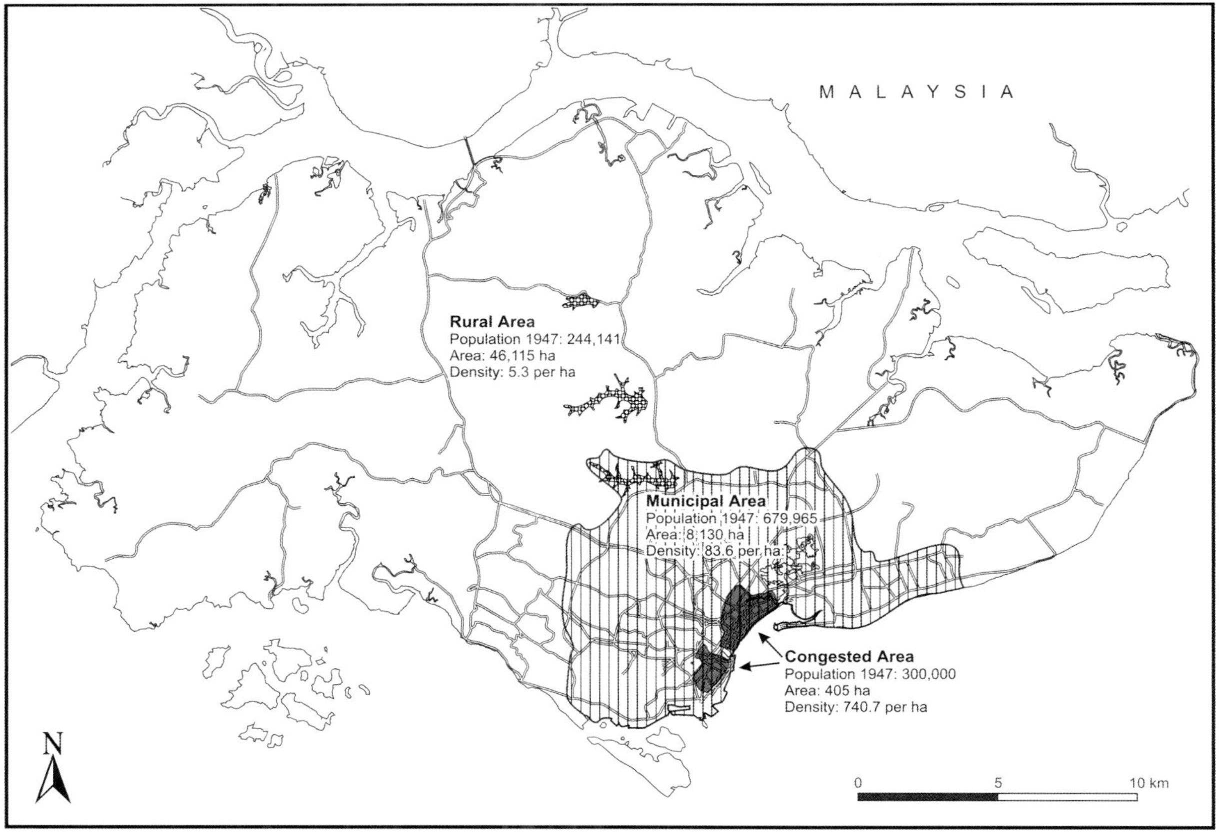
MALAYSIA
Rural Area
Population 1947: 244,141
Area: 46,115 ha
Density: 5.3 per ha
Municipal Area
Population 1947: 679,965
Area: 8,130 ha
Density: 83.6 per ha
Congested Area
Population 1947: 300,000
Area: 405 ha
Density: 740.7 per ha
N
0
5
10 km

Source: Adapted from Housing Committee (1948)

FIGURE 1.2: PRELIMINARY ISLAND PLAN, 1952

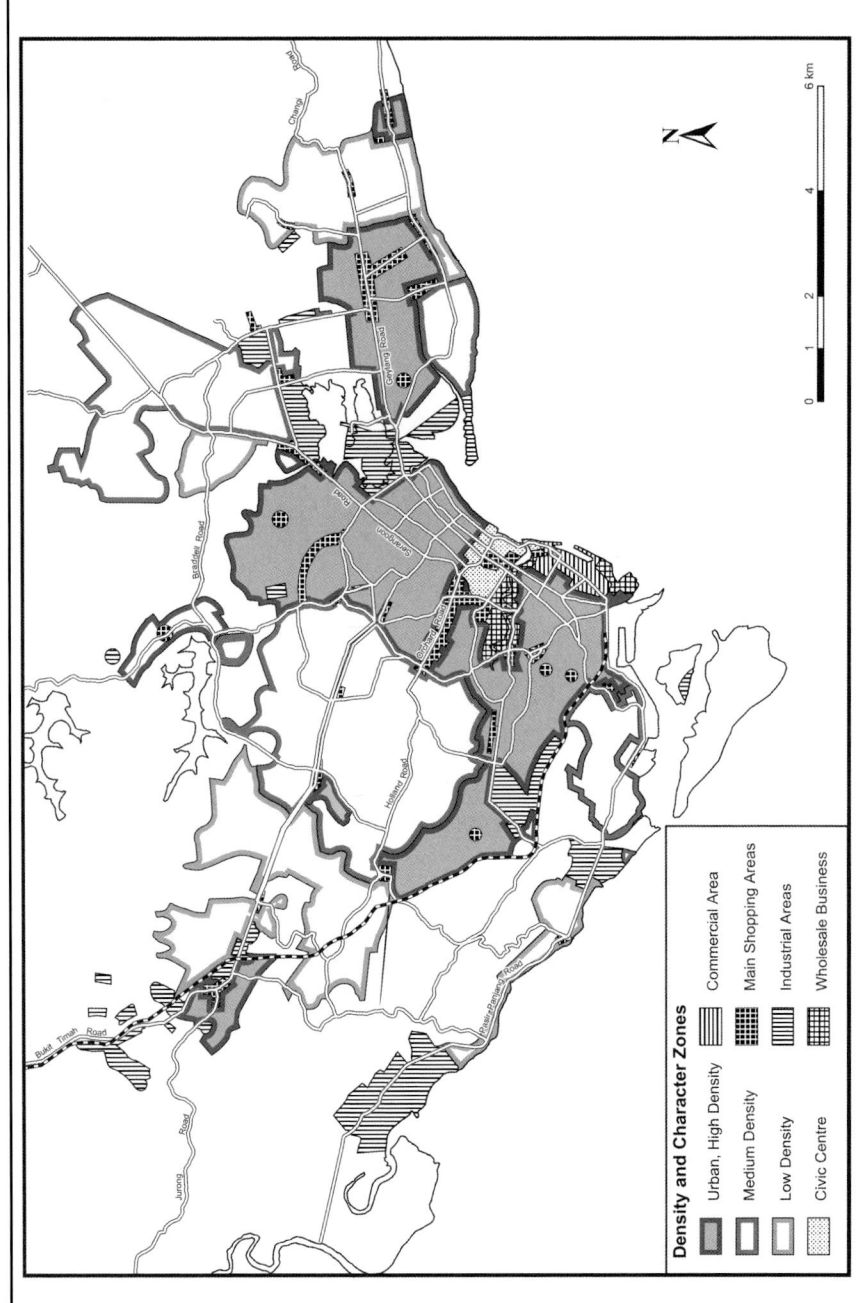

Source: Colony of Singapore (1952)

FIGURE 1.3: THE 1958 MASTER PLAN OF SINGAPORE

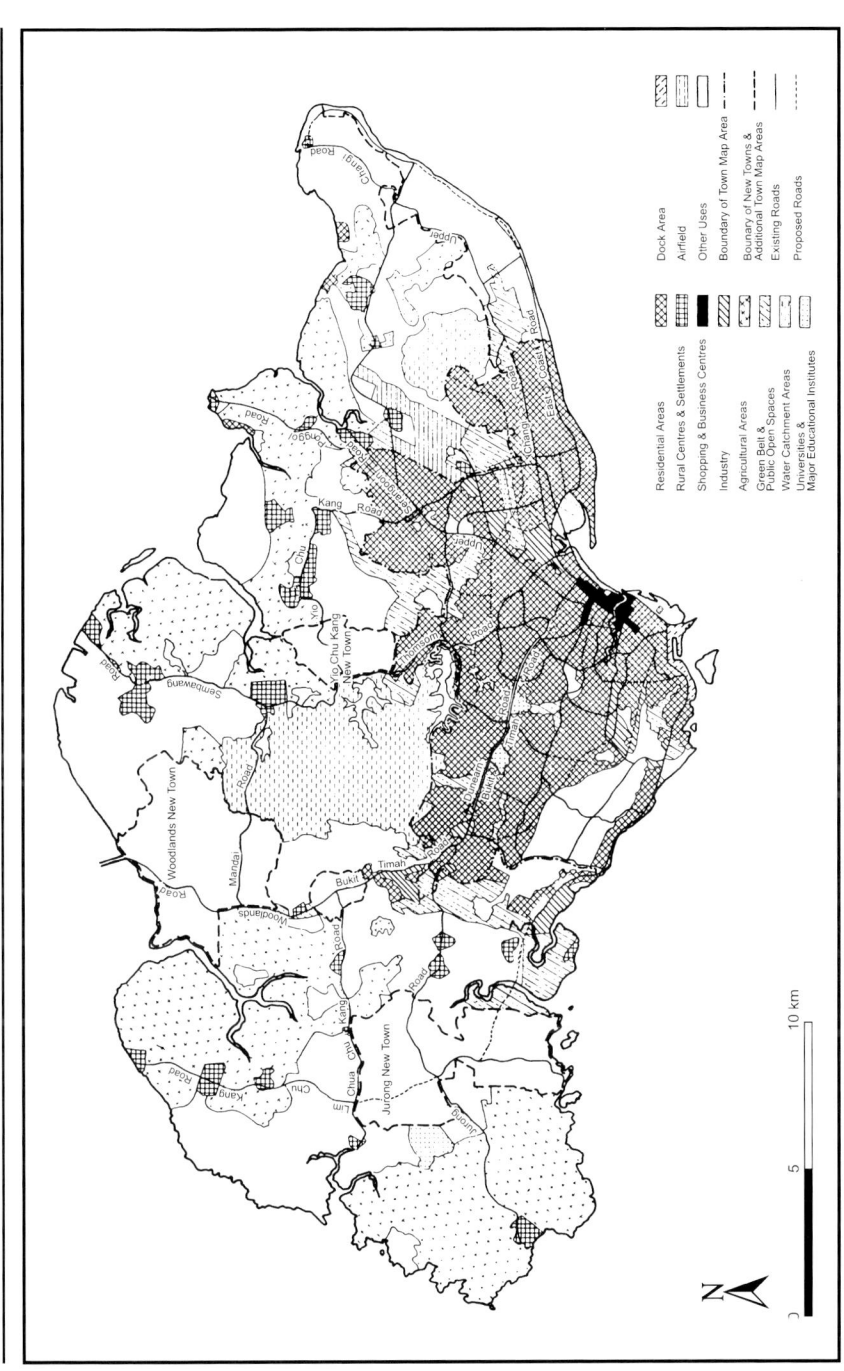

Source: State of Singapore 1963. *Annual Report of the Planning Department for 1960 and 1961*, Singapore. (adapted)

FOUR DECADES OF TRANSFORMATION

FIGURE 1.4: RING CONCEPT PLAN

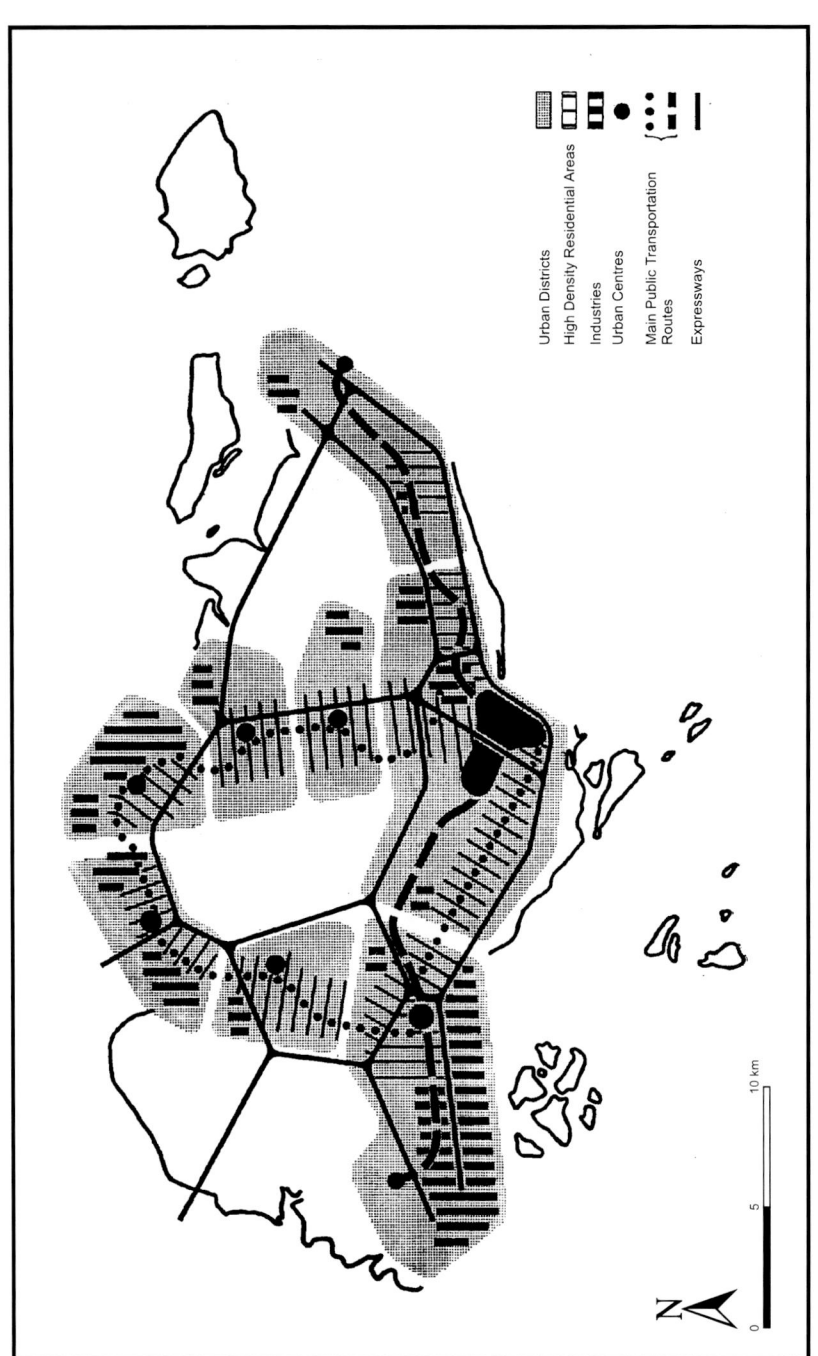

Source: MND (1970), *Annual Report, Planning Department* (adapted).

FIGURE 1.5: THE GOLDEN SHOE

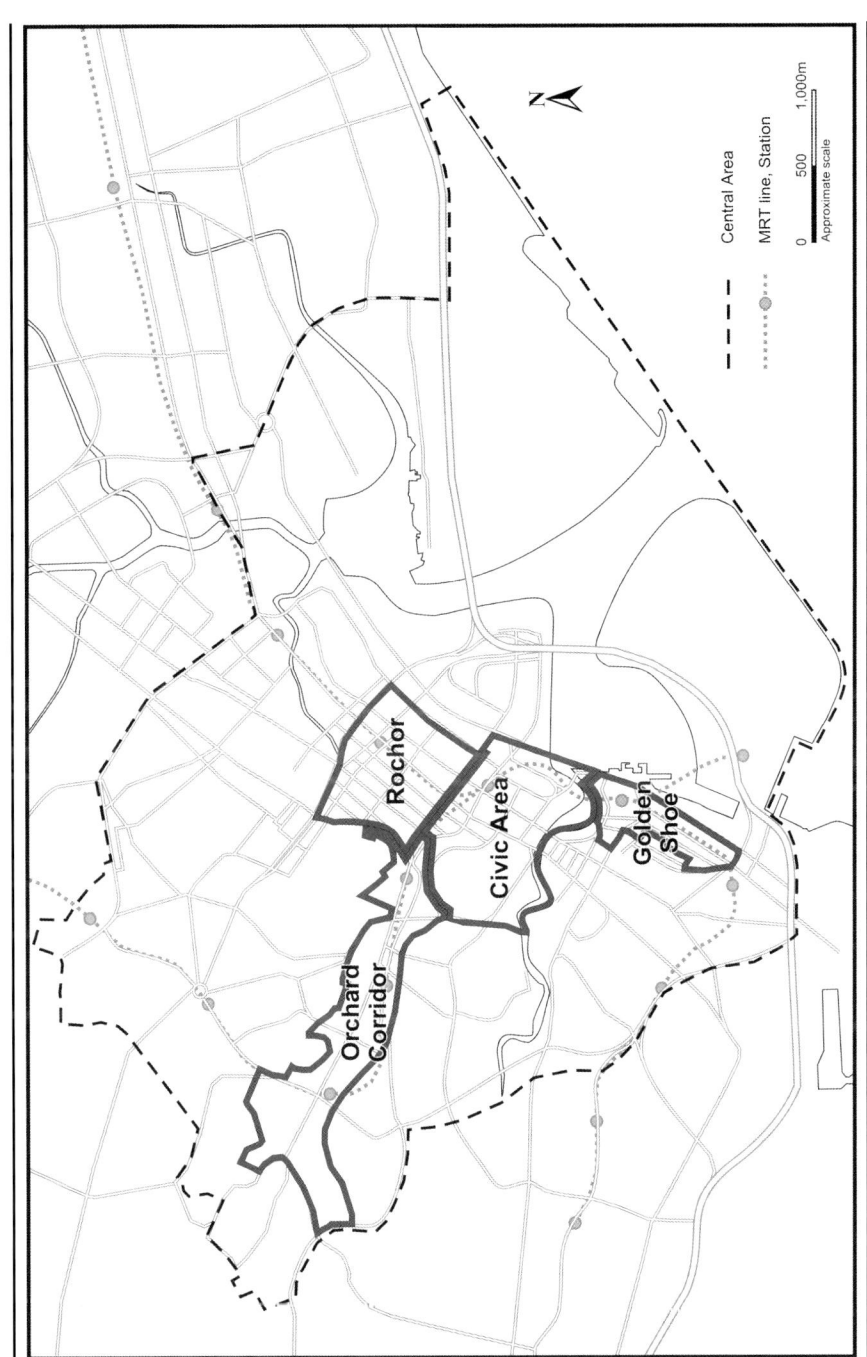

Source: URA (1989)

FIGURE 1.6A: CBD ZONE STRUCTURE PLAN, 2000–YEAR X

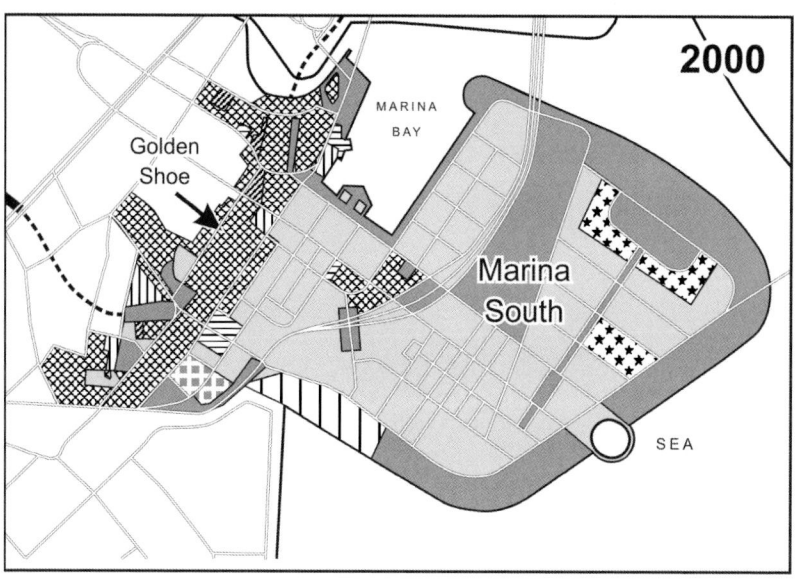

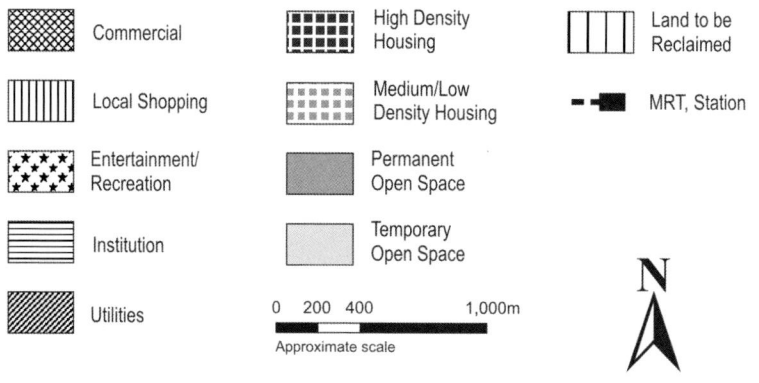

Source: URA (1992a)

FIGURE 1.6B: CBD ZONE STRUCTURE PLAN, 2000–YEAR X

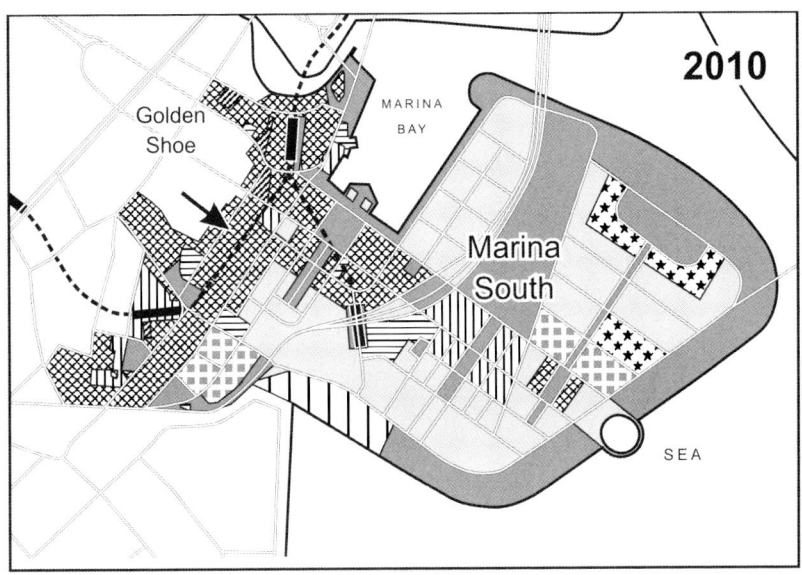

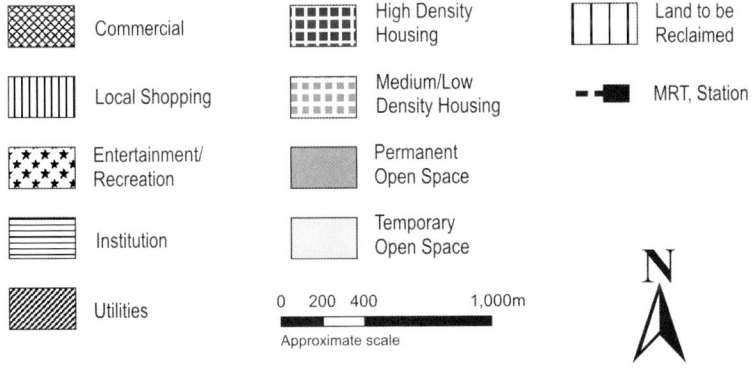

Source: URA (1992a)

FIGURE 1.6C: CBD ZONE STRUCTURE PLAN, 2000–YEAR X

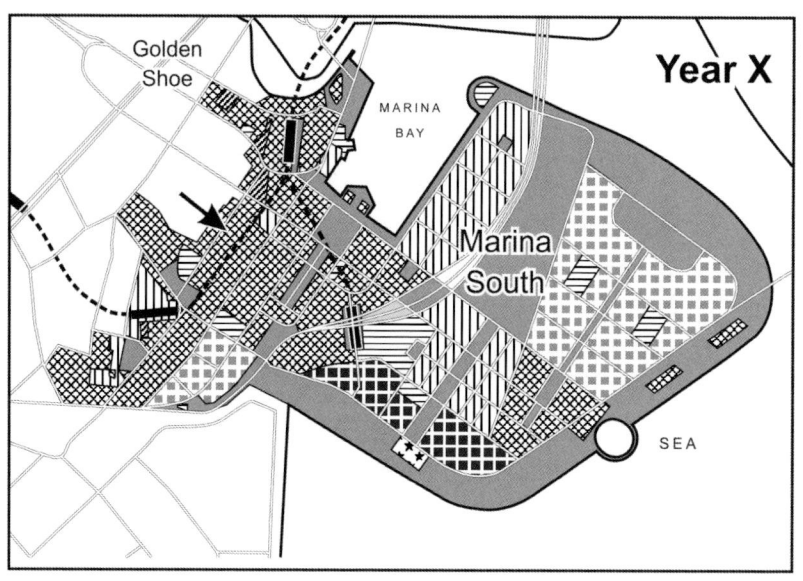

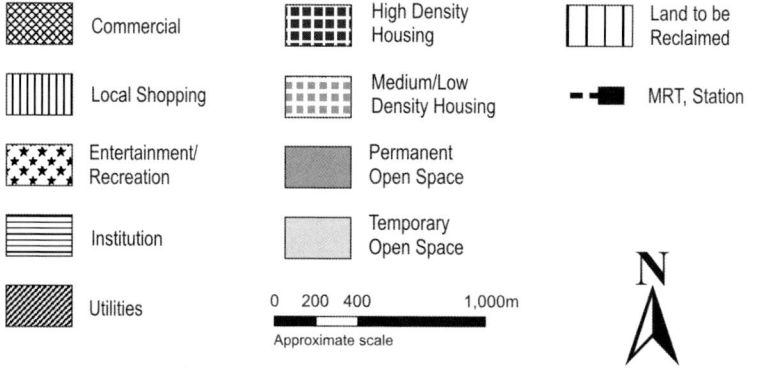

Source: URA (1992a)

FIGURE 1.7: EXPANSION OF THE CENTRAL AREA, 1958–1997

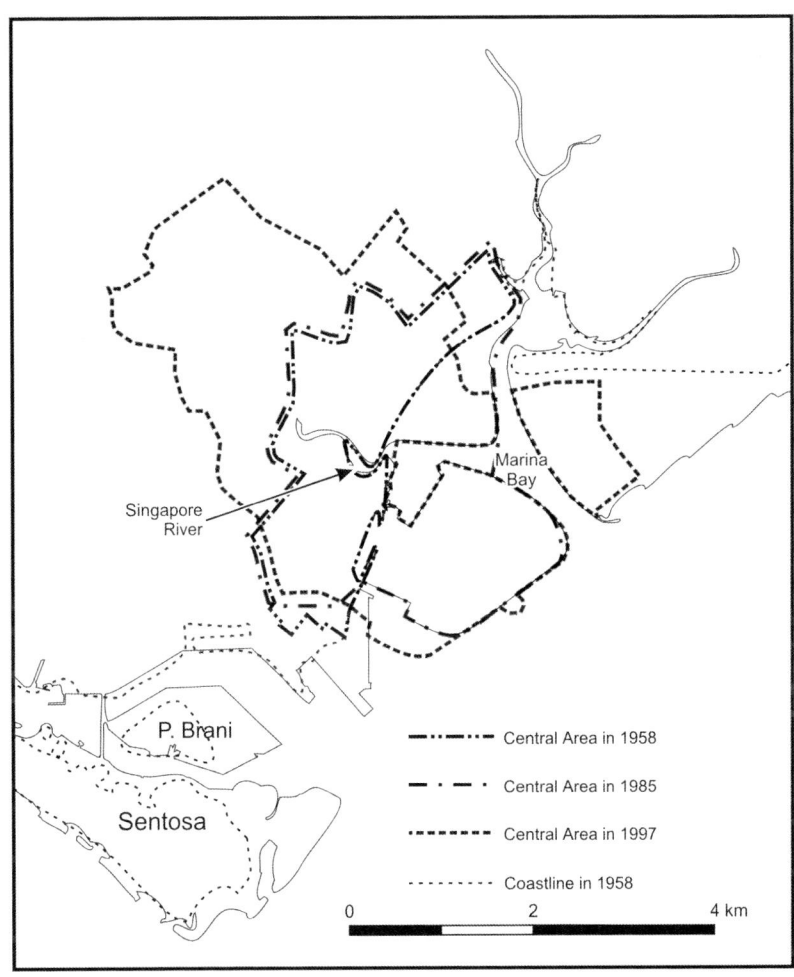

Source: Master Plan (various years)

FOUR DECADES OF TRANSFORMATION

FIGURE 2.1: INFRASTRUCTURE IN 1958

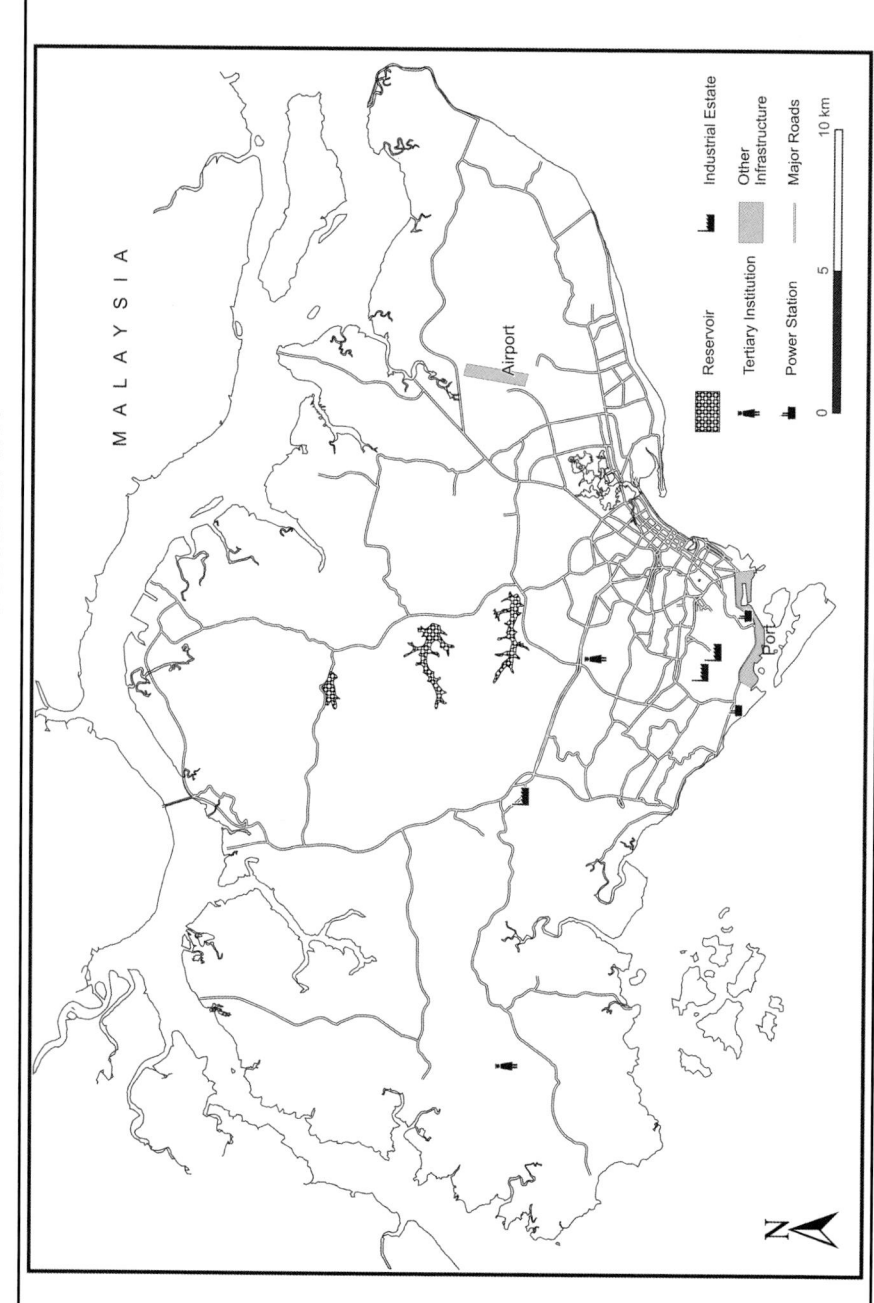

Source: Compiled from various maps.

FIGURE 2.2: INFRASTRUCTURE IN 1975

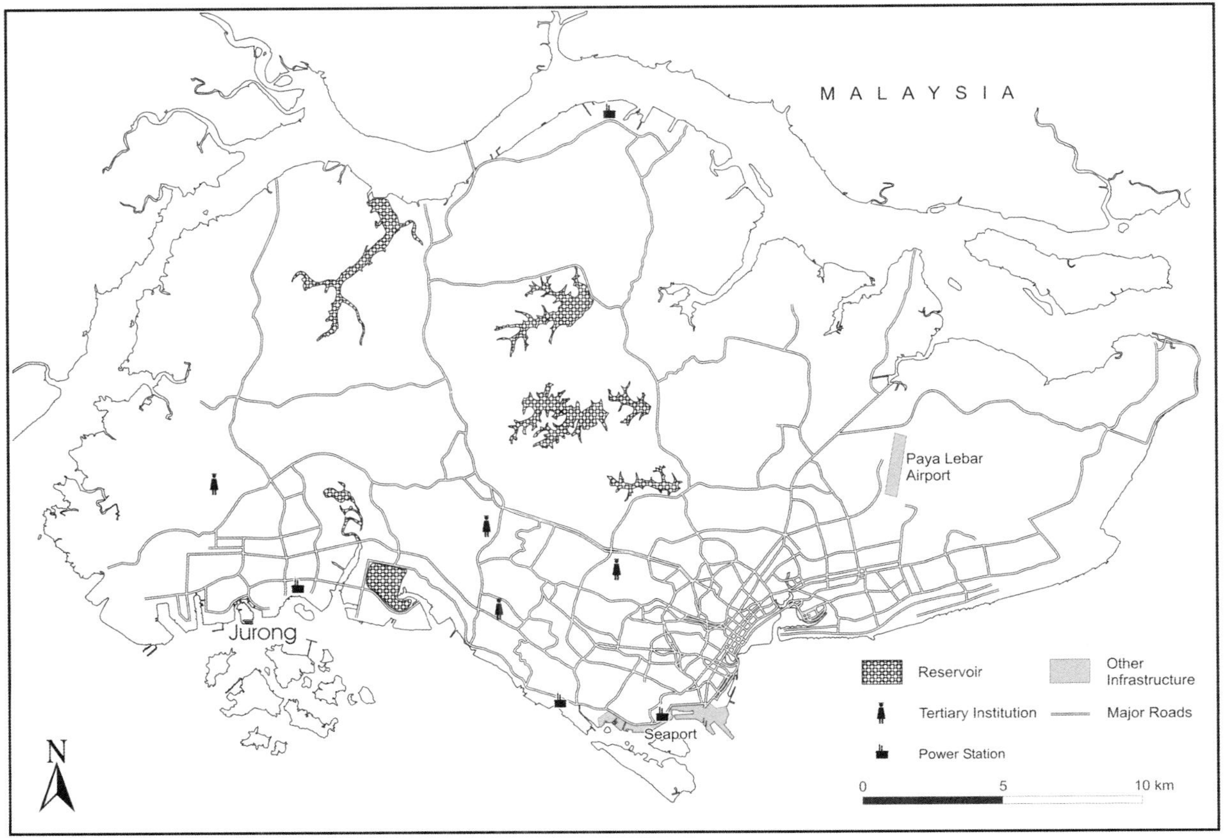

Source: Compiled from various maps.

FIGURE 2.1: INFRASTRUCTURE IN 2000

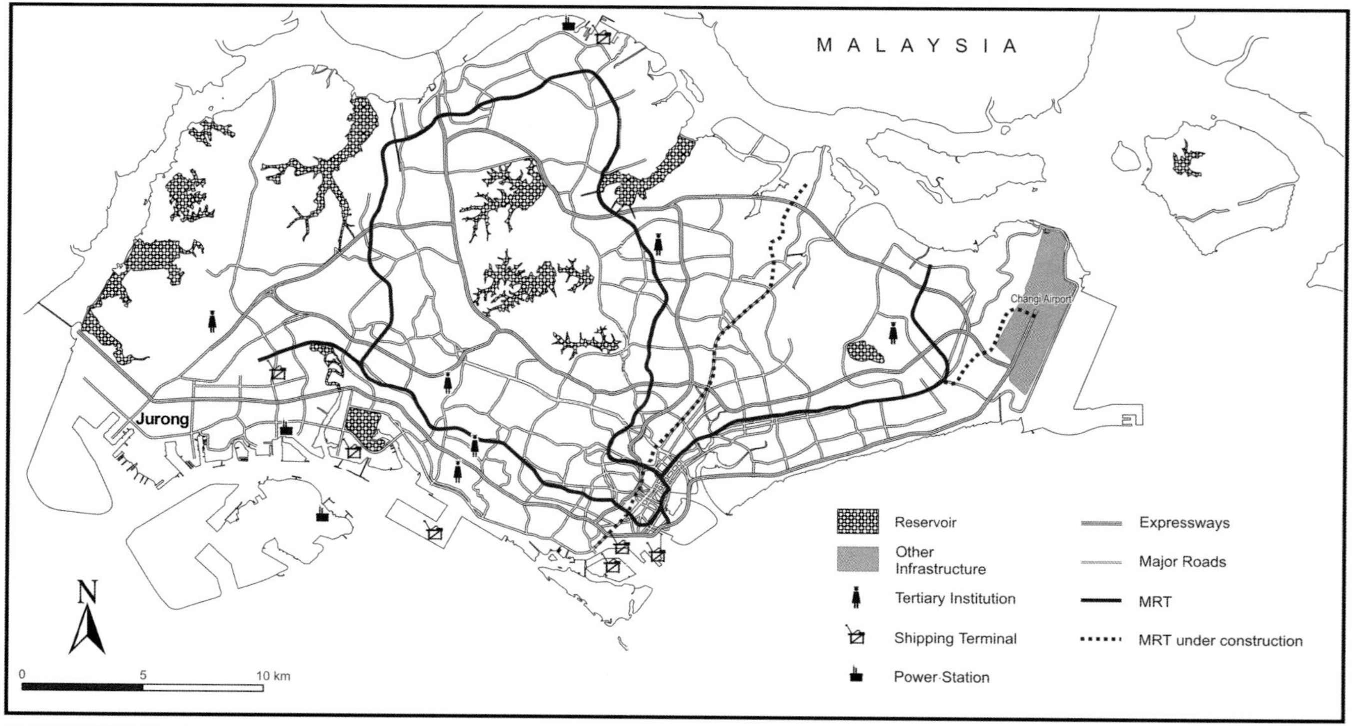

Source: Compiled from various maps.

FIGURE 2.4: RESERVOIRS AND CATCHMENT AREAS IN SINGAPORE

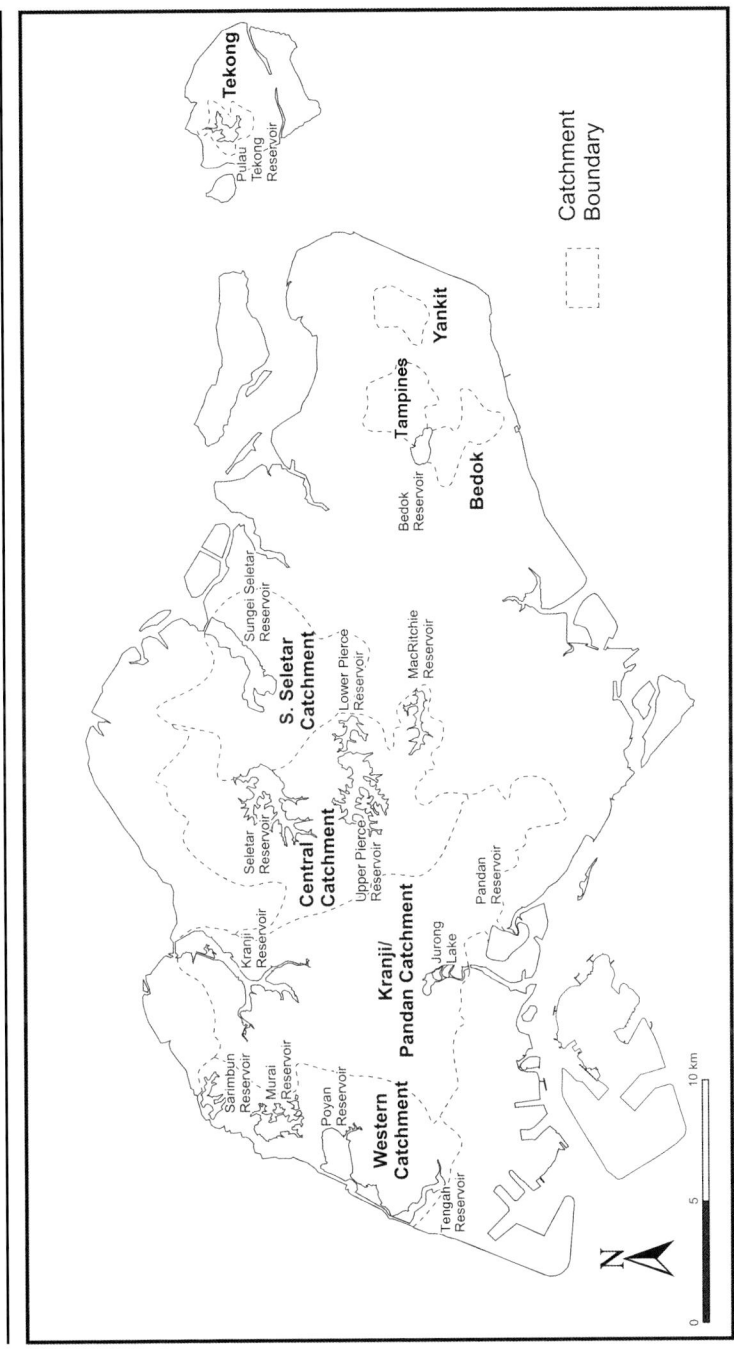

Source: Yap (1995), pp. 19, 39, adapted.

FIGURE 2.5: EXISTING SEWAGE TREATMENT PLANTS AND DEEP TUNNEL SEWERAGE SYSTEM

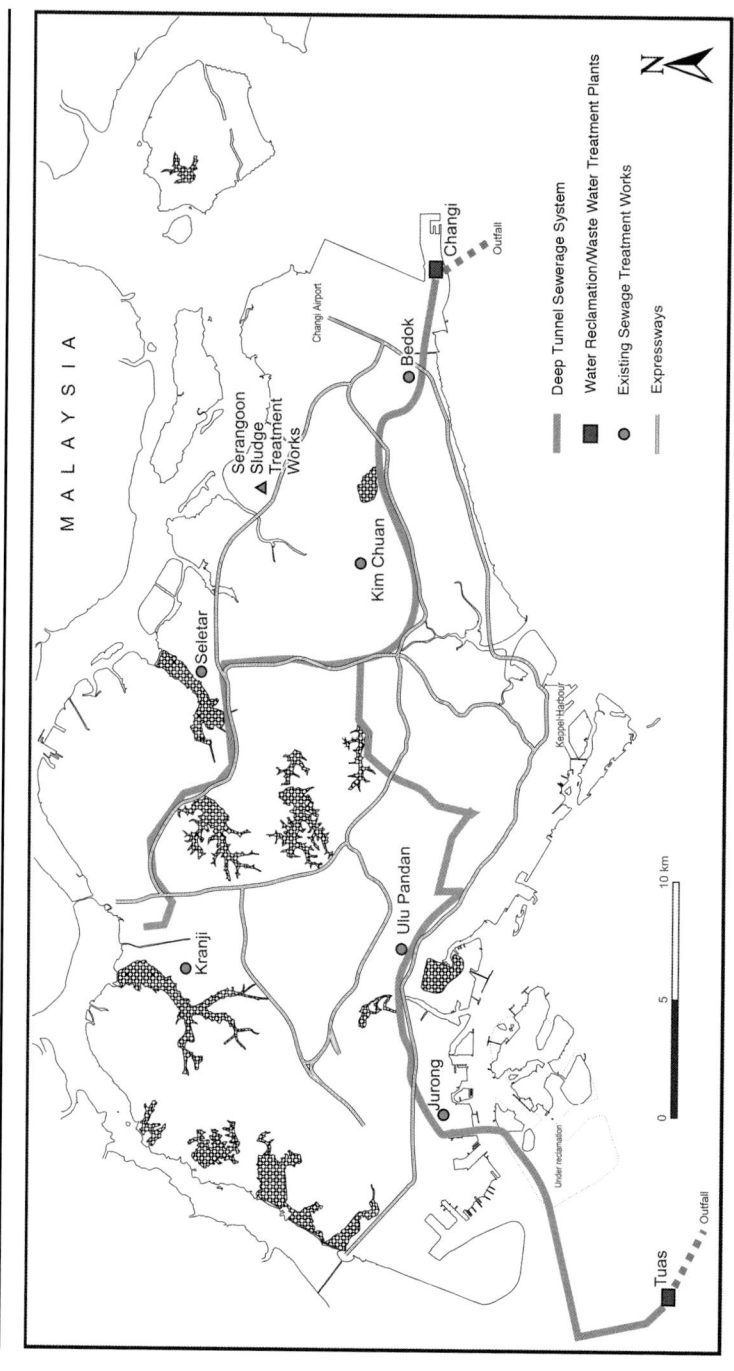

Source: Compiled from various maps.

FIGURE 2.6: REVISED 1991 CONCEPT PLAN FOR YEAR X

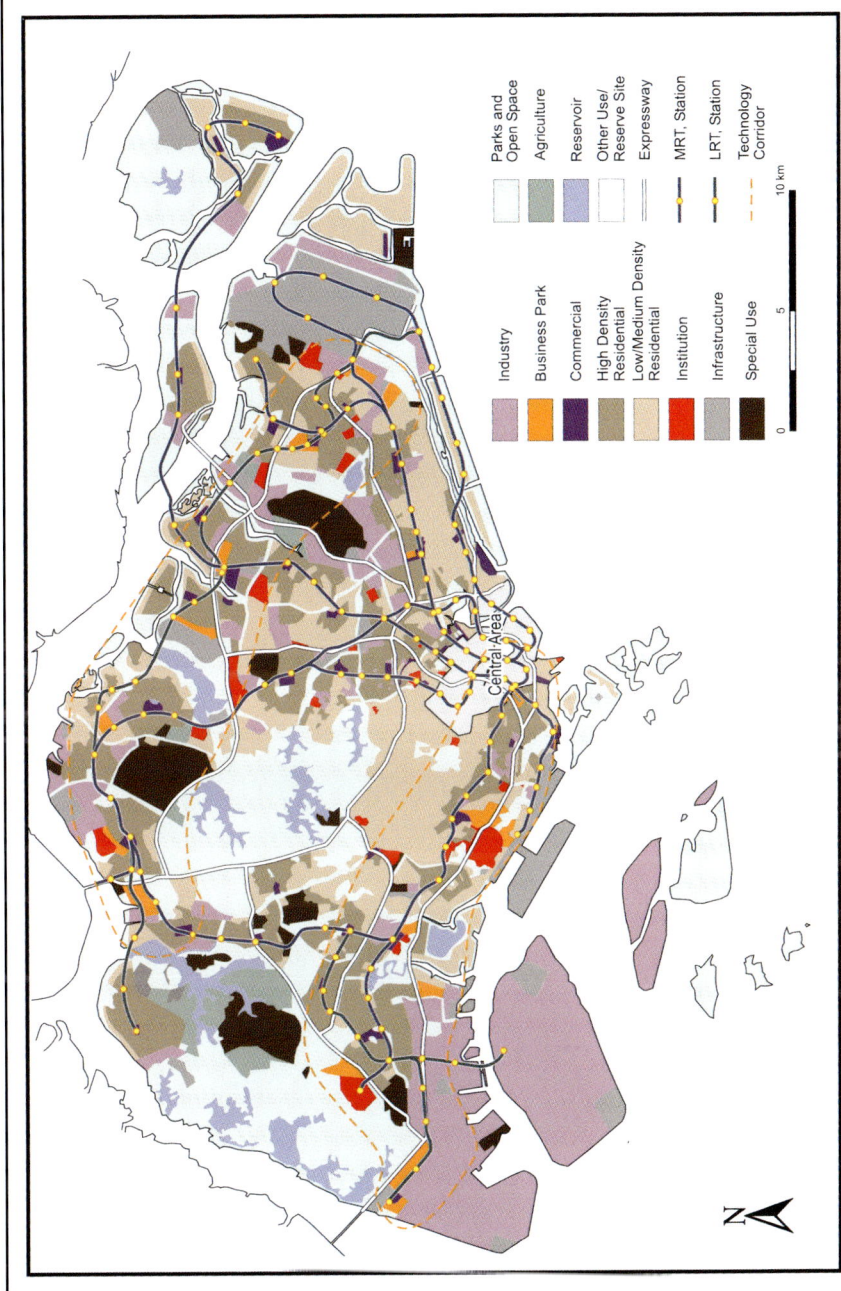

Source: URA (1992a), *Downtown Core & Portview: Development Guide Plans*, Singapore

FIGURE 3.1: JURONG IN 1958

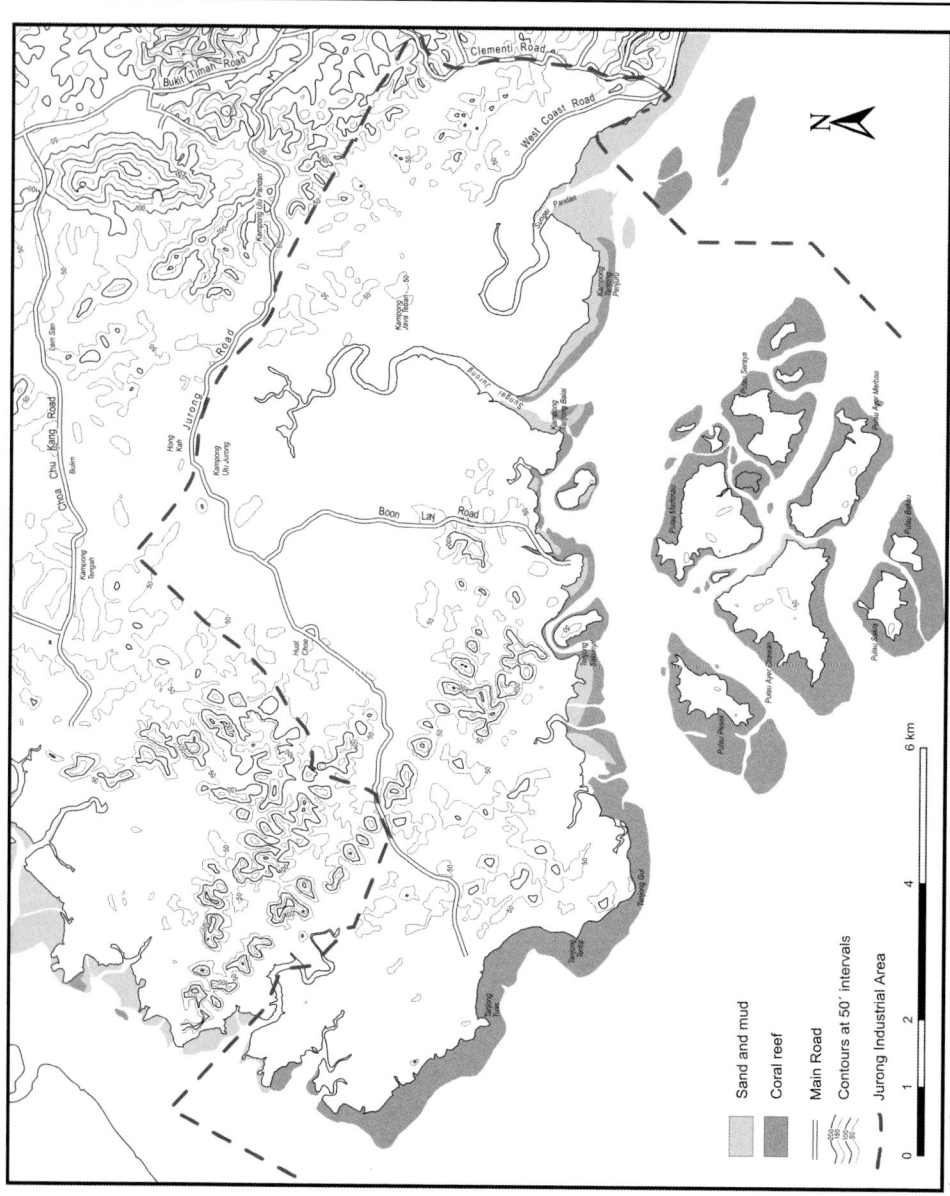

Source: Survey Department (1958)

FIGURE 3.2: JTC INDUSTRIAL ESTATES, 1970

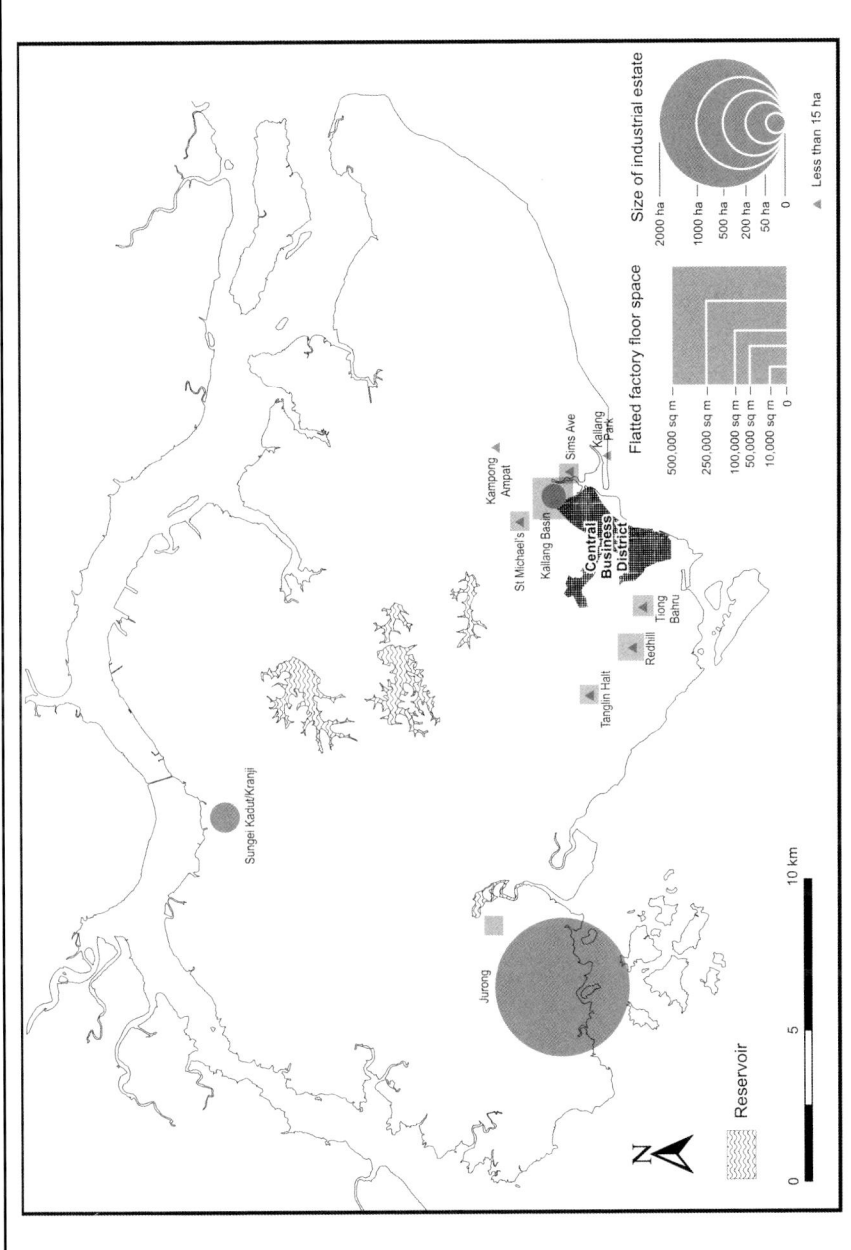

Source: JTC Annual Report (1970)

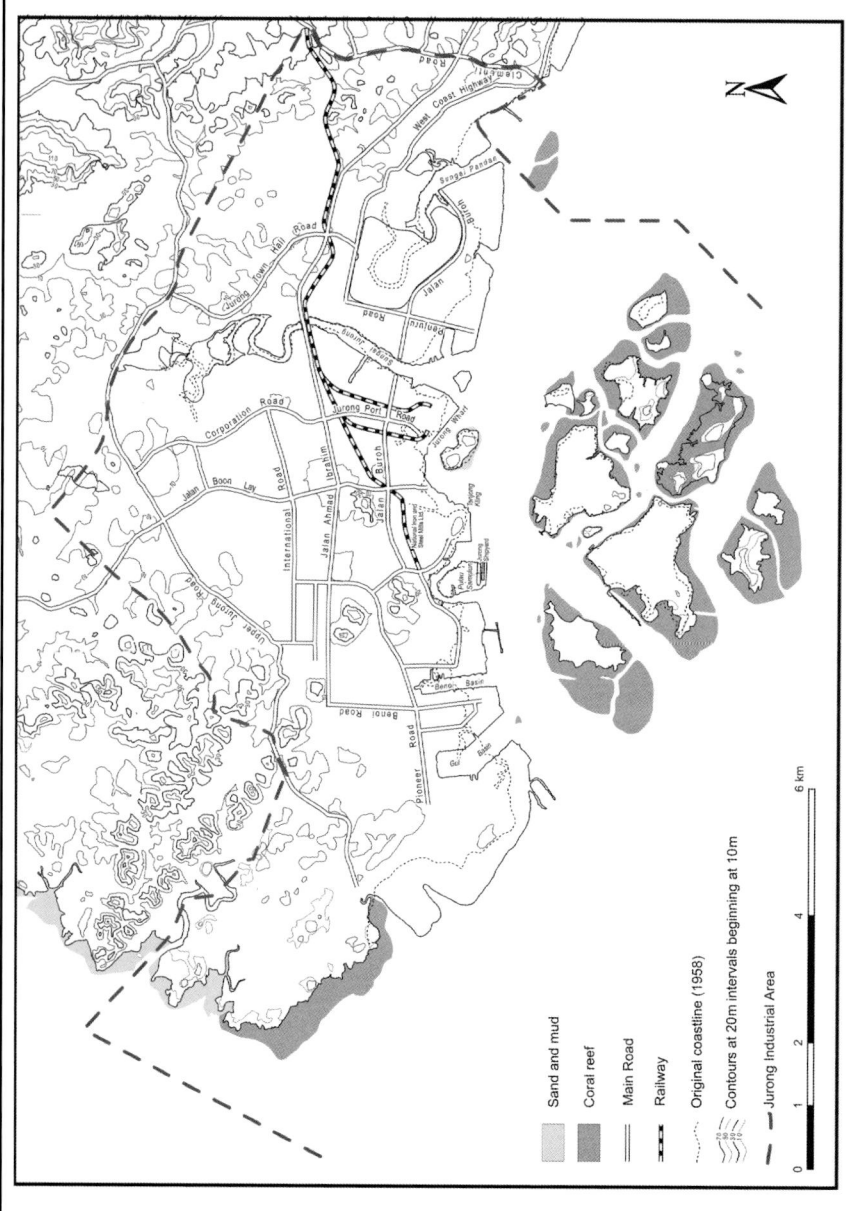

FIGURE 3.3: JURONG IN 1975

Source: Ministry of Defence (1975)

FIGURE 3.4: JTC INDUSTRIAL ESTATES, 1980

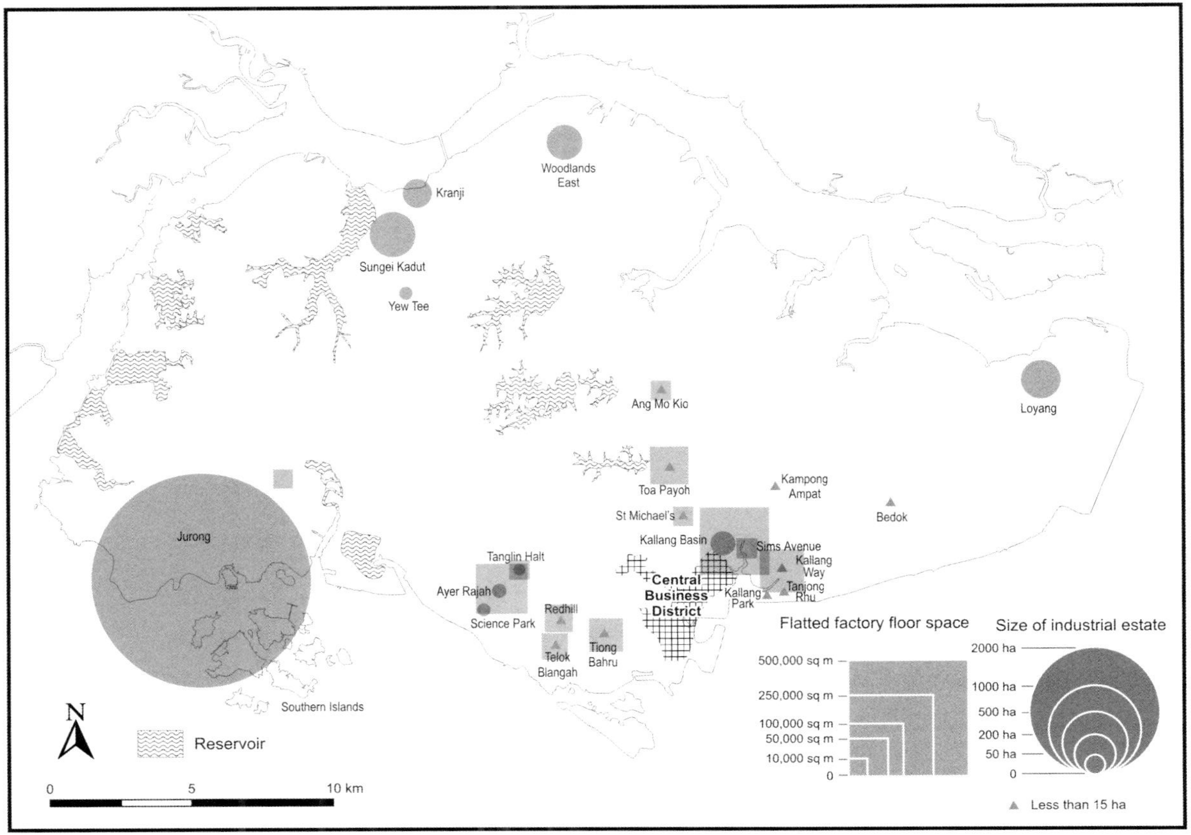

Source: JTC Annual Report (1980)

FIGURE 3.5: JTC INDUSTRIAL ESTATES, 1990

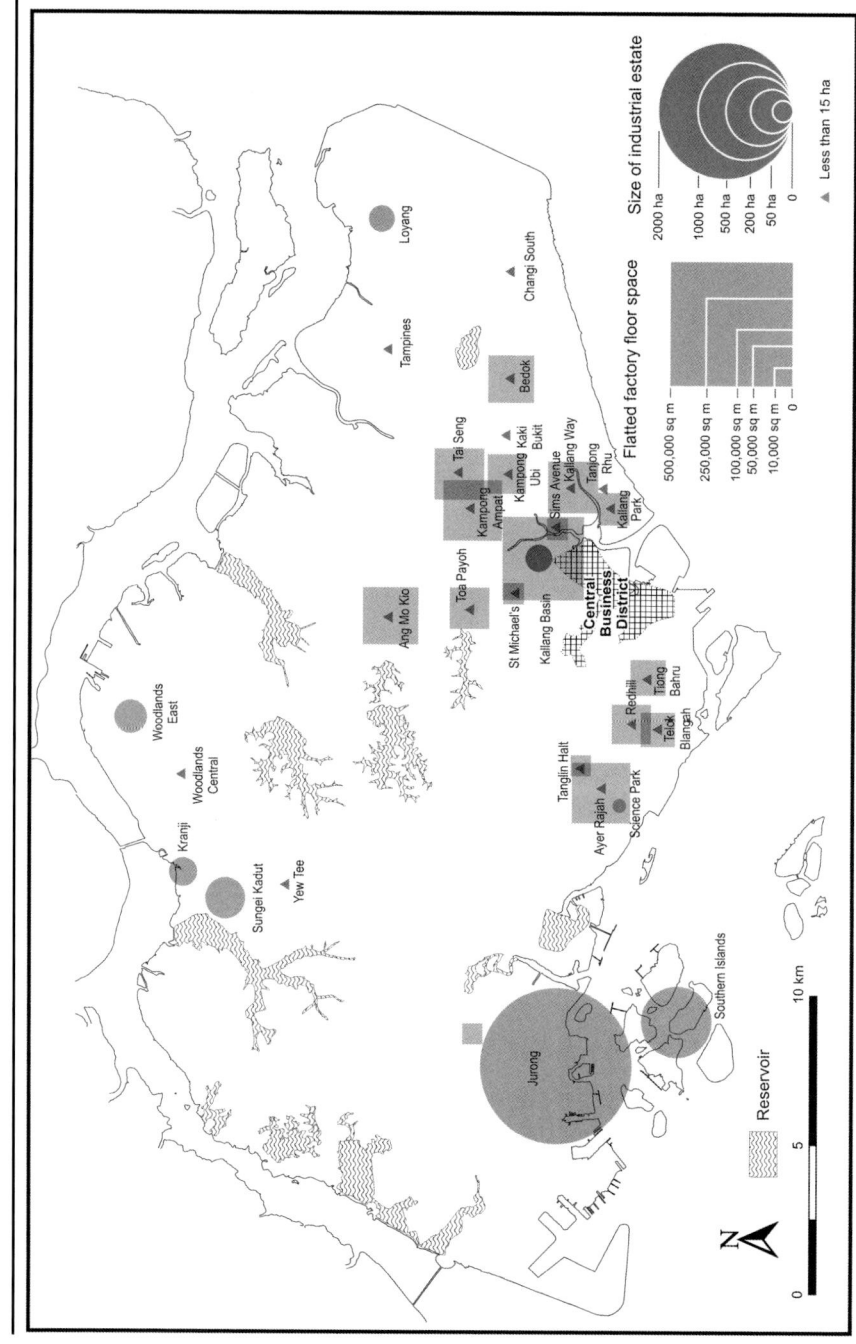

Source: JTC Annual Report (1990)

FIGURE 3.6: BUSINESS PARKS, INDUSTRY CLUSTERS AND INSTITUTES OF HIGHER LEARNING

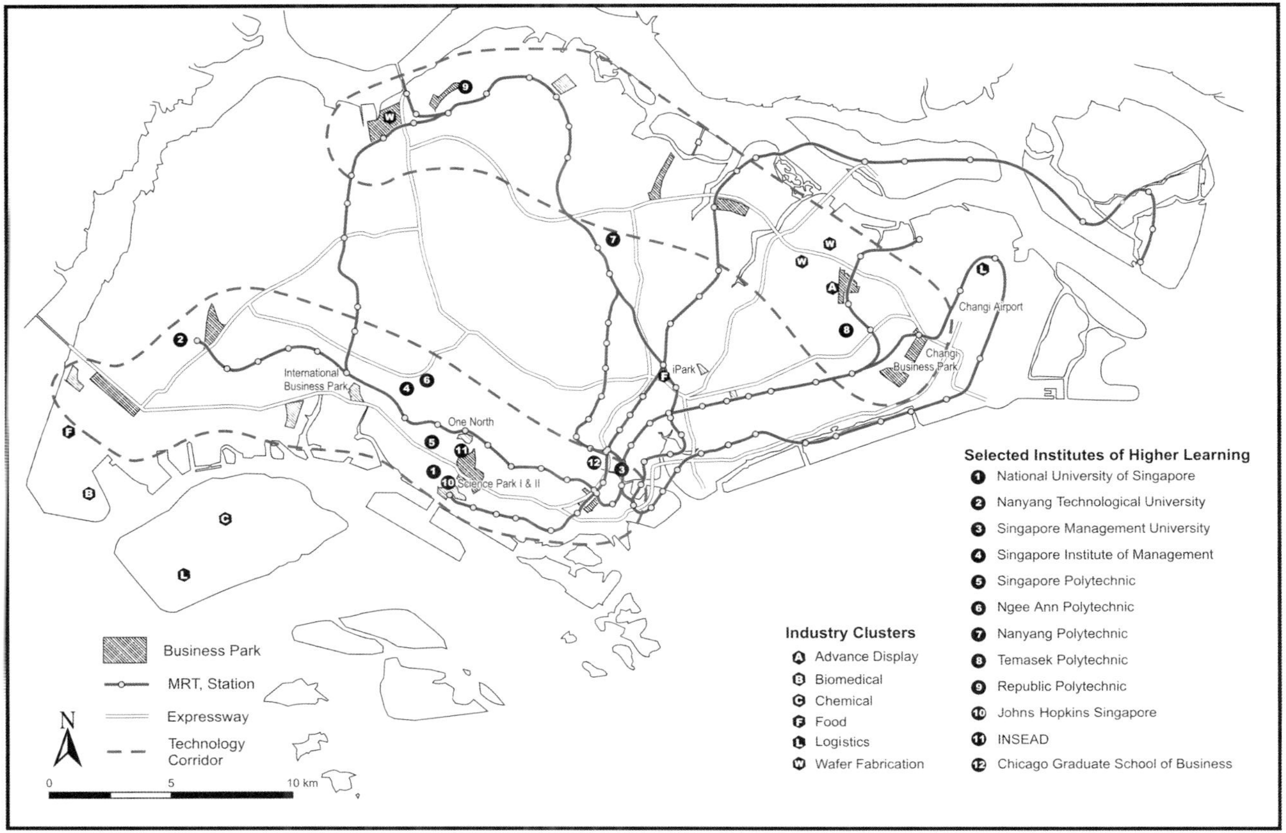

Source: URA (1992a) (Adapted).

FOUR DECADES OF TRANSFORMATION

FIGURE 3.7: JTC INDUSTRIAL ESTATES, 1998

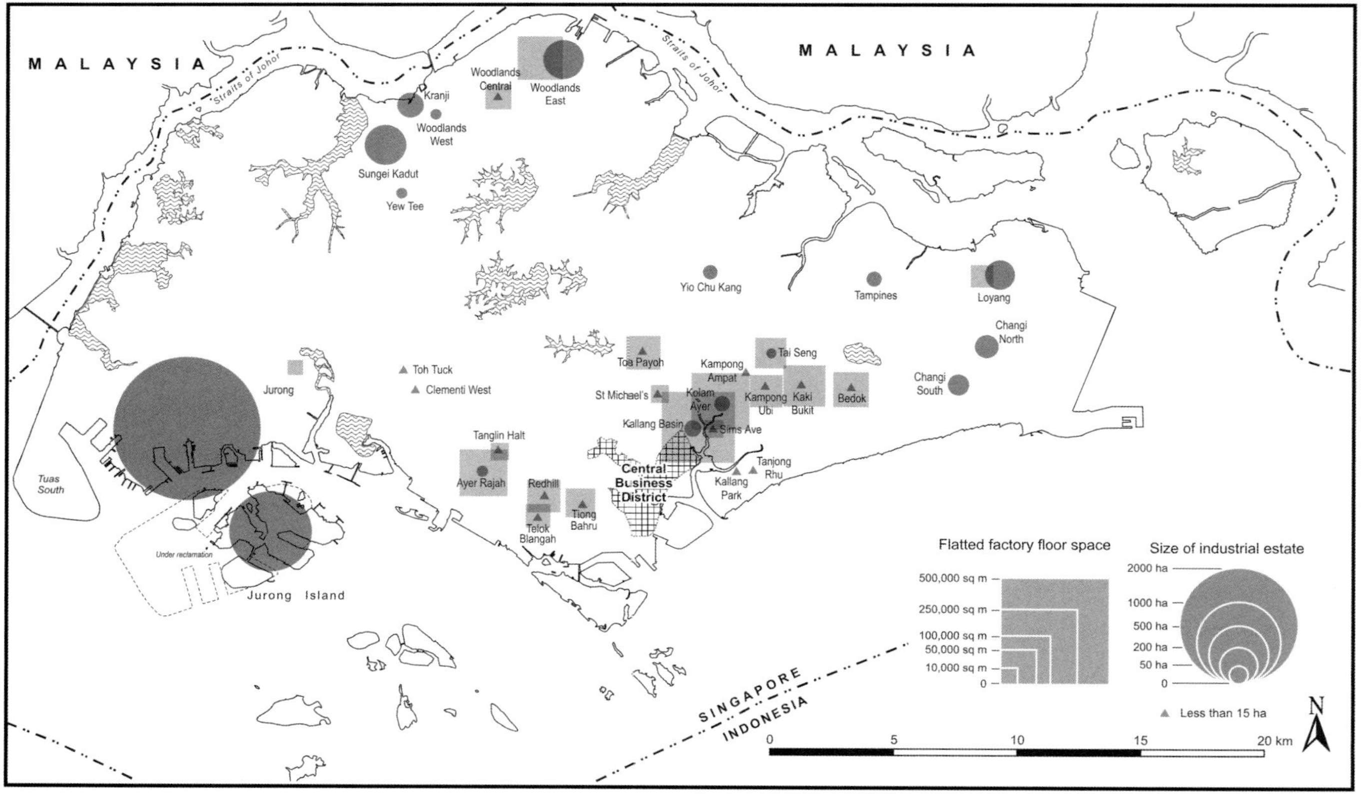

Source: JTC Annual Report (1998)

FIGURE 3.8: JURONG IN 1998

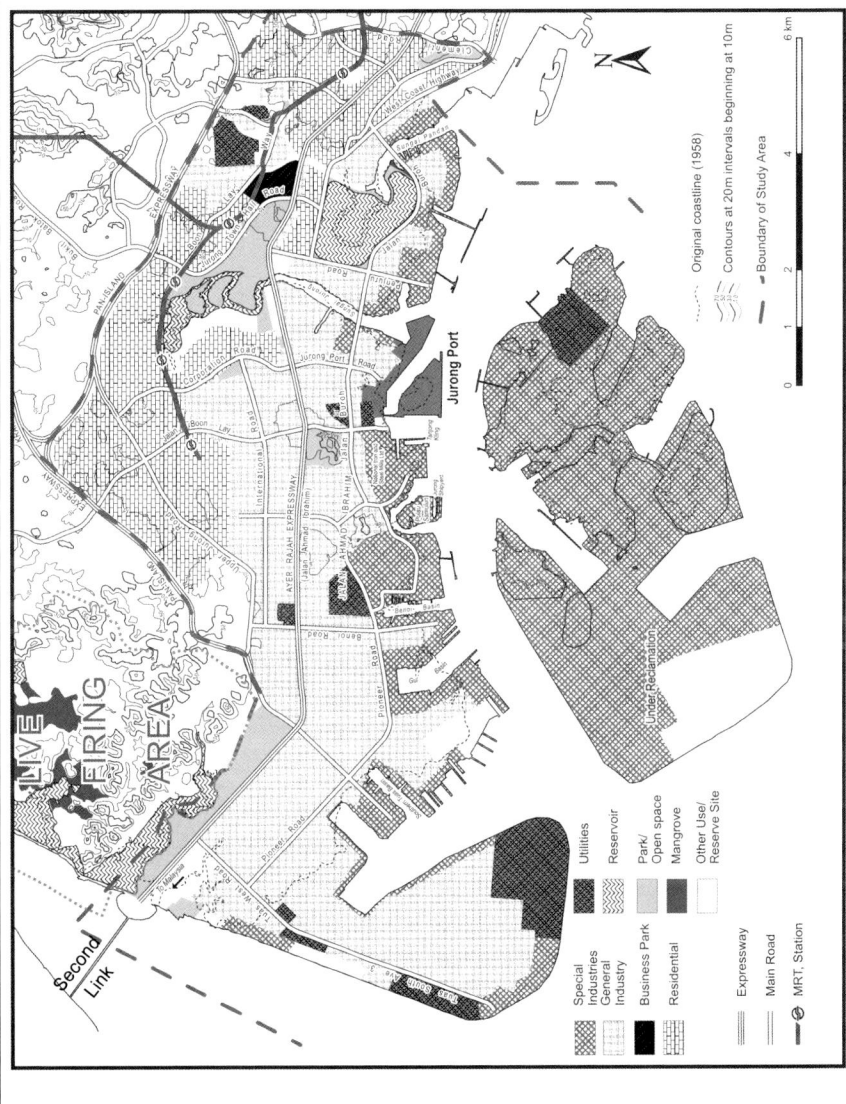

Source: Ministry of Defence (1998), JTC (unpublished map, 1998).

FIGURE 4.1A: PUBLIC HOUSING IN SINGAPORE, 1960–2000

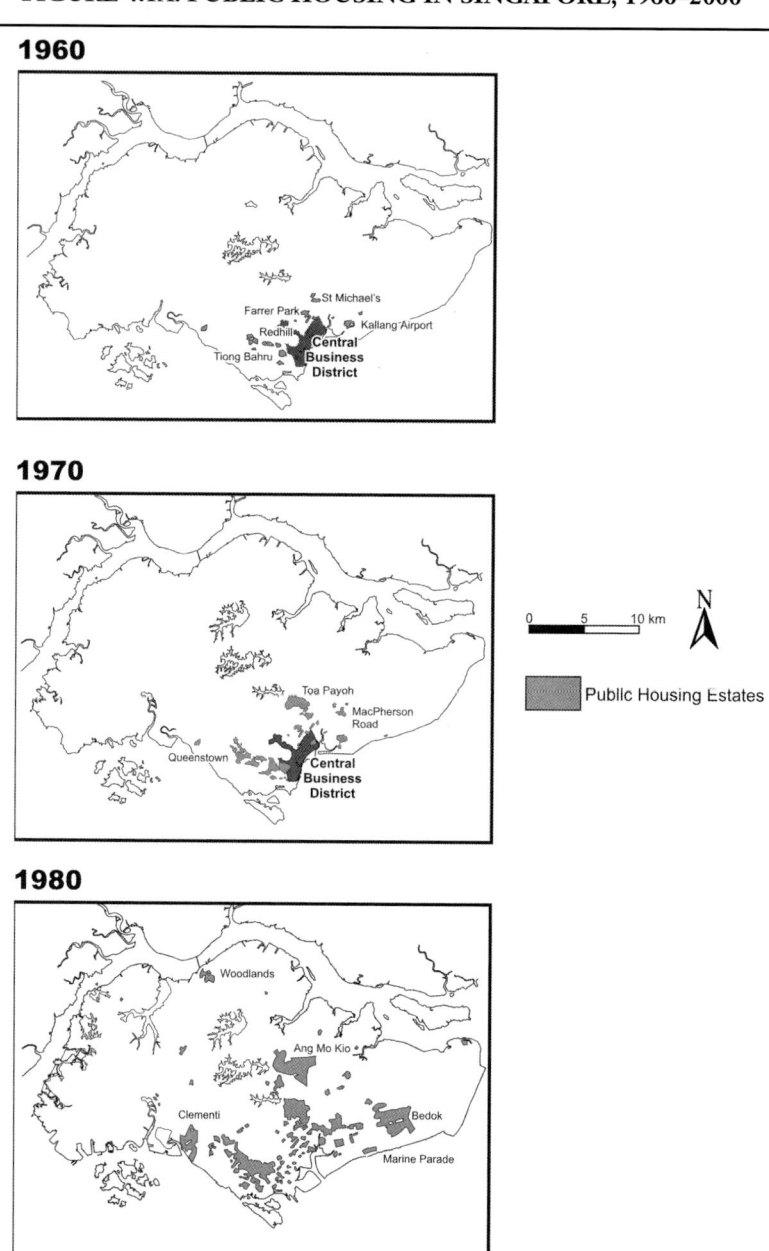

Source: HDB Annual Reports (various issues)

FIGURE 4.1B: PUBLIC HOUSING IN SINGAPORE, 1960–2000

1990

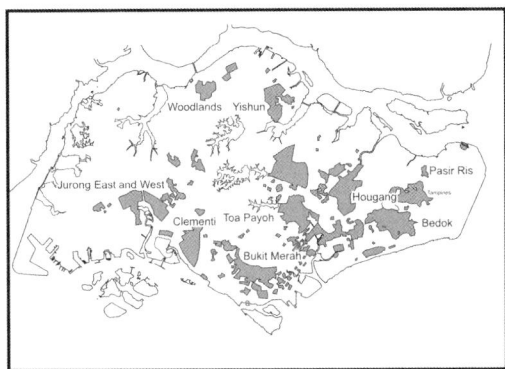

2000

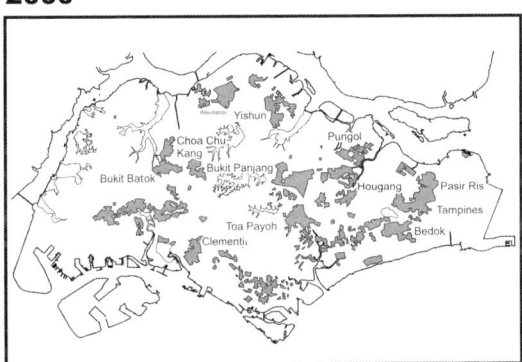

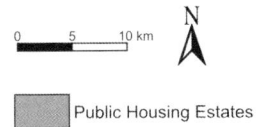

Source: HDB Annual Reports (various issues)

FOUR DECADES OF TRANSFORMATION

FIGURE 4.3: TYPE AND DISTRIBUTION OF PRIVATE RESIDENTIAL UNITS, 1999

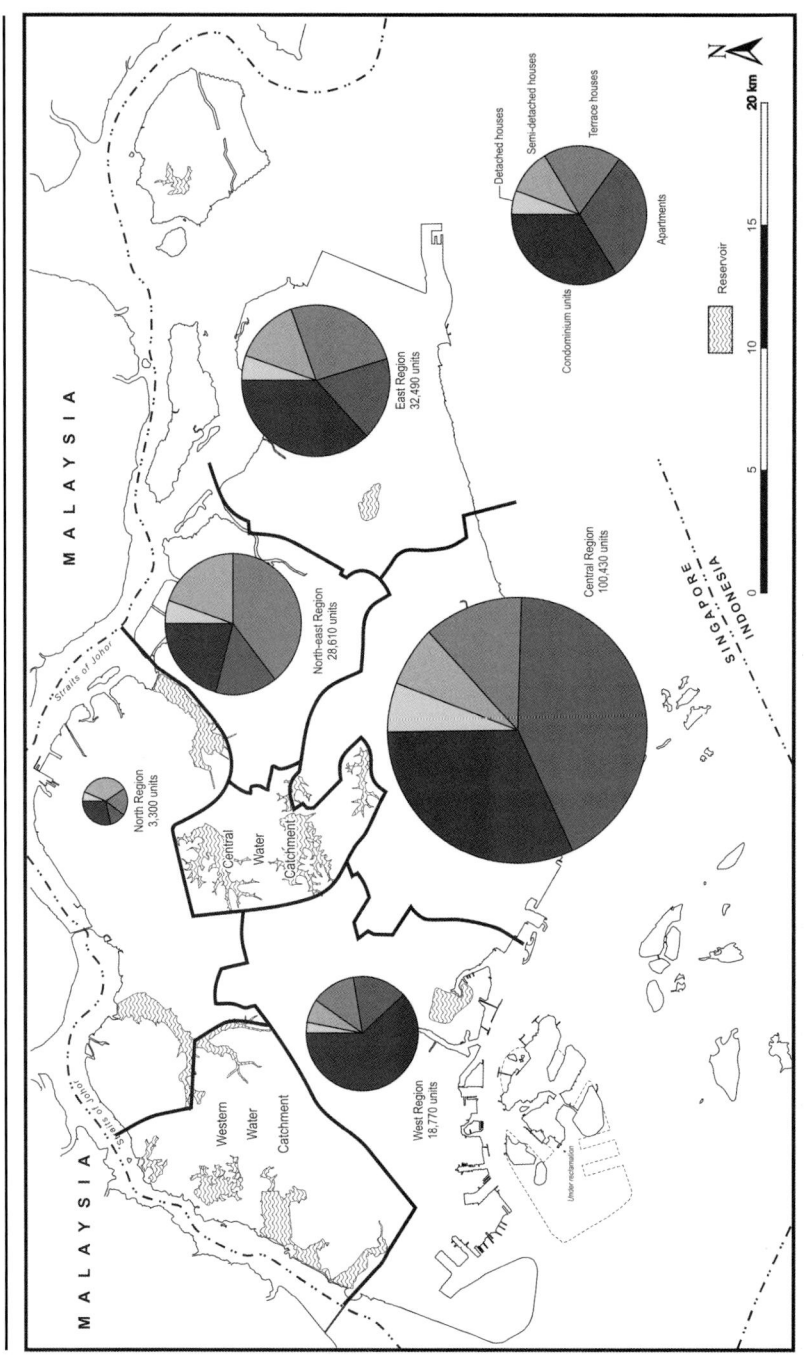

Source: Data based on URA (1999)

Figures

FIGURE 5.1A: NATURAL AREAS AND PARKS, 1958 AND 1975

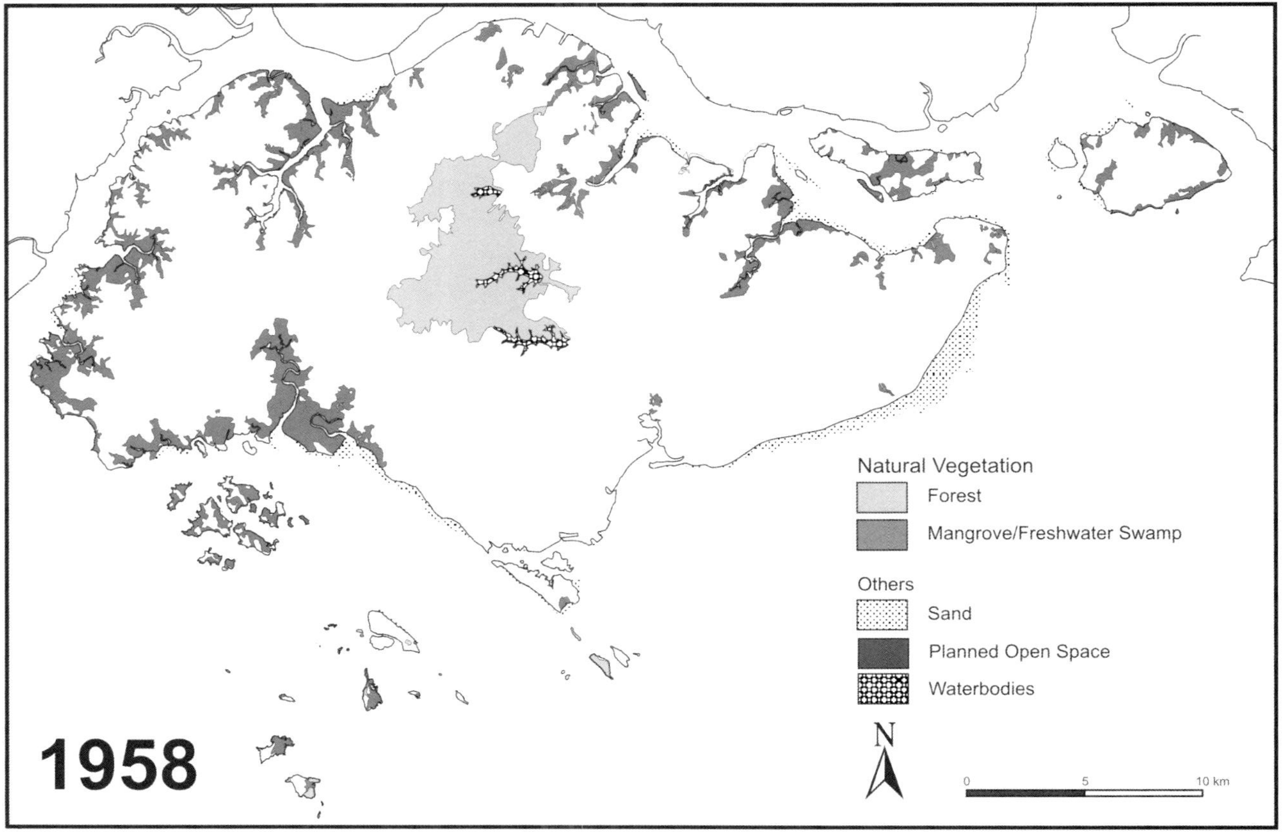

Source: Chief Surveyor, Singapore (1958)

FIGURE 5.1B: NATURAL AREAS AND PARKS, 1958 AND 1975

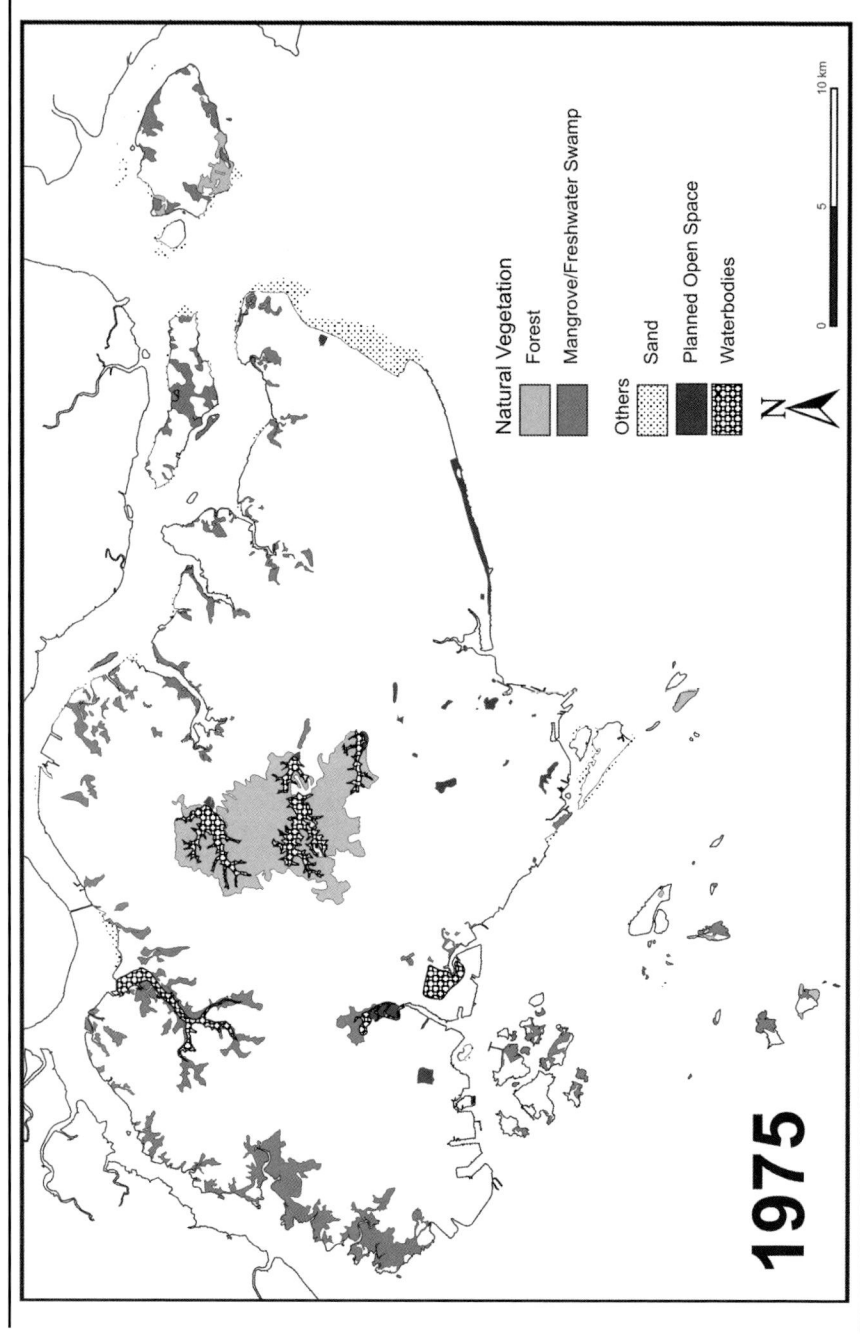

Source: Ministry of Defence (1958)

FIGURE 5.2: MAJOR PARKS AND NATURE AREAS IN SINGAPORE, 2000

Source: Ministry of Defence (1998), updated from other sources.

FOUR DECADES OF TRANSFORMATION

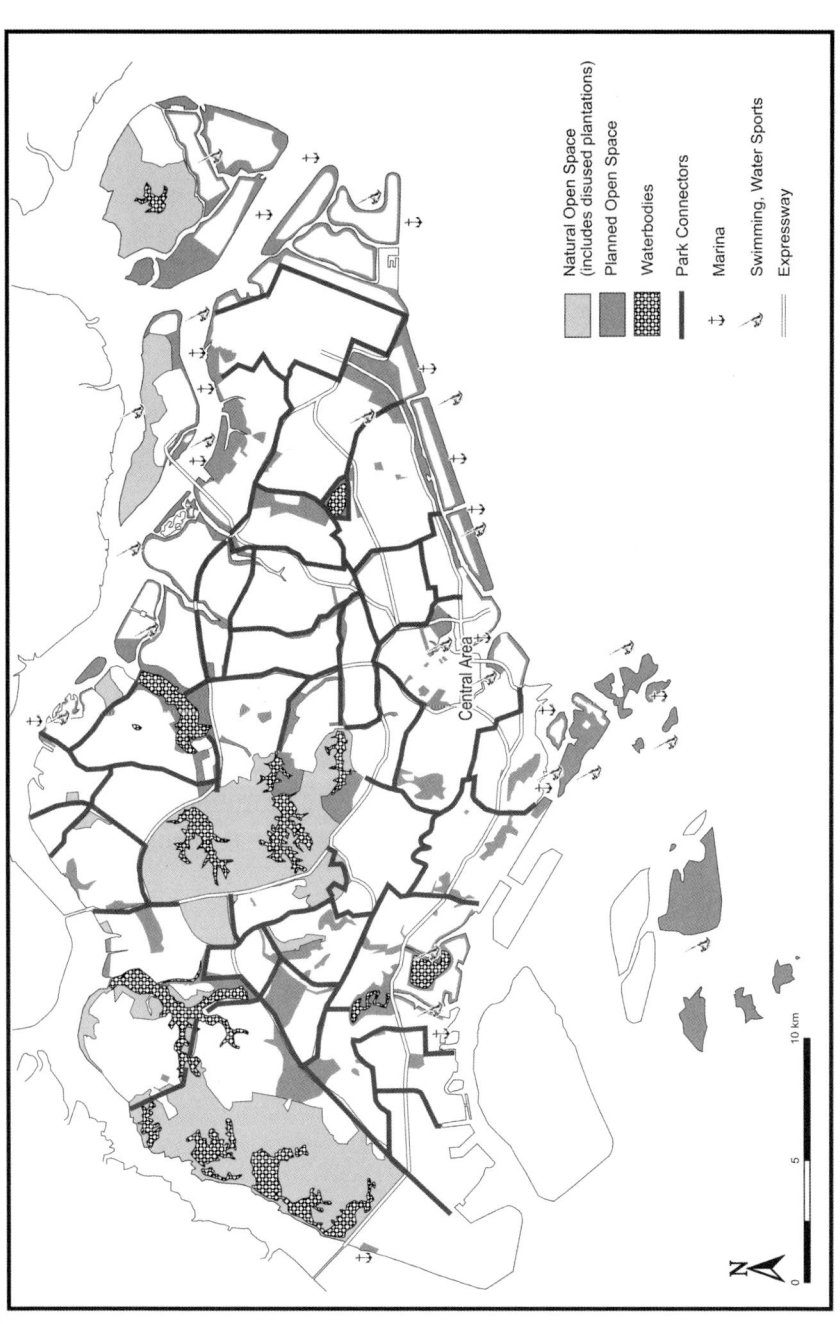

FIGURE 5.3: PROPOSED RECREATIONAL AREAS IN SINGAPORE BY YEAR X

Source: Adapted from URA (1991a)

FIGURE 5.4: CONCEPT PLAN 2001

Source: URA (2001). *The Concept Plan 2001*. Singapore

Other Titles in Geography and Environmental Research

Toponymics: A Study of Singapore Street Names
by Victor R. Savage and Brenda S. A. Yeoh

**Asian Dragons and the Green Trade:
Environment, Economics and International Law**
by Simon Tay and Daniel Esty